Praise for *Eight Theories of Justice*

Each chapter of this impressive volume sheds abundant light on the history, dynamics, and merits of key strands of ethical thought. Readers will encounter rich new connections between the major approaches to achieving justice and the deepest value commitments behind them, including revealing glimpses of the moral visions that have inspired their representative figures. Highly accessible and recommended for any audience.

—Thomas Massaro, SJ, McGinley Endowed Chair
in Religion and Society, Fordham University

In *Eight Theories of Justice: Perspectives from Philosophical and Theological Ethics*, Karen Lebacqz and Matthew Gaudet offer an accessible and pragmatic introduction to eight ethical frameworks that influence contemporary moral decision-making. This revision updates chapters devoted to well-known theories and, with chapters on communitarianism and womanist theology, widens the scope to welcome modern voices to the discussion. Lebacqz and Gaudet frame justice as a pragmatic dialogue, and this text invites readers to delve into the push and pull of the exchange of ideas. More than ever, justice is the essential dialogue for our time. Lebacqz and Gaudet have accomplished something rare—they have taken a favorite classic and have made it indispensable to the ongoing conversation.

—Grace Chan Oei, director, Center for Christian Bioethics,
Loma Linda University School of Medicine

As you try to imagine theorizing justice, test out these eight "fragments" and how Lebacqz and Gaudet have so astutely curated and interrogated them. While these eight must not be the only ones you engage in our wider, globally informed theoretical contexts, this text contributes a stimulating primer for such critical ethical discernment.

—Traci C. West, author of *Solidarity and Defiant Spirituality: Africana Lessons on Religion, Racism, and Ending Gender Violence*

Karen Lebacqz and Matthew Gaudet have enriched this already wonderful book on theories of justice. Lyrically written and carefully considered, it has inspired decades of students in my seminars and remains one of the definitive and classic texts for the study of ethics.

—Laurie Zoloth, Margaret E. Burton Professor of Religion and Ethics, University of Chicago

Eight Theories of Justice is exactly what students of philosophy and ethics need—lucid, cogent explorations of the most fundamental ways people understand and debate notions of justice. Lebacqz and Gaudet offer a highly teachable, clear, and engaging discussion of contrasting conceptions of justice, highlighting what some share and where they diverge. An essential resource for philosophers and ethicists alike. I continue to learn from Karen Lebacqz, and now Matthew Gaudet, as this work refreshes and updates a classic text and makes it incredibly relevant and useful in the present day.

—Aana Marie Vigen, professor of Christian social ethics, Loyola University Chicago

Eight Theories of Justice

Perspectives from
Philosophical and
Theological Ethics

Eight Theories of
JUSTICE

Karen Lebacqz
& Matthew J. Gaudet

FORTRESS PRESS
MINNEAPOLIS

EIGHT THEORIES OF JUSTICE
Perspectives from Philosophical and Theological Ethics

Copyright © 2025 Fortress Press. All rights reserved. Except for brief
quotations in critical articles or reviews, no part of this book may be
reproduced in any manner without prior written permission from the
publisher. Email copyright@fortresspress.com or write to Permissions,
Fortress Press, PO Box 1209, Minneapolis, MN 55440-1209.

30 29 28 27 26 25 24   1 2 3 4 5 6 7 8 9

Library of Congress Control Number: 2024947031 (print)

Cover image: 24c stamp, Justice Newspapers and Periodicals
imprint single, 1875
Cover design: Angela Griner

Print ISBN: 979-8-8898-3410-6
eBook ISBN: 979-8-8898-3411-3

Contents

Preface

The relationship between teacher and student is a special one. More than a one-way transfer of information from one who is wise to one who is less so, the best of teaching relationships comprise a mutual exchange of perspectives that leave both the teacher and the student richer for the experience.

This book is a revised and updated version of *Six Theories of Justice: Perspectives from Philosophical and Theological Ethics. Six Theories* was always intended as a teaching text, the kind of text that could facilitate the type of classroom discussion idealized above. The original *Six Theories* sought to bring together, under one cover, some important conversations about justice in philosophy and theology. The format of each chapter, with a quick review of the theory, some critical comments and questions, and a brief assessment, made the text a favorite of teachers for almost four decades.

By 2020, however, the original text showed its age. Some chapters aged better than others, but on the whole, certain elements and examples in the text clearly needed refreshing. At the same time, no other text published in the intervening years could match *Six Theories* for its clarity and organization on the topic of justice. It was a favorite of anyone who had discovered it, and they were not going to give it up easily, despite its age. Matt Gaudet's conversations with peers confirmed this. Clearly, for the sake of a whole new generation of teachers and students, *Six Theories* needed to be revised and republished for the twenty-first century. When Gaudet approached Karen Lebacqz with the idea of a revised edition, she agreed and welcomed a joint effort. We met to discuss possible revisions and discovered that we had independently arrived at almost identical lists of needed updates.

We both agreed that the text should include a chapter on communitarianism. In 1986, communitarianism was still in its infancy. It showed up in the critique section of the chapter on John Rawls but had not yet earned its own chapter. However, in the 1980s and '90s, the liberal-communitarian debates occupied certain quarters of philosophy and dueled for the attention of the left wing of American politics. Over time, the boil became a slow simmer, but the critiques that Michael Sandel and others lobbed against Rawls's early works remain trenchant. In time, Sandel shifted from debating Rawlsian philosophy to critiquing policies and structures built on liberal (and libertarian) ideas. It was clear that in the new edition, a chapter examining the pitfalls of liberal individualism, market economics, and personal liberty from a communitarian perspective was a necessary addition.

We also agreed that the chapters on Catholic social thought and liberation theology needed updating. The 1986 edition used "Economic Justice for All," a letter written by the United States Bishops Conference articulating how Catholic social teaching applied to economic disparities in the United States and globally. At the time, it was an extremely important document, especially for an American audience. "Economic Justice for All" has not been rejected, but today it is not referenced as it once was. Concurrently, Pope Francis has made noteworthy contributions to the tradition since ascending to the papacy in 2013. Both *Laudato Si'* (2015) and *Fratelli Tutti* (2020) pushed Catholic social teaching to places it had not yet gone. *Laudato Si'* challenged modern society's relationship with technology as well as its lack of meaningful relationship with the integrated global ecology. *Fratelli Tutti* took us to task for the relationships we have come to accept in our human relationships as well. More than anything, Francis's contributions to Catholic social teaching broadened the tradition from considering justice as an economic concern into one of social, environmental, and personal importance.

Similarly, at the writing of the first edition, the world was deep into the Cold War, and attention had been drawn to what was then known as the "third world" (most of what today we would call the *Global*

South)—not American-aligned liberal, capitalist democracies or Soviet-aligned communist bloc countries but the mostly impoverished rest of the world that the two superpowers fought over when resources were at stake or ignored when they were not. In that political environment, conversations on justice focused on questions of international inequality, particularly in the economic arena. Thus, Latin American liberation theology and its emphasis on class struggle had found its way into North American classrooms and media as an important countercultural movement and challenge to dominant views of justice.

Today, however, conversations about justice have shifted in important ways. James Cone and Gustavo Gutiérrez both coined the term *liberation theology* in 1968. In the North American context, especially in the United States, racism proves as significant for justice as does classism. While abolition undermined the official *system* of slavery and the civil rights movement challenged the racist *laws* of Jim Crow, the Black Lives Matter movement brought a new focus on White supremacy and the need to confront the fact that race itself is an unmistakable category for discussions of justice in modern-day America. Thus, we both felt it was necessary in the updated text not only to include but also to centralize Cone and Black liberation theology as a perspective on justice that is both necessary in the conversation and requires reckoning with as a society.

As the categories of justice widen to include race, so, too, have they come (finally) to consider the oppression of women. In the end, we chose Katie Cannon's womanist ethics as our final interlocutor. Working from Black women's experience, Cannon proposes an intersectional approach to justice that raises challenges for all the other views presented in this volume.

One final point: from the outset of this revival project, we felt burdened to find the perfect interlocutor to represent the theory represented in each chapter, and yet the harder we looked, the more we realized this was a fool's errand. In the original introduction, Lebacqz made the point that only one of the interlocutors—John Rawls—had actually set out to write a *theory* of justice. The rest offered important *perspectives* but, in large part, did not offer a comprehensive theory. Ultimately, we concluded that the category we had set for ourselves—theories of justice—was too limiting. We did not change the book title, but we did free ourselves from the burden of finding eight definitive *theories* of justice and eight perfect representatives to speak to those theories. Instead, we began to ask whose *perspective* is necessary to bring into this conversation. With this shift in focus, we were able to settle on the list above.

And so, with those adaptations, we offer our updated version. Once again, this volume is intended as a teaching text, and we offer it with our hope that both teachers and students find value in *Eight Theories of Justice: Perspectives from Philosophical and Theological Ethics*.

Matthew J. Gaudet and Karen Lebacqz, June 2024

Introduction

There may be no more urgent cry today than that for justice—and no more frequent accusation than that of injustice. But what is meant when these terms are used?

OF ELEPHANTS AND JUSTICE

Alasdair MacIntyre suggests that modern moral utterance must be understood as a series of "fragmented survivals" from the past: remnants of former ethical systems survive but without the social cohesion needed to give them force.[1] Cries for justice and accusations of injustice may appear as such fragments.

Justice is thus a bit like the proverbial elephant examined by blindfolded explorers. Each feels a different part—the foot, the ears, the tusks—and consequently, each describes the beast differently: gnarled and tough, thin and supple, smooth and hard. The elephant itself—justice—is not encompassed by any of the individual descriptions. At times, they seem incompatible, yet each contributes something to the definition.[2]

This book is about justice. Eight approaches to justice will be our blindfolded explorers. If MacIntyre's charge is true, then it is to be expected that these fragments will not be easily reconciled. There will be no single way of defining justice and no single theory of justice that satisfies all.

Indeed, the exploration is complicated at the outset because there is precious little agreement as to how the arena of justice is to be characterized and delineated.[3] The theories to be examined here are roughly in the arena of distributive justice, but one of our theorists explicitly rejects distributive justice in favor of the narrower range of commutative justice (justice in exchange). Two others add to distributive justice a notion of social justice, each with a distinctive notion of *social*. Several theories introduce liberation as a key category of justice.

Thus, the views examined here are not theories of distributive justice in a narrow sense. They are simply theories of justice—or, perhaps better, perspectives on justice. Included in their concerns are questions about allocation of goods, powers, and opportunities; about access to decision-making processes; about fundamental respect among people; and about the basic structures of society. They attend to distributive justice in a broad sense: the issue is not simply who gets how much of the pie but also what kind of pie is it to be and who is to decide.[4]

EIGHT FRAGMENTS OF JUSTICE

This book explores only eight of those fragmented survivals of moral systems regarding justice—eight ways of "making *mishpat* the measure" (Isaiah 28:17). There are many other blindfolded explorers who might have served as well. The choice of eight approaches to justice, out of all possible contenders, is not an easy task, and we make no claim that the approaches offered here are the only ones worthy of pursuit.

These eight were chosen as representatives of different schools of thought. Though four of the fragments are forms of philosophical views and four are forms of Christian theology, each offers a distinctive approach to justice. They were also chosen for accessibility: in most cases, the reader may supplement this text with a single accompanying document. Above all, they were chosen in the conviction that each raises fundamental issues for other theories of justice. Each offers a perennial challenge to other contenders.

The Utilitarian Challenge

We begin with a utilitarian challenge. Since the theory of utilitarianism was first given definitive shape more than a century ago, it has been battered and batted around until it bears the scars of age. Nevertheless, appeals to cost-benefit analyses and the near ubiquity of "do the greatest good" logic in contemporary society reveal the deep influences the theory has had on our worldview today. The perennial question "does the end justify the means?" haunts contemporary proponents of justice. The significance of utilitarianism is perhaps best attested by the fact that it provides the foil for other contemporary philosophical theories that will be considered in this volume.

John Stuart Mill's *Utilitarianism* will represent the utilitarian approach to justice here. Mill's exposition lacks the systematic development and meticulous exposition of some later utilitarians, such as Henry Sidgwick or G. E. Moore, but his approach is more readily accessible than some others. It is generally to Mill that contemporary theorists return when they wish to joust with utilitarianism. Thus, Mill's understanding of justice gives us the original challenge and sets the stage for developing a theory of justice.

A Contract Response

One jouster responding to that challenge is John Rawls. No one disputes the importance of Rawls's massive effort, *A Theory of Justice*. This work has dominated philosophical reflections on justice for half a century. There simply is no way to talk about justice today without attending to Rawls's response to the utilitarian challenge. Rawls draws on a contract model to offer a Kantian alternative to utilitarianism. He offers a defense of the liberal democratic state that takes welfare needs seriously.

An Entitlement Alternative

As utilitarianism prompted Rawls to respond, Rawls's influence has also engendered further discussion. Robert Nozick's entitlement view of justice gives voice to the concerns of many libertarians today. Where

Rawls's contract theory would permit government involvement to bring about distributive justice, Nozick sets out to show there is no moral ground for a distributive justice that demands structures of government beyond the minimal state. His *Anarchy, State, and Utopia* has become—rightly or wrongly—the theory undergirding contemporary proponents of private enterprise and minimal government. It offers a clear alternative to both utilitarian theory and Rawls.

A Communitarian Rebuttal

The communitarian gripe with all three philosophers above is that they have overvalued the role of the individual. To Rawls, Nozick, and Mill, but also to those of us living in a society built on their theories, Michael Sandel poses the question, "What has become of the common good?" For Sandel, justice is not a question of principle but of value, and when we exclude community, trust, solidarity, and relationship as measures of value for a life well lived, we have limited our understanding of justice in dangerous ways.

A Catholic Option

For all their differences, the four philosophical theories operate within a common "liberal" tradition emerging on the foundation of the European Enlightenment. They share significant assumptions regarding the role and place of the individual as the bearer of moral value and the use of reason as the grounds for any theory of justice. Although Mill argued that utilitarianism was an expression of the golden rule, and many find Rawls's concern for those who are disadvantaged compatible with Christian sympathies, none of these philosophical theories depends directly on a religious base for its concept of justice. What happens, then, when we turn to Christian tradition?

Here we begin with Catholic tradition and its multifaceted approach to social justice. We have chosen Pope Francis's writings because of their contemporary interest and his efforts to update the tradition in light of the current signs of the times. In many ways, Catholic social teaching finds certain affinities with our philosophers: like Rawls, Francis requires some preferential treatment for those at the bottom of a distribution; he also holds common cause with Sandel's pursuit of the common good and attention to the bonds between individuals. However, for Francis and the Catholic tradition, all claims to justice begin with a fundamental belief in the inviolable dignity of the human person.

A Protestant Stance

Catholic tradition always has its critics from the Protestant side. One who dominated the scene of American Protestantism during much of the twentieth century was Reinhold Niebuhr.[5] For Niebuhr, the foundation of a Christian view is love, but love must always compromise with the realities of conflict in society brought about by human sinfulness. Thus, love and justice stand in paradox and tension and result in a view that came to be known as *Christian realism*.[6]

A Liberation Challenge

In the 1960s, a new and significant challenge emerged in Christian theology. Around the world, in places where oppressed peoples did their own theological reflection, they created various forms of liberation theology.[7] We begin with a brief look at Latin American liberation theology, especially the works of Gustavo Gutiérrez, because of its dominance. In the Latin American context, economic justice loomed large, as it still does today. But in the context of the United States, the long history of racism and its effects on the Black community make a striking reference point for liberation concerns. We have therefore chosen James Cone's contributions to Black liberation theology as the representative for this chapter.[8]

A Womanist Critique

Our final theory is the womanist approach of Katie Geneva Cannon. A brief review of some central contentions of the second wave of feminism sets the stage for Cannon's womanist approach. Although Cannon did not set out to present a theory of justice—indeed, doing so might be inimical to her primary purpose—her mining of Black women's strengths in the face of triple oppression brings a distinctive approach to theories of justice and raises challenges for future work.

OF BLINDFOLDED EXPLORATION

These eight fragments are offered in the conviction that each speaks to something so fundamental that, no matter what its defects, it leaves a permanent legacy. Each figure is chosen partly as the representative of a school of thought but partly also because of the distinctive contribution of that person to their school. Each of these approaches has left, or promises to leave, a lingering mark on our understanding of justice. They may be only fragments, but they are world-shaping fragments.

All theory is part of an ongoing dialogue. Each of these approaches has been controversial. Accompanying the exposition of each theory, therefore, is a sampling of critical commentary. No doubt, the theorists or supporters from their schools would wish to rebut many of the criticisms reported here. Space precludes a full-fledged debate about each theory, and we have resisted the temptation to dispute every point of praise or criticism. Even the most recent of the theories presented here will be revised and surpassed by subsequent reflection by the time this book is in print. Readers are encouraged to explore original sources and to judge for themselves the strengths and weaknesses of each approach.

A few preliminary cautions are in order, however. First, of the eight approaches represented here, only one author—John Rawls—set out explicitly to write a theory of justice. The others had other tasks in mind, and whatever "theory" of justice is culled from their work will remain always a bit foreign to their central purposes. The views presented here are perhaps better understood as windows on justice rather than as theories per se. A window provides a frame and gives a view. It offers perspective. However, it also requires viewing through a glass and entails the inevitable distortions of that glass, not to mention the limitations of the frame.

Indeed, the fragments offered here will reflect the distortions of their social locations. One is from the nineteenth century, several are from nearly half a century ago, and only two have made contributions to this topic in the last ten years. Most did their work with direct reference to the United States, but at least one—Pope Francis—speaks to a global view. Liberationists in particular are a very diverse group, yet here they are represented by one particular and particularly controversial figure. While only one of our interlocutors is a woman, women's voices may be hidden in the background for others.[9] They are a strange group, our blindfolded explorers.

In general, we have said relatively little about their social locations or personal histories. While we recognize that social location makes an enormous difference in ethical thinking, it is our conviction that examination of the thoughts of each interlocutor may reveal important biases and limitations wrought by social location.

Further, theory has a life and an integrity of its own. Thus, our task here is to get inside each theory, to the best of our ability, and then to listen to its critics. We have before us eight descriptions of an elephant—eight proposals for doing *mishpat*, as the Hebrew Scriptures might have it. Perhaps we will find that they are not compatible. Perhaps we will find that they are. Can they speak to each other?

With all the interest in justice today, there has been precious little effort to put philosophical and theological theories into dialogue. Indeed, theological approaches to justice have not received the systematic exposition and exploration of their philosophical counterparts. This volume is but a small step toward a needed exchange in which the gifts, the assumptions, and the limitations of different views can be explored. Perhaps we shall never define the elephant accurately, but we can at least put the descriptions in juxtaposition. Perhaps as we do so, we will get some sense of the nature of the beast or at least of what is needed for further exploration.

NOTES

1 Alasdair C. MacIntyre, *After Virtue* (Notre Dame, IN: University of Notre Dame Press, 1981), 104.

2 The parable of the blind explorers and the elephant has its origins on the Indian subcontinent and finds itself in various forms in the holy texts of Buddhism, Hinduism, Jainism, and Sufism. "Blind Men and An Elephant," last edited August 28, 2024, https://en.wikipedia .org/wiki/Blind_men_and_an_elephant.

3 Joel Feinberg has proposed that traditional classifications of justice—distributive, retributive, and commutative—are not particularly helpful. See "Noncomparative Justice," in *Justice: Selected Readings*, ed. J. Feinberg and Hyman Gross (Belmont, CA: Wadsworth, 1977), 55. His proposal reflects the ambiguities to be encountered in this volume.

4 Explicitly excluded from our study is the arena of retributive justice, yet even here, John Stuart Mill does not separate the distributive from the retributive aspects of justice.

5 Niebuhr's short volume *An Interpretation of Christian Ethics* gives much of the core of his early theory, yet Niebuhr later refused to defend this work. Thus, the reader may wish to consult instead *Moral Man and Immoral Society, The Nature and Destiny of Man*, or D. B. Robertson, ed., *Love and Justice: Selections from the Shorter Writings of Reinhold Niebuhr*.

6 A more Lutheran "two kingdoms" approach is found in Emil Brunner's *Justice and the Social Order* (London: Lutterworth, 1945), and, recently, Nicholas Wolsterstorff is known for several books on justice: *Until Justice and Peace Embrace* (Grand Rapids, MI: Eerdmans, 1983), *Justice in Love* (Grand Rapids, MI: Eerdmans, 2011), *Journey toward Justice* (Grand Rapids, MI: Baker Academic, 2013). But it is Niebuhr who is strongly associated with the view called *Christian realism*, and that is why he appears here.

7 Liberation theology is often the result of groups of people working together for liberation. Thus, as Gustavo Gutierrez puts it, "it makes little difference whose name appears on articles and books." See *The Power of the Poor in History* (Maryknoll, NY: Orbis, 1983), 204.

8 In the original *Six Theories of Justice,* Karen Lebacqz chose Jose Porfirio Miranda's *Marx and the Bible* because of its explicit use of Scripture as a base for revealing the meaning of justice. However, in our American context, the firestorm created by Cone's work seems to be the most important locus for examination.

9 John Stuart Mill often attributed his inspiration to his wife, Harriet Taylor. Much contemporary liberation theology is done by women.

CHAPTER ONE

The Utilitarian Challenge

John Stuart Mill

Classical utilitarianism took root in the latter half of the nineteenth century and the early part of the twentieth. Since its inception, it has been championed successively by Jeremy Bentham, James Mill, John Stuart Mill, Henry Sidgwick, G. E. Moore, and Peter Singer. Most recently, utilitarian themes have emerged again under the branding of "effective altruism," a movement aimed at making the most "effective" choices possible.[1]

Despite its sustained influence over the years, utilitarianism in its purest form has often not been well defended. J. J. C. Smart advocated one form of utilitarianism.[2] Richard Brandt argued that another would be the most defensible form, though he did not claim to advocate it himself.[3] Nicholas Rescher proposed what he called a "chastened" utilitarianism, but his proposal for a principle of justice "distinct from" and "coequal to" utility would place him outside the realm of the classical utilitarians, for whom justice was subordinate to utility.[4]

What cannot be denied, however, is the tremendous influence the theory has had on how society has functioned for decades and continues to function today. Utilitarianism has shaped everything from classical economics to contemporary appeals to cost-benefit analysis. John Rawls summarizes it best: "During much of modern moral philosophy the predominant systematic theory has been some form of utilitarianism."[5] For our purposes in approaching theories of justice, we will use the classical approach defended by John Stuart Mill in *Utilitarianism*. Mill's exposition is of sufficient clarity and persuasiveness to set the stage for the theories of justice that dominate the landscape today.[6]

UTILITY

The basic idea of utilitarianism is simple: the right thing to do is what produces the most good. Since this is in fact the way many people approach ethical decisions, it is easy to see why the theory has had such appeal. But it deserves more detailed scrutiny.

A summary statement of the utilitarian principle is provided by Mill: "Utility or the Greatest Happiness Principle holds that actions are right in proportion as they tend to promote happiness; wrong as they tend to produce the reverse of happiness. By happiness is intended pleasure and the absence of pain."[7] Into this short statement are packed two crucial assumptions that lay the groundwork for a discussion of justice from a utilitarian perspective.

First, the goal of life is happiness. Both Mill and Jeremy Bentham before him argue this.[8] How do we know this? Bentham offers little "proof" of the assumption that happiness is the goal of life. He rests on the claim that "by the natural constitution of the human frame" we embrace these ends, and he asserts that fundamental principles are not susceptible to direct proof.[9] Mill agrees that "questions of ultimate ends are not amenable to direct proof," but he offers as argument the fact that people universally *do* desire happiness.[10] Thus, the end or goal of human life is taken to be happiness, and we know this because people do desire happiness and because doing so appears to be "natural" to us.

But what is happiness? Bentham defined it in terms of pleasure and the absence of pain. Mill expands on this by arguing explicitly for a recognition of different *kinds* of pleasure and pain. The pleasures of the intellect for Mill are not simply circumstantially more "useful" than those of the flesh but are intrinsically superior.[11] Hence, a distinction arose among utilitarians between those who consider happiness to consist primarily in pleasure and pain and those who add other goals or ends (truth, beauty). These two schools were traditionally called *hedonistic* and *ideal* utilitarianism, respectively.[12] Today, some point to a broader *pluralistic* utilitarianism describing the application of the "greatest good for the greatest number" logic across many measures of "good."[13] Increased life expectancy, rising gross domestic product, decreased abject poverty, and increasing education rates are just a few commonly touted such "goods."[14]

Second, the "rightness" of acts is determined by their contributions to happiness. This makes utilitarianism a form of teleology: the end *(telos)* determines what is right. The "right" is determined by calculating the amount of good to be produced. Thus, the "good" is prior to the "right," and the right is dependent on it.[15] As Mill puts it, actions are right in proportion as they tend to promote happiness.

But this formulation raises a question: Must the results of *each action* be calculated to determine its overall utility and therefore to decide whether it is right? At first glance, this appears to be Bentham's view. In his attempt to render a scientific basis for morality, Bentham offered a method for taking "an exact account" of the tendency of any act: "Proceed as follows. Begin with any one person of those whose interests seem most immediately to be affected by it: and take an account, 1. Of the value of each distinguishable *pleasure*. . . . 2. Of the value of *pain*. . . . 5. Sum up all the values of all the *pleasures* on the one side, and those of all the *pains* on the other. . . . 6. Take an account of the *number* of persons whose interests appear to be concerned; and repeat the above process with respect to each. . . . Take the *balance*."[16] Such a description makes it appear that every act must be subjected to a lengthy and time-consuming calculus. In the literature on utilitarianism, this approach of judging the utility of each act is called "extreme" or "act" utilitarianism.[17]

However, Bentham made it clear that he did not expect such a procedure to be "strictly pursued previously to every moral judgment."[18] Mill moves even a step further, proposing that history teaches us the "tendencies of actions" and that these historical lessons give rise to "corollaries from the principle of utility."[19] One does *not*, therefore, "endeavor to test each individual action directly by the first principle" of utility.[20] Rather, the individual act is right if it conforms to a "secondary principle" (or rule) that has been shown to have utility overall. Taking note of this argument, J. O. Urmson proposes that Mill is best classified as a "restricted" or "rule" utilitarian.[21] Most commentators have followed Urmson's lead, and the distinction between act and rule utilitarianism has become an arena for much debate and discussion.

In summary, the basic idea of utilitarianism is that actions are determined to be right or wrong depending on whether they promote happiness or good. This idea has striking implications when we turn to considerations of justice.

UTILITY AND JUSTICE

Traditional notions of justice appear to be flouted by a theory that claims the "right" act is whatever maximizes the good. Individual rights or claims would be overridden by consideration of the happiness of others. For example, if the bloodshed of a threatened race riot could be averted by framing and lynching an innocent person, it seems that the utilitarian would have to say it is "right" to do so.[22] So long as the greater good required it, all individual rights and claims would be ignored. Because of such apparent implications of utilitarian theory, issues of justice have consistently been a stumbling block for utilitarians.

Both Bentham and Mill recognized this. Indeed, Bentham's overriding concern was to render the penal system fairer and to avoid injustice in the retributive sphere.[23] We focus here on Mill's discussion of the relation between utility and distributive justice.

Mill acknowledges the strength of the feelings people have about justice and the indignation felt at instances of injustice, such as undue punishment. This very strength of feeling makes it difficult for people to see justice as a part of utility.[24] Mill therefore sets about to determine whether justice is *sui generis* or whether it is a part of utility. He concludes that it is not a separate principle arising independently but is a part of utility: "I dispute the pretensions of any theory which sets up an imaginary standard of justice not grounded on utility."[25] In so doing,

Mill follows closely in the footsteps of David Hume, whose defense of the utilitarian basis of justice is worth reviewing.

No one doubts that justice is useful to society, asserts Hume. The question is whether public utility is the *sole* origin of justice.[26] Hume attempts to show that it is by demonstrating that rules of justice do not arise in circumstances where they would not be useful. In situations of extreme deprivation, in circumstances characterized primarily by benevolence, in places where there is such an overabundance that all needs can be met without dispute, rules of justice would not be useful and therefore do not arise. The use and tendency of the virtue of justice, therefore, are "to procure happiness and security, by preserving order in society."[27] Thus, any rules of justice will depend on the particular state or condition in which people find themselves. All such rules "owe their origin and existence to that *utility*, which results to the public from their strict and regular observance."[28]

Hume does not offer a direct definition of justice. However, from his discussion, it can be seen that justice has to do with "separating" and respecting claims about private property.[29] It is where people have conflicting claims over possession in circumstances of moderate scarcity that issues of distributive justice arise. This notion of justice as dealing with *conflicting claims regarding possessions* in *circumstances of scarcity* becomes a pervasive theme throughout modern discussions.

Mill takes over Hume's basic contention that justice does not arise from a "simple, original instinct in the human breast" but arises solely out of its necessity to the support of society.[30] Justice, according to Mill, is not only a function of utility but also a "paramount obligation" due to the utility a just system engenders.[31]

Mill's path to this conclusion has three parts. First, he enumerates instances of injustice and searches for a common thread among them. Second, he attempts to discern why there is a particularly strong *feeling* about justice and whether this feeling is grounded in utility. Third, he reviews several controversial cases to show that appeals to justice will not resolve the controversy and that only calculations of utility will do so.

Mill finds six common circumstances generally agreed to be unjust: (1) depriving people of things to which they have a *legal* right, (2) depriving them of things to which they have a *moral* right, (3) people not obtaining what they *deserve*—good to those who do right and evil to those who do wrong, (4) *breaking faith* with people, (5) being *partial* (i.e., showing favor where favor does not apply), and (6) treating people *unequally*.[32]

These circumstances of injustice seem quite diverse. What is it that unifies them? The notion of legal restraint seems to run through them all, but Mill notes that this notion applies to all of morality: "duty is a thing which may be exacted from a person."[33] What, then, distinguishes justice from other kinds of duty or other aspects of morality?

To answer this question, Mill adopts Immanuel Kant's distinction between duties of perfect obligation and duties of imperfect obligation. Duties of perfect obligation generate *rights* on the part of the recipient: if I have a duty not to harm you, you have a right not to be harmed by me. Duties of imperfect obligation, on the other hand, do not give rise to corresponding rights: I have a duty to do good, but you have no "right" that I do good for you. Mill suggests that all those duties of perfect obligation that give rise to rights are the arena of justice: "Justice implies something which it is not only right to do, and wrong not to do, but which some individual person can claim from us as his moral right."[34] What distinguishes justice, then, is the notion of rights or claims. Here, Mill echoes Hume, though he does not restrict claims to the arena of property.

Whence, then, comes the special *feeling* that attaches to justice—or that is evoked by instances of injustice? According to Mill, the "sentiment of justice" is "the animal desire to repel or retaliate a hurt or damage" to oneself or to others.[35] In itself, there is nothing moral in this feeling. However, when it is subordinated to "the social sympathies" so that the desire for vengeance becomes a desire that those who infringe rules of justice should be punished, then it becomes a moral feeling. In short, behind justice lies our interest in security, "the most vital of all interests."[36] The rules of justice are therefore supported by the utility of preserving security. When one asks *why* society should defend my rights, the answer lies in the general interest of security. Justice is therefore grounded in utility.

Moreover, Mill suggests that the most intense feelings are raised around certain types of injustice, to wit, "acts of wrongful aggression or wrongful exercise of power over someone" and then acts of "wrongfully withholding from him something which is his due."[37] Such wrongful withholding includes the withholding of good. Thus, such common standards of justice as "good for good and evil for evil" are easily encompassed in the utilitarian perspective. And if each is to get what is deserved, then a concept of equal treatment follows: "It necessarily follows that society should treat all equally well who have deserved equally well of *it*. . . . This is the highest abstract standard of social and distributive justice."[38] Strong feelings and commonly accepted standards of justice are therefore explained by the utilitarian view.

Indeed, the utilitarian view will not only explain accepted standards but also help adjudicate among them. Mill offers three examples of social conflict where the requirements of justice are under dispute and generally accepted standards cannot settle the claims. One of these is the question of whether remuneration should be based on contribution or effort. Appealing to justice will not solve the issue, for some think justice requires reward for contribution, and others think it requires reward for effort. How, then, do we decide what justice really requires? "From these confusions there is no other mode of extrication than the utilitarian."[39] Justice is ultimately dependent on utility because conflicts in the common rules of justice can be adjudicated only by reference to utility.

Hence, Mill concludes, "Justice is a name for certain classes of moral rules which concern the essentials of human well-being more nearly, and are therefore of more absolute obligation, than any other rules for the guidance of life; and the notion which we have found to be of the essence of the idea of justice—that of a right residing in an individual—implies and testifies to this more binding obligation."[40]

REVIEW

Mill's approach to justice rests on an analysis of the commonsense and moral sensitivities of his day. He begins with those things considered unjust in his own society, and he presumes universal verity for those considerations. His focus is on actions, not on systems or structures per se. His examples are largely at the microlevel; no clear distinctions are made between interpersonal injustices and larger social injustices. He accepts an understanding of justice as dealing with personal claims or rights and attempts to undergird those claims with a utilitarian argument.

Hence, for Mill, there can be no theory of justice separate from the demands of utility. *Justice* is the term given to those rules that protect claims considered essential to the well-being of society—claims to have promises kept, to be treated equally, and so forth. But those claims are subject to the dictates of a utilitarian calculus; they can be overridden when the "greater good" demands it. Similarly, any conflicts among the rules of justice that protect those claims are also subject to the dictates of a utilitarian calculus and can be overridden. Justice depends on utility and does not contradict utility.

The essential features of justice in the utilitarian scheme are these: It acknowledges the existence of individual *rights* that are to be supported by society.[41] It permits—indeed, for Mill, it requires—*rules* determined to be for the good of society to ensure compliance with certain stringent obligations and to protect individual rights. It can incorporate notions of *equal treatment* and *desert*. But, most important, justice is not *sui generis* but is dependent on social *utility* for its foundation. Hence, all rules of justice, including equality, can bow to the demands of utility: "Each person maintains that equality is the dictate of justice, except where he thinks that expediency requires inequality."[42] Whatever does the greatest overall good will be "just."

CRITIQUE

Since the time of Mill's defense of the relation between utility and justice, utilitarian theory has undergone considerable controversy and revision. We cannot review all that development here. We will confine our critique to those aspects of utilitarianism that raise questions from the perspective of a concern for justice. Does utilitarianism give an adequate account of justice, or does it violate concepts of justice?

The problems for the act utilitarian are legion. If we are to judge the "right" thing to do in each instance by calculating what will do the most good overall, then there are numerous circumstances in which the "right" act will violate accepted standards of justice. As W. D. Ross pointed out, and others have elaborated, act utilitarianism appears to require that we break a promise or even harm someone any time more "good" could be accomplished by doing so.[43] This, suggests Ross, is absurd. It clearly violates our felt sense of what is right to do: "Do we really think that the production of the slightest balance of good, no matter who will enjoy it, by the breach of a promise frees us from the obligation to keep our promise?"[44]

In a similar vein, John Rawls argues that classical utilitarianism violates the demands of justice by permitting losses to some to be compensated by gains to others: "It may be expedient but it is not just that some should have less in order that others may prosper."[45] Utilitarianism appears not to respect differences among persons.[46]

Others have also argued that utilitarianism ignores the personal character of duty. Ross charges that "if the only duty is to produce the maximum of good, the question who is to have the good—whether it is myself, or my benefactor, or a person to whom we have made a promise— should make no difference."[47] But, of course, it does make a difference.

Indeed, Richard Brandt suggests that the act utilitarian must face the paradox of having to spend her income on charity rather than on her family if it will do more good. Similarly, if she has promised to pay the child next door twenty-five dollars for mowing the lawn, she must renege on the promise if she could do more good by giving the twenty-five dollars to charity. Even accounting for the child's sense of loss, anger, and disillusionment, there are surely circumstances in which the greater good would be done by breaking the promise. Indeed, act utilitarian theory would appear to go so far as to require that she kill her elderly grandfather if she can prevent his suffering and bring about great good for those who would inherit his estate.[48] As Alan Donagan charges, "Act-utilitarianism . . . outrages moral intuition at almost every turn."[49]

Since Mill himself declared that breaking faith or promises is one of the recognized instances of injustice, it is quite clear that he would not have intended utilitarianism to countenance such possibilities. This suggests that rule utilitarianism may have significant advantages over act utilitarianism when it comes to justice. For the rule utilitarian, rules are established on grounds of their overall utility. Then the "rightness" of each act is assessed by seeing whether it concurs with a rule, not by assessing the consequences of the act per se. The rule utilitarian can permit such secondary rules as "keep promises," or "do not kill," or "provide for your family." Thus, rule utilitarianism avoids some of the obvious problems that act utilitarianism encounters in the arena of justice.

Yet rule utilitarianism is not without its difficulties. First, how are "rules" to be understood? Bentham and Mill made no distinctions at all between act and rule utilitarianism; they simply referred to tendencies of acts.[50] Mill clearly supported secondary rules to be derived from the great principle of utility. Yet it is not clear just what *sort* of rules he had in mind, nor what sort are most defensible. Some think that his rules were merely rules of thumb—generalizations from experience that would be helpful in the circumstances but could be overridden at any time by the direct application of the primary principle of utility. Thus, "keep promises" would be a helpful rule of thumb but would not necessarily tell us whether to keep a specific promise. A rule utilitarianism based on rules of thumb easily collapses into act utilitarianism since rules are always subject to being overridden by the immediate application of the principle of utility.

However, as John Rawls points out in a celebrated essay, "Two Concepts of Rules," this is only one way to understand how rules might function in a utilitarian approach.[51] Not all rules are "summary rules" that can be reconsidered at any moment. Some rules are "practice" rules: they define a practice, such that the practice does not exist apart from its rules. Games such as baseball are of this sort—the game does not exist apart from the rules that define it. Rawls argues that promising is a practice. Rules about promising, therefore, are not liable to be set aside at any moment, "for unless there were already the understanding that one keeps one's promises as part of the practice itself, there couldn't have been any cases of promising."[52] That is, promises could not exist apart from the rules that say they are to be kept; that is part of the meaning of a promise.[53]

Now, if utilitarian rules are of this "practice" sort, then they will not be liable to being overridden in the instance. At first glance, this would appear to get rule utilitarianism out of the dilemmas of act utilitarianism. However, the attempt is not altogether successful. As David Lyons notes, the practice must be justified by its utility. But suppose there is an instance within the practice where more utility would seem to be achieved by breaking the rules of the practice (e.g., by breaking a promise). Lyons suggests that each such case implies that there is a "subclass" within the practice that ought to be permitted as an exception to it. In short, the practice itself may not yield as much utility as would a different definition of the practice that permitted certain exceptions. But then this means that the practice cannot be justified on grounds of utility since in fact it does not yield as much utility as another, similar practice would. Hence, every exception to the practice threatens to undermine the utilitarian justification for the practice itself.[54]

Further, there is always the possibility that secondary principles, even "practice" rules, can conflict with each other. What is one to do, then? For example, in the arena of distributive justice, rewarding people for *effort* will tend toward greater utility by providing incentives. Yet rewarding for *contribution* will avert resentment and thus encourage industry. It is entirely possible, then, that a rule utilitarian system will produce two subsidiary rules, one rewarding for effort and the other for contribution. What is the rule utilitarian to do when these conflict?

In such a circumstance, either there must be additional priority rules for determining what to do in cases of conflicts among rules, or the rule utilitarian falls back on an act utilitarian escape: do whatever will produce the most good in *this* circumstance. In the first instance, rule utilitarianism becomes absurdly burdened with subsidiary rules and becomes ultimately impossible to learn and hence to follow.[55] This suggests that the obvious secondary rule is the utilitarian principle itself: when rules conflict, do whatever would produce the most good in the circumstances. This appears to be the solution Mill proposed in his case about conflicting rules of justice in remuneration. But then even "practice" rule utilitarianism seems ultimately to collapse into act utilitarianism, at least in cases of conflicting rules.[56] It may be for that reason that H. J. McCloskey calls rule utilitarianism a "half-hearted" utilitarianism.[57]

Moreover, critics charge that some rules good for society would require acts generally not considered to be obligatory or required by justice. For instance, it might promote utility to have a rule that all members of society should put aside a small portion of their income to support those who have no desire to work for their living.[58] Yet, generally, such acts would be considered acts of "beneficence" rather than of "justice"; they would fit Kant's category (adopted by Mill) of "imperfect" rather than "perfect" obligation. How does utilitarianism propose to draw the line between justice and beneficence, obligation and supererogation?[59]

Perhaps even more fundamental than these criticisms are the possible conflicts within the utilitarian formula itself. Mill was quite clear that the utilitarian standard was not the agent's own happiness but "the greatest amount of happiness altogether."[60] The calculator of happiness is to be "strictly impartial" between his own happiness and that of others.[61] Indeed, the principle of utility "is a mere form of words without rational signification unless one person's happiness . . . is counted for exactly as much as another's."[62]

But this then gives rise to a problem: Is it the greatest *good* that is to be done or the greatest good *for the greatest number*? Classical utilitarians have used both formulae, seemingly without regard to the possible conflicts between them. But conflicts there are, as Nicholas Rescher pointedly shows. Take the following two distribution schemes:

	Scheme I			Scheme II	
A receives	8 units		A receives	4 units	
B	1		B	4	
C	1		C	1	

Scheme I does the "greatest good" overall, but Scheme II does the "greatest good for the greatest number." Which is required by the utilitarian formula? Are we to honor the greater number or the overall maximum utility?[63]

The problem is seen in sharp relief when we consider the possibility that we might increase *overall* utility or happiness simply by increasing the number of people on earth. Yet the *average* happiness of each might be lowered considerably as the population rose.[64] For instance, a society consisting of ten people with two units of happiness each has a total utility of twenty units, whereas a society consisting of forty people with one unit of happiness each has a total utility of forty units. Does the utilitarian formula require that we add to the population so as to increase overall utility even at the cost of average happiness?[65]

Clearly, this is not what is intended, and some have proposed that the maximum overall utility should be interpreted precisely in terms of *average* utility. To do so, it appears to avoid some problems encountered by the classical utilitarian formula.[66]

But the average utility has its problems. While it seems to work well in the previous example, consider the following example:

	Scheme I			**Scheme II**
A receives	6 units		A receives	5 units
B	6		B	5
C	6		C	5
D	1		D	4
E	1		E	1

Our intuitive sense is that scheme II is more just. But taking average utility gives no way to choose between them since the average utility in each case is four units.

With yet another slight modification, average utility can be shown to be counterintuitive:

	Scheme I			**Scheme II**
A receives	6 units		A receives	4 units
B	6		B	4
C	6		C	4
D	1		D	3
E	1		E	3

Again, scheme II seems the more just. Yet it yields an average utility of only 3.6 units compared to an average utility of 4 units in scheme I. Modifying utilitarianism to focus on average utility does not seem to solve the problem of violations of our intuitive sense of justice. Concern for the average happiness does not solve the problem of gaps between those at the top and those at the bottom.

Both classical and average utility therefore appear to leave open the possibility that some will be sacrificed for the sake of others. The possibility that some might be deprived in order that others might experience great happiness "offends our sense of justice," declares Rescher.[67] Hence, he proposes that we need some sort of utility floor to ensure that none is pushed below the point of survival or minimal utility in order that others may gain.

But even when all are at or above a utility floor, the utilitarian formula appears to countenance serious inequities. Take, for example, the following two schemes, where one unit is the utility floor:

	Scheme I		**Scheme II**	
A receives	2 units		A receives	1 unit
B	2		B	1
C	3		C	6
D	3		D	6
E	3		E	6

From the perspectives of both overall utility and the greatest good for the greatest number, scheme II is clearly superior. Yet unless we have some reason to think that C, D, and E *ought* to get such disproportionately large shares, our instincts tell us that scheme I is more just.[68] Whether given as the greatest good or as the greatest good for the greatest number, therefore, utilitarianism appears to provide no guarantees against grossly inequitable distributions.

This takes us to what Rescher calls the "decisive and fatal" objection to the principle of utility, taken alone, as a standard for justice.[69] In the paragraph above, we raised the question of whether there might be some reason to think that persons C, D, and E "ought" to receive more than persons A and B. This notion of ought or desert is fundamental to justice and appears to be ignored by the utilitarian approach.

If all the potential recipients of a distribution scheme are equally deserving, then the utilitarian approach of counting up happinesses and unhappinesses and maximizing the total good may be the most just way to deal with the situation. But, as Rescher argues, "human actions . . . are inherently claim-modifying; they . . . engender merit and demerit."[70] Real people in a real world act, and as they act, they create claims (merit or demerit) for themselves—or possibly claims on the part of others (e.g., by making a promise). To ignore such claims is to deny justice in a very fundamental sense.

Indeed, to maximize happiness for five bad people while three good people go unhappy seems to some the very antithesis of justice. As Ross puts it, "Suppose that *A* is a very good and *B* a very bad man, should I then . . . think it self-evidently right to produce 1001 units of good for *B* rather than 1000 for *A*? Surely not. I should be sensible of a *prima facie* duty of justice, i.e., of producing a distribution of goods in proportion to merit, which is not outweighed by such a slight disparity in the total goods to be produced."[71]

One need not accept the thesis that justice means distribution *solely* in terms of virtue in order to give virtue and vice some "claim" in the distribution process. Since the time of Aristotle, philosophers have generally accepted that justice requires, at least to some extent, distribution in accord with virtue or moral excellence. Maximizing happiness does not always seem good in itself.[72]

Thus, Rescher argues the strong thesis that "distributive justice consists in the treatment of people *according to their legitimate claims*" and concludes that "a doctrine of distribution that is not predicated upon a judicious accommodation of claims is not a theory of distributive justice."[73]

Critics of utilitarianism do not agree on the range of legitimate claims.[74] Rescher finds seven such claims that have held an honored place in history. One of these is indeed the utilitarian standard of distributing in accord with what is in the public interest or for the common good.

However, there are six additional claims—need, contribution, effort, ability, the market values of supply and demand, and equality.[75] Our purpose here is not to explore or defend all of these claims but merely to suggest that if justice can be shown to require attention to any one of them outside the utilitarian canon, and if utilitarianism can be shown not to account adequately for that one, then utility alone does not suffice to give justice.

Mill would have responded to such a charge that utilitarianism is here misunderstood. As noted above, the principle of utility permits secondary principles—indeed, for Mill, it requires them. Among these will be such principles as "evil for evil" and "good for good." Thus, notions of desert appear to be handled by a rule utilitarian scheme. Mill can simply argue that distributions ignoring claims would frustrate normal expectations and therefore undermine society.[76] In short, what is unjust cannot be truly useful or happiness-maximizing, though it may appear so at first glance.

Putting aside the general objections to rule utilitarianism noted above, does such a rule utilitarian approach solve the difficulty? Following Rescher and other critics, we think not. First, one cannot show that a recognition of claims would *always* be required as a component of utility. The rule utilitarian must be willing to permit the possibility that a utilitarian system of rules would *not* incorporate some of the claims enumerated above. Second, to say that such claims arise because they are useful and then to say that utility requires that they be part of justice is circular reasoning. If there is no standard of justice independent of utility, why should such "normal expectations" arise in the first place?[77]

Then there is the difficult issue of how the utility of frustrating such normal expectations is to be judged. Indeed, a problem common to both act and rule utilitarianism is how the *value* of different goods and evils is to be assessed.[78] Utilitarianism requires not only predictions of the future, which are notoriously inaccurate, but also some way to measure different values—or happinesses—against each other: "The point of the concept of *utility* is to quantify diverse sorts of personal happiness."[79]

But some goods seem incommensurable with others. How does one weigh the harm of the disappointment experienced by the child for whom a promise is broken against the good done by giving food for subsistence to a poor family? For his part, Bentham's utilitarianism tried to avoid this problem by reducing everything to units of pleasure (hedons) and pain (dolors).[80] Mill's hierarchy of pleasures purposefully eliminates this simplicity from utilitarianism. The problem of incommensurability is further exacerbated as even more measures of good are added to pluralistic utilitarianism.

Mill argues that when comparing the value of different pleasures, the individual who has experienced both will know from experience which is greater: "It is better to be a human being dissatisfied than a pig satisfied; better to be Socrates dissatisfied than a fool satisfied. And if the fool, or the pig, are of a different opinion, it is because they only know their own side of the question."[81] But in this assertion, Mill does not recognize the cultural limitations of the value judgments incorporated into utilitarian assertions. For example, Sidgwick argues *against* the notion that those who are rich should distribute their superfluous wealth among those who are poor on the grounds that "the happiness of all is on the whole most promoted by maintaining, in adults generally (except married women), the expectation that each will be thrown on his own resources for the supply of his own wants."[82] In an ethical system where the right depends on calculations of the good, those calculations are always subject to cultural limitations.

Finally, the utilitarian approach, which focuses so exclusively on the *results* of distribution, appears to neglect another important aspect of justice: the *procedures* for distribution.[83] To be sure, a rule utilitarian is likely to accept equal opportunity or openness of positions or some other procedural safeguards as part of the subsidiary rules of justice justified by the principle of utility.[84] However, as noted above, such equalities are always vulnerable to the greater utility of inequality of access or opportunity: "All persons are deemed to have a *right* to equality of treatment, except when some recognized social expediency requires the reverse."[85]

ASSESSMENT

In spite of all these criticisms and objections, "the utilitarian theory of distribution is impressive."[86] As Brandt notes, the kinds of things that emerge as relevant in a utilitarian approach really *are* relevant to issues of justice. So it would not be fair to leave the utilitarians without indicating some of the strengths of utilitarian concerns.[87]

Those strengths appear to lie precisely at the point where a narrow calculus of justice in terms of what is "due" to persons will actually limit rather than enhance their life chances. Many authors distinguish between a narrow and a wider sense of justice (or between *justice* and *fairness* or some other cognate terms). Justice in the narrow sense deals with claims, merit, and distribution in accord with what is "due" to persons. It focuses almost exclusively on the allocation aspect of distributive justice: who is to receive what.

But a theory of distributive justice that focuses exclusively on the *allocation* of goods and neglects the link between *production* and allocation makes a serious mistake. Consider, for example, the following two schemes:

Scheme I		Scheme II	
A receives	3 units	A receives	5 units
B	3	B	5
C	3	C	6

Assuming the parties have equal claims, from the perspective of distributive justice, narrowly conceived, the first scheme is more just. All parties have received equally, in accord with their claims.

But surely they might prefer the second scheme, in which goods are not distributed equally, but everyone receives a larger share. If an unequal distribution of goods (e.g., through special incentives) creates more good for all, then it seems at least better, if not more just, in the narrow sense. What is available to be distributed can be affected by the pattern of distribution itself: by permitting some to have more than others even when their claims may be equal, incentives can be created so that more goods are produced and the life chances of all are enhanced.

This is precisely the strength of classical utilitarianism, which saw that justice in a narrow sense of the exact honoring of claims might be sacrificed for utility in the sense of greater happiness for all. As Rescher puts it, "Justice in its fullest expression requires that account be taken also of the common good."[88] What seems unjust in a narrow sense may still be just in the wider sense.[89] Thus, even such a staunch defender of claims as Rescher finds some justification for allocations of goods based not on claims but on social utility.

Indeed, several authors conclude that justice in its broadest sense requires attention both to fairness in the narrower sense and to utility. Brandt notes that systems that distribute income most equally generally do not provide the most incentive for production and hence the most chance for increasing the goods available to all. He therefore concludes that both equality and utility appear to be required for justice.[90] Rescher also gives utility a place in a larger understanding of justice: "Our thesis is that justice (in the narrow sense) and the general good of utilitarianism must be *coordinated* with one another, and that just this constitutes justice in its wider sense."[91]

While classical utilitarianism may not always provide for our best understanding of justice in the narrower sense, it adds an important dimension to any full theory of justice. It therefore raises a serious challenge and sets an important agenda for all who would attempt a theory of justice. It is precisely that agenda that is addressed by John Rawls.

NOTES

1 Effective altruism is the view that humans need to be selective about how they spend their limited time and resources; hence, they should use data to decide how to do the most good, whether choosing a charitable donation or a career.

2 J. J. C. Smart, "Extreme and Restricted Utilitarianism," in *Contemporary Utilitarianism*, ed. Michael D. Bayles (New York: Doubleday, 1968), 99–141.

3 Richard B. Brandt, "Toward a Credible Form of Utilitarianism," in Bayles, *Contemporary Utilitarianism*, 143–186.

4　Nicholas Rescher, *Distributive Justice: A Constructive Critique of the Utilitarian Theory of Distribution* (Indianapolis: Bobbs-Merrill, 1966), x.

5　John Rawls, *A Theory of Justice* (Cambridge, MA: Harvard University Press, 1971), preface.

6　John Stuart Mill, *Utilitarianism* (New York: Bobbs-Merrill, 1957).

7　Mill, *Utilitarianism*, 10.

8　For Jeremy Bentham's argument, see *An Introduction to the Principles of Morals and Legislation*, ed. J. H. Burns and H. L. A. Hart (London: Methuen, 1982), 11–12.

9　Bentham, *An Introduction*, 13.

10　Mill, *Utilitarianism*, 7 and 48. However, Henry Sidgwick later argued that this is not a "proof" of utilitarianism; he drew his defense of the theory largely on the basis of its coherence with and ability to systematize the maxims of "common sense." See *The Methods of Ethics* (London: Macmillan, 1962), 419–420.

11　Mill, *Utilitarianism*, 12.

12　See David Lyons, *Forms and Limits of Utilitarianism* (Oxford: Clarendon, 1965), 9. W. D. Ross in *The Right and the Good* (Oxford: Clarendon, 1930), 17, argues that "ideal" utilitarianism is logically the more basic of the two.

13　See "Consequentialism." In *Stanford Encyclopedia of Philosophy*, accessed August 26, 2024, https://plato.stanford.edu/entries/consequentialism/.

14　While such measures have been used by governments for years, recently they have also been urged by the "effective altruism" movement. Effective altruists seem to seek any measure that is intuitively considered "good." They make the point that "we need to prioritize between different ways to improve the world," but how priorities are set and incommensurate goods are compared and weighed is left to a vague notion of "expected value" that does not adequately deal with the question. (Max Dalton, "The Effectiveness Mindset," July 1, 2022, https://forum.effectivealtruism.org/posts/5nkeh7LWFYQ9YGdLS/the -effectiveness-mindset.)

15　Teleology is contrasted with deontology, in which the right is prior to the good. The theory of John Rawls, to be considered in the next chapter, is a form of deontology.

16　Bentham, *An Introduction*, 39–40.

17　See Smart, "Extreme and Restricted Utilitarianism."

18　Bentham, *An Introduction*, 40.

19　Mill, *Utilitarianism*, 30–31.

20　Mill, *Utilitarianism*, 31.

21　J. O. Urmson, "The Interpretation of the Moral Philosophy of J. S. Mill," in Bayles, *Contemporary Utilitarianism*.

22　H. J. McCloskey, "A Non-Utilitarian Approach to Punishment," in Bayles, *Contemporary Utilitarianism*, 239–259, argues that the act-utilitarian is committed to such a position. However, T. L. S. Sprigge, "A Utilitarian

Reply to Dr. McCloskey," in Bayles, *Contemporary Utilitarianism*, 261–269, defends utilitarianism against the charge.

23 Bentham, *An Introduction*, 1. While Bentham notes that "the business of government is to promote the happiness of the society, by punishing and rewarding," his exclusive interest in punishment takes him away from the arena of reward, which is more the arena of distributive justice.

24 Mill, *Utilitarianism*, 53.

25 Mill, *Utilitarianism*, 73.

26 David Hume, "Of Justice" (section 3 of *An Enquiry Concerning the Principles of Morals*, first published in 1751), reprinted in J. Feinberg and H. Gross, *Justice: Selected Readings* (Belmont, CA: Wadsworth, 1977), 75.

27 Hume, "Of Justice," 76. Note that Hume deals with justice not as a set of principles for distribution but as a *virtue*: "the cautious, jealous virtue of justice" (75).

28 Hume, "Of Justice," 77. Sidgwick criticizes Hume at this point, arguing that what Hume calls "justice" is really nothing but "order" (*The Methods of Ethics*, 440). Rawls argues that Hume is not a true utilitarian since what he calls "utility" really amounts to a form of common good rather than a strict utilitarian calculus in which the good of some compensates for losses to others (*A Theory of Justice*, §6).

29 Hume, "Of Justice," 78, declares that it is "requisite, for the peace and interest of society, that men's possessions should be separated." Elsewhere, he speaks of establishing rules for property "which are, on the whole, most *useful* and *beneficial*" (79).

30 Hume, "Of Justice," 81–82.

31 Mill, *Utilitarianism*, 78.

32 Mill, *Utilitarianism*, 54–57.

33 Mill, *Utilitarianism*, 60.

34 Mill, *Utilitarianism*, 62.

35 Mill, *Utilitarianism*, 65. It is interesting to note here that Sidgwick takes almost exactly the opposite approach. He suggests that justice arises from the "natural impulse to requite benefits," focusing on reward instead of punishment or vengeance as the foundation of justice. Indeed, Sidgwick's approach leads him to suggest that the real foundation for justice is gratitude. See *The Methods of Ethics*, bk. 3, chap. 5, *Justice* (New York: Dover, 1966), 279.

36 Mill, *Utilitarianism*, 67.

37 Mill, *Utilitarianism*, 74.

38 Mill, *Utilitarianism*, 76.

39 Mill, *Utilitarianism*, 72. Mill does not show *how* the utilitarian formula helps to solve the problem any better than the various appeals to "justice." He merely *asserts* that this is the case.

40 Mill, *Utilitarianism*, 73.

41 Among the strongest of those rights for Mill were basic rights of liberty (see *On Liberty*). Clearly, Mill envisioned no basic conflict between the "greatest good" overall and the protection of fundamental liberties such as freedom of thought.

42 Mill, *Utilitarianism*, 57.

43 Ross, *The Right and the Good*, chap. 2.

44 Ross, *The Right and the Good*, 38.

45 Rawls, *A Theory of Justice*, §3; see also §1: "justice denies that loss of freedom for some is made right by a greater good shared by others."

46 Rawls, *A Theory of Justice*, §5.

47 Ross, *The Right and the Good*, 22.

48 Brandt, "Toward a Credible Form of Utilitarianism," 147. Smart, "Extreme and Restricted Utilitarianism," 111, following Sidgwick, might argue in response that such acts are indeed *right,* though they are to be *condemned:* "a right action may be rationally condemned."

49 Alan Donagan, "Is There a Credible Form of Utilitarianism?" in Bayles, *Contemporary Utilitarianism*, 198. Lyons makes the same point in a more subdued manner: "no pure utilitarian theory can account for some of our strongest convictions" (*Forms and Limits*, xi).

50 Mill, *Utilitarianism*, 10; Bentham, *An Introduction*, 11–12.

51 John Rawls, "Two Concepts of Rules," in Bayles, *Contemporary Utilitarianism*, 59–98.

52 Rawls, "Two Concepts," 95.

53 Lyons, however, has argued (*Forms and Limits*, 193) that promises do not constitute a "practice" in the way Rawls intends.

54 Lyons, *Forms and Limits*, 184–186.

55 Brandt, "Toward a Credible Form of Utilitarianism," 164–165, argues that rules must be learnable.

56 As J. J. C. Smart puts it ("Extreme and Restricted Utilitarianism," 115), "If 'act optimifically' is itself one of our rules then there will always be a conflict of rules whenever to keep a rule is not itself optimific. If this is so, restricted utilitarianism collapses into extreme utilitarianism." While Smart here argues for the priority of extreme or act-utilitarianism because of this "collapse," others have seen the collapse as a fault of rule-utilitarianism that renders it no better than act-utilitarianism. See, for example, H. J. McCloskey, "An Examination of Restricted Utilitarianism," in Bayles, *Contemporary Utilitarianism*, 124–127; see also Lyons, *Forms and Limits*.

57 McCloskey, "A Non-Utilitarian Approach to Punishment," 253.

58 Donagan, "Is There a Credible Form of Utilitarianism?" 194–195.

59 Sidgwick, *The Methods of Ethics*, 492, appears to acknowledge this. He suggests, however, that it is "practically expedient" to retain the distinction.

60 Mill, *Utilitarianism*, 15–16.

61 Mill, *Utilitarianism*, 22.

62 Mill, *Utilitarianism*, 76.

63 Cf. Rescher, *Distributive Justice*, 25.

64 Cf. Sidgwick, *The Methods of Ethics*, 415.

65 Rescher, *Distributive Justice*, 27.

66 See the discussion in Rawls, *A Theory of Justice*, §27.

67 Rescher, *Distributive Justice*, 29.

68 Cf. Rescher, *Distributive Justice*, 31. Rescher proposes as an equity principle a rule of "least square deviation from the average" (32).

69 Rescher, *Distributive Justice*, 48.

70 Rescher, *Distributive Justice*, 56.

71 Ross, *The Right and the Good*, 35.

72 Rescher, *Distributive Justice*, 54.

73 Rescher, *Distributive Justice*, 82 and 63.

74 According to A. D. Woozley, for example, A. M. Honore includes in the list of claims the concept of "special relations," which does not appear on Rescher's list and which Woozley himself is disinclined to accept; see Woozley, "Injustice," in *Studies in Ethics*, American Philosophical Quarterly Monograph Series no. 7, ed. Nicholas Rescher (Oxford: Basil Blackwell, 1973).

75 Rescher, *Distributive Justice*, 73.

76 This is, in fact, the argument that Sidgwick makes. The breaking of a promise, he suggests, disappoints deeply held expectations, which is an evil (*The Methods of Ethics*, 443). Sidgwick also explicitly acknowledges a notion of justice as reward for merit; the requital of desert, he suggests, "constitutes the chief element of Ideal Justice" (283).

77 Lyons (*Forms and Limits*, 172) argues, for example, that the utilitarian might wish to support justice by arguing that the one who does not contribute to an enterprise and nonetheless wishes to benefit from that enterprise "sets a bad example." But then the utilitarian has presupposed that it is "wrong" to benefit without contributing. That is, some notion of justice is there prior to the utilitarian calculus.

78 Cf. Ross, *The Right and the Good*, 23; Rawls, *A Theory of Justice*, §15.

79 Rescher, *Distributive Justice*, 10.

80 Though it's never made entirely clear by Bentham, it seems to be that one dolor is the equivalent of one negative hedon, thus making even pleasure and pain commensurable. Assigning hedon and dolor values to particular experiences is more difficult in practice, however, which is probably why Mill abandoned the attempt.

81 Mill, *Utilitarianism*, 12.

82 Sidgwick, *The Methods of Ethics*, 436.

83 Lyons, *Forms and Limits*, 162. Note that Lyons suggests that fairness can be a prerequisite for achieving utility (e.g., in order to obtain a full house, extra theater seats must be divided; a fair division will ensure use of the seats) [169–170].

84 Richard B. Brandt, *Ethical Theory* (Englewood Cliffs, NJ: Prentice-Hall, 1959), 425.

85 Mill, *Utilitarianism*, 77–78.

86 Brandt, *Ethical Theory*, 422.

87 In a fascinating essay, Joel Feinberg discusses the justice of judgments. Untrue assessments of one's merits and demerits are, according to Feinberg, a primary instance of injustice. We shall attempt here to be as "fair" as possible to those approaches and theories under consideration! See Joel Feinberg, "Noncomparative Justice," in Feinberg and Gross, *Justice: Selected Readings*.

88 Rescher, *Distributive Justice*, 92.

89 Indeed, Rescher (*Distributive Justice*, 106–107) proposes that the rules of distributive justice may differ depending on the type of economy. In an economy of scarcity (e.g., where there is not enough to provide a minimal level for all), seeming inequities may be optimal (so that some, at least, survive); in an economy of sufficiency, equity and distribution in accord with claims would be the just approach; in an economy of abundance, some inequities may "pay for themselves" by increasing the goods available for distribution and serving justice in the larger sense.

90 Brandt, *Ethical Theory*, 430–431.

91 Rescher, *Distributive Justice*, 102.

CHAPTER TWO

A Contract Response

John Rawls

Whatever its shortcomings, classical utilitarianism sets an important agenda for other theories of justice. The strengths of utilitarianism in the arena of justice are two: (1) it provides—in theory, at least—a concrete method for making difficult decisions, and (2) it recognizes the importance of happiness or the general good as part of a theory of justice. Yet we also saw that utilitarianism presents problems for justice: it appears not to honor individual persons, and it has implications that are often "counterintuitive, sometimes manifestly abhorrent."[1]

The task that John Rawls sets himself in *A Theory of Justice* is to propose an alternative theory of justice not only that takes persons seriously and does not risk their well-being or rights for the sake of others' good but that also offers a concrete method for making the most fundamental decisions about distributive justice.[2] Rawls's focus is on the basic structure of society, not the rightness or wrongness of particular actions or even of particular institutions. The intuitive notion is that the basic structure of society favors some starting positions over others, and that these inequalities have lingering effects on our chances in life.[3] Principles of justice are needed to regulate the basic structure so as to mitigate such unfair advantages. Rawls seeks a way to locate such principles without presuming agreement on the goals or ends that people might have for their lives. In a pluralistic society, there is not likely to be agreement about such ends, so a method for deriving principles must be devised that works on only a few basic assumptions (e.g., that whatever our goals in life might be, we want more of the basic goods of life). Rawls calls the result *justice as fairness.*

THE VEIL OF IGNORANCE

Justice as fairness has its roots in two places: the social contract theories of John Locke and Jean-Jacques Rousseau and the deontology of Immanuel Kant. The basic idea is astonishingly simple, though its working out in theory is rather complex. Rawls's aim is to use the concept of a social contract to give a procedural interpretation to Kant's notion of autonomous choice as the basis for ethical principles. Principles for justice (and moral philosophy in general) are to be the outcome of rational choice.[4]

In essence, the approach is this: Imagine a group of people who are going to choose principles for assessing the justice of basic structures of society. Clearly, if the principles are to be just, they must be chosen in a situation that is itself fair. That is, no one must be allowed to dominate the choice or to use to unfair advantage such contingencies as natural endowments or social position.[5] Hence, principles of justice will be the result of fair choice—justice as fairness.[6]

How, then, do we make the circumstances of choice—the original position from which the parties choose—fair? Rawls proposes that the representative persons in the original position choose from behind a "veil of ignorance."[7] The veil of ignorance and other stipulations of the original position become the linchpins of the system: "the idea of the initial situation is central to the whole theory and other basic notions are defined in terms of it."[8]

The veil of ignorance means that the parties choosing principles lack certain kinds of knowledge that might make the bargaining process unfair.[9] They do not know what position they hold in society or what their own particular goals or life plans might be. They do not know what society they belong to or what generation they are. Such particular kinds of knowledge always make it possible for persons to skew principles in their own favor. This would clearly not be fair, and so there must be an adequate veil of ignorance to remove such possibilities.

What the parties do know are two things. First, their society will be subject to the "circumstances of justice."[10] This means it is characterized by cooperation but also by conflict.[11] Along lines suggested earlier by Hume, Rawls proposes that circumstances of justice obtain "whenever mutually disinterested persons put forward conflicting claims to the division of social advantages under conditions of moderate scarcity."[12] Questions of justice arise in situations of scarcity and conflict of interest.

Second, they must know something about economic theory, something about social organization, and something about human psychology.[13] In short, they must know enough about human society to be able to make some predictions about the likelihood that the principles chosen can be strictly adhered to without undue stress or "strains of commitment."[14]

Moreover, the parties are mutually disinterested.[15] That is, they take no *particular* interest in each other's aims and purposes, whatever those might be. They are also rational, knowing that they want more of the primary goods of life if possible.[16] And they are not "envious"—that is, they prefer to gain in primary goods even if others gain more than they do.[17]

In short, we have a circumstance in which people do not know their specific life plans but know only that they are likely to want more of those basic goods that help to support any life plan. They enter the bargain with a view to furthering their own interests in obtaining such goods but without the kind of envy that would make them refuse gain for themselves accompanied by greater gain for others. They are ignorant of the kinds of things that would give them an unfair advantage in any bargaining position. Under these stipulations, the hypothetical contract can proceed.

They are then offered a choice of a range of principles for the distribution of rights and duties and of the benefits and burdens of social cooperation. These principles will govern the basic structure of society—the network of institutions that determines, to a large extent, what their life chances will be. It should be noted here that they also choose for a "well-ordered society," that is, for a society in which they can expect that the concept of justice chosen is public and that people comply strictly with its requirements.[18] Which principles will they choose?

PRINCIPLES OF JUSTICE

Rawls argues that under such conditions, the parties choosing in the original position would select two principles of justice. First, they would be concerned to secure their equal liberty, and they would establish a principle to that effect: "Each person is to have an equal right to the most extensive total system of equal basic liberties compatible with a similar system of liberty for all."[19] That is, they would separate out basic human liberties and secure them against any unequal division.

Indeed, Rawls argues that, except under very stringent circumstances, the parties in the original position would never want to permit any compromising of basic liberties for the sake of other social or economic benefits. Thus, not only is equal liberty the first principle, but it also stands in serial (lexical) order so that liberty can be restricted only for the sake of liberty and not for the sake of economic or other social gains.[20]

Next comes the question of whether they would permit any inequalities in income, wealth, power, and so on. Here, it might seem as though the obvious answer is no. That is, people choosing principles from an initial situation of equal ignorance and not knowing what their position in society will be might choose to ensure that goods are always divided equally.[21] Indeed, if society were a zero-sum game in which the size of the store of goods to be distributed could never be increased, this is precisely what Rawls says they would do.[22]

However, human society is not a zero-sum game. Through the efforts of social cooperation, it is possible to increase the quantity of goods to be distributed. For example, suppose there is a shoe factory with five workers, each currently earning $40,000 per year.[23] One of these workers has a particularly arduous task, and it is because of the time required for that task that a bottleneck occurs and production is held at current levels. Now it might be possible to induce this person to work faster by paying $50,000 per year (or to attract to the job a more skilled person than could be attracted by $40,000). If the increased productivity releases the bottleneck overall, so that the net income of the company is now $230,000, then there is a utility surplus of $20,000 (net income less salaries). This surplus could be divided among the other workers, bringing their salaries up to $45,000. Incomes are no longer equal, but everyone is better off.

Given that human society works this way and that the parties in the original position would know such general facts about society, surely they would choose the unequal incomes represented by the increased salaries here.[24] This was, of course, precisely the challenge raised by utilitarianism: justice in its full sense seems to require some accounting for the total *amount* of good as well as for its allocation.

However, utilitarianism might stipulate that justice is done even if one person loses in the transition, as long as the greater good for the greater number or the greater net good is done. Suppose the rearrangement of the shoe factory puts one person's salary at $37,500, while others move to $47,500 and one moves to $50,000. Under the utilitarian scheme, this represents the greater net good and the greater good for the greater number, but one person is worse off.

Why would persons in the original position choose a principle that might make them *worse* off than they were before? Rawls argues that the parties in the original position would not choose the utilitarian principle.[25] Since they are concerned to protect their own interests, they would not risk lesser income only for the benefit of others. Rather, they would choose a principle such as the following: "Social and economic inequalities, for example inequalities of wealth and authority, are just only if they result in compensating benefits for everyone, and in particular for the least advantaged members of society."[26] Called the *difference principle*, this principle becomes the core of Rawls's substantive theory of justice. It permits some inequalities in distribution but only those that protect or improve the position of the least advantaged in society.

Choice of the difference principle over a principle such as maximizing average utility rests on one of the more controversial aspects of Rawls's theory: his adoption of the strategy of "maximin." In brief, this strategy stipulates that the parties in the original position would choose in such a way as to "maximize the minimum."[27]

The choice of maximin as a strategy can be understood this way: Suppose I am in this original bargain. I do not know who I will be in society or what kind of a society I may encounter when the veil of ignorance is lifted. With no way of calculating my chances of being the least advantaged, it is reasonable for me to act protectively to preserve the position of the least advantaged member of society since that person might be me. Thus, I will permit inequalities only if they work to the benefit of the least advantaged. Hence, I will try to avoid the worst results and maximize the minimum. Thus, I am concerned not merely that any inequalities result in compensating benefits for everyone but especially that they result in benefits for the least advantaged. The strategy of maximin is thus "the vital bridge linking the rules of justice with the conditions described by the original position."[28]

Moreover, those in the original position would want to be sure that any inequalities of position and power are not locked in for all time but are subject to fair competition and open to all persons to try for them. Though they would be willing to permit social inequalities that work to their advantage, they will stipulate that such inequalities be attached to positions open to all on a liberal principle of "fair equality of opportunity."[29] Finally, since they are not sure to which generation they belong, they will require that one generation not squander resources but enact a just savings principle toward the good of future generations.

Thus, the final formulation of Rawls's second principle of justice for institutions is as follows:

> Social and economic inequalities are to be arranged so that they are both
> (a) to the greatest benefit of the least advantaged, consistent with the just savings principle, and
> (b) attached to offices and positions open to all under conditions of fair equality of opportunity.[30]

Added to the principle of equal liberty, we now have the two principles that form the core of Rawls's theory of justice for the basic structures of society.

These two principles are a special case of the general concept of justice. The general concept is that social values "are to be distributed equally unless an unequal distribution of any, or all, of these values is to everyone's advantage."[31] In contrast to the utilitarian "greatest good" criterion, Rawls's conception requires that *each person* benefit from any social inequalities.[32] The requirement that *each* person benefit becomes the requirement that the *least advantaged* benefit under the stipulations of maximin in the original position.

The full theory, therefore, takes the form of a fundamental affirmation of liberty and a limited acceptance of certain inequalities, judged from the perspective of their impact on the position of those least advantaged.[33] These principles are those that would be chosen by autonomous individuals situated in a "fair" setting. They are thus, in Rawls's view, "categorical imperatives" expressing the autonomy of "free and equal rational beings."[34] Most importantly, perhaps, the principles that would be chosen are *not* those of classical utilitarianism or its numerous revisions.

JUSTIFICATION

If Rawls is right, then the two principles cited above are those that would be chosen by parties in the original position as principles for distributing rights and duties, burdens and benefits. But are these principles *just?* Does the fact that they are chosen mean they are right? To ask this question is to ask about the justification for the principles.

The answer to the question may be given in several ways. First, justice as fairness yields pure procedural justice. In pure procedural justice, there is no standard for deciding what is "just" apart from the procedure itself.[35] Justice applies not to the outcome but to the system.[36] Rawls develops this concept in discussing the place of equal opportunity as a principle of justice. However, it may also apply to justice as fairness as a theory: whatever is chosen by the parties in the original position is just simply by virtue of being the outcome of the decision procedure. Thus, if the parties do in fact choose Rawls's two principles, then these are the principles that provide justice.

Much depends, therefore, on the original position and the strictures established around the choice procedure. Here Rawls proposes two constraints to assess the fairness of the procedure. The first is that the premises introduced into the original position should be as "weak" as possible and should be widely accepted.[37] Only those things that are generally agreed to constitute "fair" or "minimal" assumptions should be necessary in the original position. Hence, for example, we cannot propose that everyone share a particular goal or life plan, for this would require some strong assumptions about the human good; however, we can propose that each party will have their own life plan and will seek certain primary goods as means necessary to that life plan. Thus, "the conditions embodied in the description of the original position are ones that we do in fact accept."[38]

The second constraint or qualification is a method of assessment called *reflective equilibrium*.[39] This method involves testing the description of the original position by seeing whether it yields principles that really do match our considered convictions about justice. Do the principles that arise seem to require what is fair when we deliberate about it? If not, then we can either change our considered convictions (pruning or stretching them as the principles might require) or alter the stipulations about the original position until it yields new principles that give us a better match. With this back-and-forth method of testing, "eventually we shall find a description of the initial situation that both expresses reasonable conditions and yields principles which match our considered judgments duly pruned and adjusted."[40]

The second and third parts of *A Theory of Justice* are devoted largely to testing out the implications of the principles: Do they yield social institutions that match our considered convictions about justice?[41] Do they offer a vision of a well-ordered and fair society? Rawls argues that the principles, worked out in social institutions, would help us to discard those ordinary precepts of justice that are not helpful on a fundamental level and would confirm other common suppositions about justice.

Perhaps most important here is his rejection of any concept of distribution in accord with virtue; all legitimate expectations are shown to be based on social institutions, not on such factors as the contingencies of birth or advantages of upbringing.[42]

The final test of the theory depends on the coherence of all these elements together: the original position, the arguments for the principles chosen, the kinds of institutional arrangements that they might engender, and the fit between these arrangements and our considered convictions of justice.

REVIEW

Justice as fairness provides a clear contrast to the utilitarian view. Principles of justice are derived not by assessing the utility of actions (or of tendencies of actions) but by rational choice in a fair setting. Those principles are geared toward the basic structure of society, not toward every act or every level where justice is a concern. Rawls deals with the macrolevel rather than the microlevel. A *Theory of Justice* offers a complex and subtle theory based on a striking insight about the potential for using the social contract as a foundation for a theory of justice.[43]

Most importantly, where Mill's utilitarian approach leaves the individual vulnerable to the demands of the greater good of others, Rawls's principles clearly protect those who are least advantaged. No tradeoffs are allowed between their liberty or well-being and the well-being of others. Basic liberties must be distributed equally and cannot be sacrificed for the sake of economic gain. While income and social status, power and privilege may be distributed unequally, such unequal distribution is allowed only where it renders the least advantaged better off than they would otherwise be.

CRITIQUE

Does the theory succeed? The voluminous criticism that arose in scarcely more than a decade testifies to the importance of Rawls's theory.[44] It also suggests there may be serious flaws in justice as fairness. A sampling of the critical commentary directed toward Rawls's method, principles, and justification will illuminate problem areas and also demonstrate the divergence among critics.

Method

Rawls's contract method has been criticized from a number of angles. Some of these will be dealt with below in the discussion of justification. Several others deserve separate attention.

Justice as fairness is meant to set up a situation in which principles for justice are the outcome of rational choice by self-interested actors. The original position, with its veil of ignorance, is to remove those particularities that would bias choices. Hence, the principles chosen need not presume particular concepts of the good but presume only a minimum about human nature, namely, that people are free, equal, and rational. Does the original position succeed in providing the kind of neutrality desired?

Several critics argue that it does not. Marxist critics charge that Rawls's basic definition of human nature and of human society has built into it some deep biases about nature and society.[45] Milton Fisk asserts that the concept of humans as free, equal, and rational is not a neutral concept.[46] In a Marxist perspective, human nature cannot be defined entirely apart from social class. Nor is a "well-ordered" society necessarily the goal in terms of which justice is to be defined, given Marxist assumptions about class struggle. Thus, Rawls's attempt to take an ahistorical, "world" perspective is antithetical to some basic Marxist assumptions.

A related critique challenges Rawls's implicit epistemology. The veil of ignorance is intended to remove particular knowledge, but the parties in the original position are still presumed to have general knowledge about such areas as politics and economic theory. Is this possible? Robert Paul Wolff charges there can be no such "general" knowledge that is not itself based on particular knowledge.[47] Which theories about economics would be known? Any such theories have biases already built into them. Thus, it is not possible for the parties in the original position to have unbiased general knowledge; all general knowledge is based on and reveals particularities and biases.

Michael Sandel maintains that Rawls's theory depends on an unsubstantiated notion of the choosing self. Rawls attempts to adapt Kant's autonomous self. The principles are to reflect the choice of this self and to be categorical imperatives expressing the nature of persons as free, equal, and rational, but there must be no overriding ends that direct the choices made. Hence, the selves who do the choosing must always stand at a certain distance from their ends and goals: they have goals, but they are not defined by them. Ultimately, this means that the self becomes invulnerable—it is not changed by its experiences or by its cooperation with others. This is a very limited view of the self, charges Sandel, and does not account for some important aspects of community and self-knowledge: "If utilitarianism fails to take seriously our distinctness, justice as fairness fails to take seriously our commonality."[48]

Several critics note that under the circumstances of the veil of ignorance, the contract really becomes a kind of individual rationality "writ large."[49] Since the veil of ignorance removes the distinguishing features of the parties to the point where their decision would be unanimous, there is a sense in which they can be collapsed into one person. Rawls himself recognizes this. He proposes that the contract is really a "perspective" that can be adopted by anyone willing to put themselves under the requisite veil of ignorance.[50]

However, one of Rawls's criticisms of utilitarianism is that it uses an ideal-observer approach that derives social principles as though they were equivalent to the choices made by a single person. "There is no reason," says Rawls, "to suppose that the principles which should regulate an association of [people] is [sic] simply an extension of the principle of choice for one [person]."[51] Yet this is precisely what happens once the contract is collapsed into the perspective of a single person.

Rawls's principles have been accused of lacking any mechanism for rectification for existing injustices, especially across generations. Environmental advocates, especially, have critiqued Rawls's mechanism for intergenerational justice—the just savings principle—for providing no means to respond when prior generations have destroyed environmental conditions and depleted natural resources.[52]

Finally, critics charge that Rawls's theory is essentially circular. The argument depends on the particular circumstances chosen for the original position. These are manipulated to yield the two principles since Rawls himself acknowledges that a slight variation would yield a form of utilitarian principle. As James S. Fishkin puts it, "Adoption of one particular procedure can always be challenged on the ground that it is biased toward X's convictions rather than Y's."[53]

Principles

This leads us to the question of whether Rawls's method would indeed yield his principles. Rawls's two principles and their lexical ordering have also come under close scrutiny and are found wanting by many critics.[54]

The Principle of Equal Liberty

H. L. A. Hart raises several criticisms regarding Rawls's principle of equal liberty. As posed, and with the lexical order in effect, this principle permits restrictions on liberty only for the sake of a more *extensive* system of liberties, but liberties can conflict. When they do, appeals to the *extent* of the system of liberty may not resolve the conflict. Rather, what is needed are judgments about the relative *value* of the two liberties at stake.[55] Since reasonable people may differ as to these liberties, appealing to the judgment of a rational person in the original position does not solve the problem.

Moreover, our considered convictions about justice include many instances in which liberty must be curtailed in order to avoid harm to others (e.g., in legislation regarding pollution). It would be "extraordinary," says Hart, if Rawls meant to exclude such instances from permissible restrictions on liberty.[56]

Finally, Hart notes that every liberty is a two-edged sword: I receive benefits from exercising a liberty myself but must also bear the burdens of others exercising it. The choice of a principle of liberty depends on a judgment that the benefits from having the liberty will outweigh the harm of having others exercise the same liberty.[57] Would those in the original position then choose Rawls's principle regarding liberty? "It does not follow that a liberty which can only be obtained by an individual at the price of its general distribution through society is one that a rational person would still want."[58]

The Lexical Ordering

Other criticisms are directed not at the first principle per se but at its relation to the second principle.

First, some challenge the presumed independence of the two principles. Rawls appears to presume that inequalities in the economic arena do not affect the equality of basic liberties. Rawls recognizes that economic inequalities can affect one's ability to *exercise* a liberty; he calls this ability "the worth of liberty."[59] However, though the worth of liberty may be affected by economic inequalities, he argues that the liberties themselves can nonetheless be distributed equally.

Norman Daniels retorts, "Equal liberty without equal worth of liberty is a worthless abstraction."[60] Further, he asserts that "our historical experience . . . is that inequalities of wealth and accompanying inequalities in powers tend to produce inequalities of liberty."[61] Moreover, those with more wealth influence political systems and systems of liberty in various ways (e.g., through control of schools). Hence, Daniels asserts, social theory and historical experience suggest that political liberties cannot be separated from economic inequalities in the way Rawls wishes, and those in the original position would not choose principles that assume such a separation.

Related criticisms are levied by Brian Barry and Bruce Ackerman. The lexical ordering of the two principles appears to require that we would always choose a situation of slightly more equal liberty rather than a situation of greater economic justice. This, Barry suggests, is not likely to be the choice of those in the original position.[62] Ackerman charges that Rawls's lexical ordering of the principles reflects a kind of tunnel vision with regard to values: "a program involving the welfare of millions will fail to engage the contractarian's attention, let alone concern, so long as it does not trench upon his precious rights."[63]

The Difference Principle

However, for our purposes, it is the difference principle that is central. Many authors consider it to be the core of Rawls's thought. Just as many find it wanting as a principle of justice. The criticisms are so numerous and varied that only a few can be noted here.

First, assuming the principle is accepted, there are problems of application. How are the "least advantaged" to be identified? Rawls proposes that position and power generally attach to income and wealth, and therefore that income is a sufficient measure. Wolff argues that this is not proven, and Benjamin Barber and Brian Barry note that Rawls's theory fails to account for racial discrimination or other characteristics not necessarily correlated with income but correlated with disadvantage in society.[64]

More fundamental are the attacks on maximin as a decision strategy. The reasoning behind the difference principle depends on the peculiar features of maximin. Rawls argues that it is rational for those in the original position to choose such a protective strategy. However, Barber argues that the choice of maximin depends not simply on *rationality* but on a particular kind of *psychology* (i.e., an unwillingness to take risks).[65] Since those in the original position are not supposed to have a particular temperament, it cannot be presumed that they would be so cautious.

Moreover, the strategy of maximin requires that we care little for what we receive, above a certain minimum; otherwise, we would choose a principle that takes more risk but offers the possibility of a larger gain. Thomas Nagel argues that this is not "rational" per se: for many life plans, it is precisely the amounts above the minimum that are so crucial.[66]

R. M. Hare suggests that the most reasonable response to a situation of uncertainty is not maximin but a strategy called *insufficient reason*: where I have insufficient reason to know what position I might hold, I assume that I have *equal chances* of holding any of the possible positions.

But in this case, as Rawls admits, the parties would likely choose a principle of average utility as their principle of justice. Rawls excludes insufficient reason as a mode of reasoning open to the parties in the original position. Hare charges that he does so not because rationality requires it but only to avoid the obvious utilitarian outcome.[67] Responding to the same issue, Wolff suggests that if the parties really cannot estimate the likelihood of their being in any position, then "neither maximin nor any other rule makes the slightest sense."[68]

Several authors propose that under the conditions of the original position and the veil of ignorance, the choice that would make the most sense is not maximin (and, hence, the difference principle) but a rule setting a floor and then permitting some risk-taking above that floor. The arguments offered for maximin really are good arguments for ensuring against calamity, but once a floor is established, those in the original position might choose to take their chances on maximizing their expectations.[69]

Wolff argues further that the difference principle is counterintuitive: Why *not* choose a principle that benefited everyone *except* the least advantaged?[70] T. M. Scanlon points out that the difference principle does not deal with the situation where the position of the least-well-off group is not improved but the number of persons in that group is reduced.[71] Richard W. Miller proposes that the difference principle would involve too many "strains of commitment" for capitalists at the top and hence would not be chosen by those in the original position, who must worry about whether the principles chosen can be adhered to without undue stress.[72]

All these arguments suggest that Rawls has not adequately defended the choice of the difference principle or perhaps that his principle needs yet other modifications. Most crucial, of course, are the arguments asserting that the difference principle is not *fair*. Barry argues there is nothing in the difference principle itself that would prevent a distribution of goods according to race.[73] Thus, it does not offhand avoid violations of some of our most deeply held convictions about justice.

Others argue that it is not fair to those on top. Just as utilitarianism appears to permit the sacrifice of some for the sake of others, so does the difference principle: those at the top may receive benefits only if those at the bottom do so as well. Robert Nozick's criticism is the most biting here. First, he argues that goods are not "manna from heaven" but products of a productive process.[74] Nozick argues that precisely because the utility surplus that can be created through special incentives involves additional effort on the part of some, they are entitled to part of that utility surplus. The surplus cannot simply be distributed as though no one deserved any part of it. The difference principle, which looks only at relative levels of income rather than at contribution to the productive process, appears to ignore these important questions.[75] Indeed, he argues that those on the bottom of the social scale already receive the greatest advantages from social cooperation and that it would be absurd to suggest that justice requires them to be given any more.[76]

Second, Nozick proposes that we imagine those best off saying to those worst off, "Look, you gain from this cooperative venture; therefore, we will participate only if we get as much as possible." If these terms seem "outrageous," suggests Nozick, then surely the difference principle is also outrageous, for this is exactly what it requires, in reverse.[77] In short, the difference principle appears to violate a Kantian norm and use some people as means to others' ends. The fact that it uses those better off to help those worse off does not make it any more "just" than a utilitarian scheme that uses the worse off to benefit the better off.

Rawls might respond that those who are better off also gain from the social venture. However, as Sandel notes, this response seems to depend on the notion that talents are "owned" by the community, and this notion is not substantiated, nor does it concur with the individualistic bases of Rawls's theory.[78]

Jeffrey H. Reiman defends the difference principle at this point.[79] He acknowledges that at first glance, this principle does not appear to allow "only reciprocal advantages," as Rawls claims. However, he proposes that if distributions are understood in terms of labor rather than goods or money, the difference principle is not only defensible but indeed would be chosen over free market or other principles.

Reiman's basic argument is this: The social product gained by cooperative endeavor is really the product of different people's labor. Thus, when goods are distributed, what is really being distributed are the proportions in which individuals work for each other. The question of just distribution is, therefore, the question of reasonable terms for the exchange of labor. When, for example, is it reasonable to exchange t hours of A's labor for $t + n$ hours of B's labor?

Clearly, the answer is: when B receives more than she would by a direct exchange of $t + n$ hours. Thus, if A can be induced to turn out twenty-four loaves of bread in eight hours by being given sixteen cups of sugar in return, then even if it takes B sixteen hours to produce the sugar, B is getting more bread than she would at a straight one-unit-per-hour rate (i.e., B gets twenty-four loaves instead of sixteen loaves). Seen in this light, suggests Reiman, the difference principle does not "confiscate" A's goods and give them to B but merely prevents A from taking B's (greater) labor without giving B anything in return. Thus, it does not require "sacrifice" from A or "use" A, as Nozick would claim, but merely prevents A from exploiting B's labor.

However, others find the difference principle unjust not to those on top but to those on the bottom. The notion that normal operations of the market benefit those on the bottom through a chain connection with benefits at the top is a "living fossil," charges Barry.[80] Rawls argues that gross inequalities will not happen between the top and bottom layers; however, Fishkin notes there is no adequate empirical base for ruling out such a possibility.[81]

Justification

Finally, questions and challenges are raised about the justification for the two principles of justice. Some challenge whether Rawls has really adopted pure procedural justice, in which the procedure determines the result. Wolff suggests that if Rawls truly used pure procedural justice, he could not claim to know in advance which principles would be chosen. Thus, the choice of two principles undermines Rawls's claim to pure procedural justice.[82] David Lyons asserts that Rawls *does* have an independent standard of justice—the standard of fairness that is built into the original position.[83]

In essence, this amounts to a challenge that the premises grounding the original position are not as "weak" as Rawls claims. Others join in this challenge. For example, Sandel asks why Rawls considers "mutual disinterest" a weak assumption.[84] He argues that Rawls's theory ultimately rests on a particular understanding of human nature—the invulnerable self who always stands apart from one's experiences. This is not a "weak" assumption. The charge that Rawls manipulates the original situation so as to get his chosen principles also undermines his claims for pure procedural justice.

Others question whether pure procedural justice is itself a fallacious theory. The fact that principles are *chosen*, even under fair circumstances, does not necessarily mean they are *just*. Ronald Dworkin notes, for instance, that my (autonomous, fair) agreement to sell a painting for one hundred dollars on Monday does not make that a fair price on Wednesday when I discover that the painting is a masterpiece.[85] As Sandel puts it, "If the parties to the original contract *choose* the principles of justice, what is to say that they have chosen *rightly*?"[86] He notes that traditional contract theorists turned to natural law to provide an independent standard. But this, of course, is precisely what Rawls does not want to do. He wants the principles to be fair, simply because they are the outcome of rational choice under certain conditions.

Indeed, David Lyons proposes that Rawls does have an independent standard. His principles are a rational departure from egalitarianism. But then it seems as though strict equality is the real standard of justice, and Rawls's principles are an "amalgam of a moral egalitarianism and a non-moral acceptance of beneficial inequalities."[87] In short, being chosen in the original position is not synonymous with being just.[88]

Of course, Rawls might respond to this charge that the choices made in the original position are to be tested against our considered convictions. The requirement of coherence between the principles chosen and our ordinary judgments is the second check and balance for the justice of the principles. This claim also is challenged.

Hare asserts that Rawls simply uses his own intuitions as a check and balance: "Since the theoretical structure is tailored at every point to fit Rawls' intuitions, it is hardly surprising that its normative consequences fit them too."[89] Because of the intuitive elements that enter into such a test, Lyons proposes that it can never be conclusive.[90] Several critics charge that the coherence test and the notion of pure procedural justice are not only a strange juxtaposition but indeed contradictory: If the theory is pure procedural justice, why should a coherence test be needed at all? And if the principles are justified by their coherence with our considered convictions, why should we need the elaborate mechanism of the original position? These two parts of Rawls's theory do not seem well integrated at the level of justification of his principles.[91]

Finally, some critics charge that Rawls's theory is apolitical, ahistorical, and lacking in the kind of empirical data that would be needed to test out the implications of the principles and provide a genuine check on our considered convictions. As Wolff puts it, "The empirical specificity needed to lend any plausibility to it [is] . . . drained away."[92]

ASSESSMENT

Nevertheless, in spite of all the criticisms raised—or perhaps precisely because so much scholarly time and energy have been devoted to analyzing and responding to this theory—*A Theory of Justice* promises to leave a lasting legacy. Like the utilitarian theory to which it responds, it raises fundamental challenges and sets the agenda for the next generation of reflections on distributive justice. As one of Rawls's staunchest critics puts it, "It is a mark of John Rawls' achievement that I must begin with a critique of contractarian theory."[93]

Wolff proposes that "the real value of a philosophical position lies almost entirely in the depth, the penetration, and the power of its central insight."[94] In this regard, Rawls's theory appears to have two central insights, corresponding to the two parts of the theory: its contract method and its principles.[95] Each raises a fundamental challenge and future agenda.

Is it possible to construct a theory of justice that does not presume a single good or end for humankind? Where utilitarians posited happiness, or some balance of pleasure and pain, as the good that formed the ground of justice, Rawls's method is intended to derive principles for justice without asserting any single goal and without making justice dependent on that goal. Such an attempt would appear to be increasingly important in a pluralistic world where different goods are posited by different people. If the method works, it offers the possibility of an approach to justice that depends only on human freedom, equality, and rationality. While critics may consider these "strong" assumptions, they are assumptions sufficiently widely shared today to offer the hope of a common grounding for justice.[96]

Moreover, if Rawls's movement from method to principles works, or if the principles themselves are accepted, then this common ground for justice would appear to require protections for the least advantaged in society. While critics may find fault with the reasoning used to formulate Rawls's principles, the challenge raised by those principles to any future theory of justice is their stress on the position of the least advantaged. The requirements of equal rights, and of only those social and economic inequalities that make the least advantaged better off than they would have been otherwise, provide a standard that can be used to judge social policy and have a strong intuitive appeal to many in our contemporary world.

Thus, whether one takes the "power" of Rawls's central insight to reside in his contractarian method or in his elaboration of the two principles that protect the least advantaged, it is clear that this theory is sufficiently powerful to set a future agenda for some time to come. It certainly set the agenda for Robert Nozick, who differs with Rawls not only in method but most particularly in understanding the substance of justice.

NOTES

1 Robert Paul Wolff, *Understanding Rawls: A Reconstruction and Critique of A Theory of Justice* (Princeton, NJ: Princeton University Press, 1977), 11.

2 John Rawls, *A Theory of Justice* (Cambridge, MA: Harvard University Press, 1971). Rawls intends to provide an alternative to the two major theories that dominated the early part of this century: utilitarianism, on the one hand, and deontological intuitive theories, on the other. However, it is clear that utilitarianism sets the major agenda for his work.

3 Rawls, *A Theory of Justice*, §2.

4 Rawls, *A Theory of Justice*, §3.

5 Rawls notes that basic structures in society always favor some starting positions and thus incorporate inequalities (*A Theory of Justice*, §2). His overriding concern is to "look for a conception of justice that nullifies the accidents of natural endowment and the contingencies of social circumstance" (§3).

6 Rawls, *A Theory of Justice*, §3.

7 Rawls, *A Theory of Justice*, §3.

8 Rawls, *A Theory of Justice*, §78.

9 Rawls, *A Theory of Justice*, §24.

10 Rawls, *A Theory of Justice*, §24.

11 Rawls, *A Theory of Justice*, §22.

12 Rawls, *A Theory of Justice*, §22.

13 Rawls, *A Theory of Justice*, §24.

14 Rawls, *A Theory of Justice*, §29.

15 Rawls, *A Theory of Justice*, §25.

16 Rawls, *A Theory of Justice*, §25.

17 Rawls, *A Theory of Justice*, §25. *Envy* is used here in a somewhat technical sense, in which it can be distinguished from jealousy. Robert Nozick (*Anarchy, State, and Utopia* [New York: Basic Books, 1974], 239) proposes that the envious person prefers that neither have a good rather than that the other have it while she or he does not.

18 Rawls, *A Theory of Justice*, §2. Rawls notes explicitly that he is looking for an "ideal" situation of justice because the "nature and aims of a perfectly just society is the fundamental part of the theory of justice." Taking this "ideal" approach has the advantage of avoiding questions about compensatory or reparative justice.

19 Rawls, *A Theory of Justice*, §46.

20 Rawls distinguishes two circumstances under which liberty might be limited. A less extensive liberty for all is sometimes permissible in the interest of strengthening the total system of liberty. A less than equal liberty must be acceptable to those with the lesser liberty, presumably because it strengthens their future liberties. Rawls does acknowledge that under circumstances of extreme duress, there may be times when people would prefer greater economic gains to liberty; however, these are only for situations of dire stress (§82).

21 This is indeed what Rawls suggests they would initially consider (Rawls, *A Theory of Justice*, §26).

22 Rawls, *A Theory of Justice*, §81.

23 The figures have been changed here, but we are indebted to Wolff for the basic example (*Understanding Rawls*, 30–31).

24 Cf. Rawls, *A Theory of Justice*, §26.

25 "It hardly seems likely that persons who view themselves as equals, entitled to press their claims upon one another, would agree to a principle which

may require lesser life prospects for some simply for the sake of a greater sum of advantages enjoyed by others" (Rawls, *A Theory of Justice*, §3).

26 Rawls, *A Theory of Justice*, §3.

27 Rawls, *A Theory of Justice*, §26.

28 Benjamin R. Barber, "Justifying Justice: Problems of Psychology, Politics, and Measurement in Rawls," in *Reading Rawls*, ed. Norman Daniels (New York: Basic Books, n.d.), 297.

29 Rawls, *A Theory of Justice*, §13.

30 Rawls, *A Theory of Justice*, §46.

31 Rawls, *A Theory of Justice*, §11.

32 Social cooperation requires reciprocal advantages, claims Rawls (§6). He suggests that the utilitarian approach requires too much identification with the plight of others (§31).

33 A complete theory of justice requires principles not only for institutional arrangements but also for individuals. Here Rawls proposes a principle of fairness that requires we do what the rules of fair institutions would require and a range of "natural duties" such as nonmaleficence, beneficence, etc. (*A Theory of Justice*, §19). The important question regarding the relationship between such principles and those for institutions simply cannot be addressed here. At least one critic, William A. Galston (*Justice and the Human Good* [Chicago: University of Chicago Press, 1980], 4), argues that political life cannot be separated from "natural" duties.

34 Rawls, *A Theory of Justice*, §40. Rawls asserts, "Properly understood, then, the desire to act justly derives in part from the desire to express most fully what we are or can be, namely, free and equal rational beings with a liberty to choose."

35 "Pure" procedural justice is distinguished from "perfect" and "imperfect" procedural justice. In each of the latter cases, there is an independent standard for assessing the justice of the outcome, and the only question is whether the procedures are guaranteed to give that outcome. For example, justice in criminal law requires that only the truly guilty be found guilty; however, the court system does not guarantee that result, so it is an instance of "imperfect" procedural justice. In "pure" procedural justice, there is no such independent standard for determining the justice of the results. Whatever results from the procedure is "just" by definition (Rawls, *A Theory of Justice*, §14).

36 Distributive justice, says Rawls (§14), is not the same as "allocative" justice. That is, justice is not determined by looking at some pattern or end-state of goods but by looking at the procedures involved in the basic structures of society.

37 Rawls, *A Theory of Justice*, §4.

38 Rawls, *A Theory of Justice*, §4.

39 Rawls, *A Theory of Justice*, §9.

40 Rawls, *A Theory of Justice*, §4.

41 For example, Rawls proposes a four-stage implementation procedure for the application of principles to the various aspects of political and social life (*A Theory of Justice*, part II).

42 Rawls, *A Theory of Justice*, §48.

43 In the revised edition of *A Theory of Justice* (Cambridge, MA: Harvard University Press, 1999), Rawls makes minor adjustments that do not affect the basic outline presented here. In *Political Liberalism* (New York: Columbia University Press, 1993), he addressed what he considered a flaw in the original—namely, the assumption that the principles were for a "well-ordered" society. Recognizing that a pluralistic democracy could contain competing and irreconcilable comprehensive doctrines of what constitutes the good life, Rawls limited his theory of justice to being a *political* conception, but the mainstays of the theory remain: the original position, the veil of ignorance, and the two principles in their lexical order. In *The Law of Peoples* (Cambridge, MA: Harvard University Press, 1999), Rawls extended his theory to the international community, resulting in eight principles for international cooperation but retaining the original position and veil of ignorance as central concepts. These later works do not require significant changes in the presentation of Rawls's basic contract theory of justice.

44 Several volumes are devoted entirely to a critique of Rawls, and others take Rawls as the epitome of contemporary liberal theory. For the former, see Daniels, *Reading Rawls*; Wolff, *Understanding Rawls*; and Brian Barry, *The Liberal Theory of Justice: A Critical Examination of the Principal Doctrines in* A Theory of Justice *by John Rawls* (Oxford: Oxford University Press, 1973). For the latter, see Michael J. Sandel, *Liberalism and the Limits of Justice* (Cambridge: Cambridge University Press, 1982); and George Parkin Grant, *English Speaking Justice* (Notre Dame, IN: Notre Dame University Press, 1985).

45 See Milton Fisk, "History and Reason in Rawls' Moral Theory," and Richard W. Miller, "Rawls and Marxism," both in Daniels, *Reading Rawls*. Note, however, that there is at least one Marxist defense of Rawls: Jeffrey H. Reiman, "The Labor Theory of the Difference Principle," *Philosophy and Public Affairs* 12, no. 2 (Spring 1983), 133–159.

46 Fisk, "History and Reason," 57.

47 Wolff, *Understanding Rawls*, 122–123.

48 Sandel, *Liberalism*, 174. Bruce Ackerman makes the same criticism, suggesting that Rawls operates on a "false individualism" that fails to acknowledge cultural influences on the self. See Bruce J. Ackerman, *Social Justice in the Liberal State* (New Haven, CT: Yale University Press, 1980), 345. Sandel and George Parkin Grant also charge that Rawls's alliance of Kant and contract theory is an uneasy alliance at best. The "circumstances of justice," which Rawls adopts from Hume, are empirical judgments. Thus, for Sandel, Rawls cannot claim that justice is the first virtue of social institutions but

only of institutions in those societies that have certain characteristics that fit Humean assumptions. Not only may there be other virtues for society, but justice--as a narrow kind of calculation of interests--may even be a vice on occasion. Grant argues that Rawls tries to derive fairness from self-interest, while the "very core of Kant's thought is his sharp division between self-interest and fairness" (*English Speaking Justice*, 99).

49 Galston, *Justice and the Human Good*, 115.

50 Rawls, *A Theory of Justice*, §24.

51 Rawls, *A Theory of Justice*, §6.

52 See Sarah Kenehan, "Rawls, Rectification, and Global Climate Change," *Journal of Social Philosophy* 45, no. 2 (Summer 2014): 252–269, https://doi.org/10.1111/josp.12062; Robert V. Bartlett and Walter F. Baber, "Ethics and Environmental Policy in Democratic Governance," *Public Integrity* 7, no. 3 (Summer 2005): 219–240.

53 James S. Fishkin, *Justice, Equal Opportunity, and the Family* (New Haven, CT: Yale University, 1983), 183.

54 Rawls (*A Theory of Justice*, §3) explicitly argues that one might reject the method and nonetheless accept the principles of justice as fairness.

55 H. L. A. Hart, "Rawls on Liberty and Its Priority," in Daniels, *Reading Rawls*, 240.

56 Hart, "Rawls on Liberty," 245. It is not altogether clear that the "natural duties" of beneficence and nonmaleficence will always fill the gap.

57 Barry (*The Liberal Theory of Justice*, 117) makes an analogous argument about social goods: though it is true that in general we want more of the basic goods, he suggests that we would not always want more if the price is that others also have more. It may be better to be poor in a poor society than rich in a rich one.

58 Hart, "Rawls on Liberty," 248. Hart also questions whether it would be rational for those in the original position to choose such a limiting principle when they are not sure what the circumstances of society will be. If they are not sure which stage their society has reached, why would they choose to limit liberty only for the sake of liberty?

59 Rawls, *A Theory of Justice*, §32.

60 Norman Daniels, "Equal Liberty and Unequal Worth of Liberty," in Daniels, *Reading Rawls*, 263.

61 Daniels, "Equal Liberty," 256.

62 Barry, *The Liberal Theory*, 52, 60–61.

63 Ackerman, *Social Justice*, 341.

64 Wolff, *Understanding Rawls*, 134–135; Barber, "Justifying Justice," 303; Barry, *The Liberal Theory*, 45–47.

65 Barber, "Justifying Justice," 298.

66 Thomas Nagel, "Rawls on Justice," in Daniels, *Reading Rawls*, 12; see also Barry, *The Liberal Theory*, 97.

67 R. M. Hare, "Rawls' Theory of Justice," in Daniels, *Reading Rawls*, 104. Others argue that under the conditions of the original position––and possibly even with the maximin strategy––the parties would choose some variant of utilitarianism. That is, for all of Rawls's criticism of utilitarianism, he has not shown that under the ideal conditions of the "well-ordered society" it is any less appealing than his difference principle. See, e.g., David Lyons, "Nature and Soundness of the Contract and Coherence Arguments," in Daniels, *Reading Rawls*, 166.

68 Wolff, *Understanding Rawls*, 161. Hare concurs, "The truth is that it is a wide open question how the [people in the original position] would choose" ("Rawls' Theory of Justice," 106).

69 Hare, "Rawls' Theory of Justice," 104–106; Miller, "Rawls and Marxism," 223; and Nagel, "Rawls on Justice," 12. Barry (*The Liberal Theory*, 104) also criticizes maximin for not guaranteeing a satisfactory minimum.

70 Wolff, *Understanding Rawls*, 69–70. Wolff notes that the requirement to benefit the least well advantaged solves a problem of prioritizing. If the requirement is simply that "all" must benefit, there are possible solutions where everyone would benefit but where the benefits would be distributed differently. How would the parties choose between such solutions? Requiring that the least advantaged benefit most solves this prioritizing problem (see 39–43). However, it brings other, counterintuitive implications.

71 T. M. Scanlon, "Rawls' Theory of Justice," Daniels, in *Reading Rawls*, 195.

72 Miller, "Rawls and Marxism," 214.

73 Barry, *The Liberal Theory*, 16–17.

74 Nozick, *Anarchy, State, and Utopia*, 198. Similarly, Wolff (*Understanding Rawls*, 207) asserts that the game theory on which Rawls's approach is based is an inadequate model because it "treats the goods to be distributed as exogenously given."

75 Nozick, *Anarchy, State, and Utopia*, 198. The question of entitlement is the subject of the next chapter.

76 Nozick, *Anarchy, State, and Utopia*, 192–195.

77 Nozick, *Anarchy, State, and Utopia*, 195. Nagel ("Rawls on Justice," 13) makes the same charge.

78 Sandel, *Liberalism*, 78 and 102. Indeed, Sandel argues (149) that at crucial points, Rawls depends on a notion of a communal self, which he has explicitly rejected. Otherwise, for example, there is no way to defend his notion that our talents and natural attributes are not "ours" but belong in some way to the community.

79 Reiman, "The Labor Theory."

80 Barry, *The Liberal Theory*, 111.

81 Rawls, *A Theory of Justice*, §26; Fishkin, *Justice*, 15.

82 Wolff, *Understanding Rawls*, 178. Nozick (*Anarchy, State, and Utopia*, 203) argues that Rawls's procedure guarantees a focus on end-state principles

since each person calculates their probable end-state. The theory therefore prevents derivation of historical, process-oriented principles.

83 As David Lyons (*Forms and Limits of Utilitarianism* [Oxford: Clarendon, 1965], 159) puts it, "The contract argument rests upon an unargued commitment to fairness and impartiality."

84 Sandel, *Liberalism*, 46. Sandel asserts, "What we need is an account of what exactly constrains the descriptive assumptions appropriate to the initial situation."

85 Ronald Dworkin, "The Original Position," in Daniels, *Reading Rawls*, 19.

86 Sandel, *Liberalism*, 119; Lyons (*Forms and Limits*, 153) makes a similar comment: "Those principles seem miscast as principles *of justice* even if they can be supported by the argument from rational self-interest."

87 Lyons, *Forms and Limits*, 153.

88 Indeed, Hare ("Rawls' Theory of Justice," 86) suggests that Rawls is "foisting" a set of moral views on his readers by trying to equate the two.

89 Hare, "Rawls' Theory of Justice," 84.

90 Lyons, *Forms and Limits*, 146.

91 See Dworkin, "The Original Position," 24; Lyons, *Forms and Limits*, 148; and Wolff, *Understanding Rawls*, 180–191.

92 Wolff, *Understanding Rawls*, 195; see also Barber, "Justifying Justice," 310.

93 Ackerman, *Social Justice*, 336.

94 Wolff, *Understanding Rawls*, 7. We concur, though one must also acknowledge the importance of the detailed elaboration of the central insight that Rawls provides in the latter two sections of the book.

95 Wolff (*Understanding Rawls*, 16) appears to take Rawls's contract method as his central insight. We are more inclined to agree with Nagel that it is the *principles*, and not the contract method per se, that will leave a lasting agenda. See Nagel, "Rawls on Justice," 15.

96 Moreover, Rawls would appear to avoid the relativism of other approaches that attempt to be pluralistic. For example, in *Spheres of Justice: A Defense of Pluralism and Equality* (New York: Basic Books, 1983), Michael Walzer argues for a plurality of principles of justice corresponding to different "spheres." There is no central guiding principle (4). However, this leaves the reader wondering why particular practices are chosen as examples of justice in the different spheres and why other practices would not be considered just. Rawls attempts to respond to this sort of relativism by providing a point from which the justice of the basic system can be assessed.

CHAPTER THREE

An Entitlement Alternative

Robert Nozick

If Rawls is right, and justice requires that the basic structures of society be arranged so as to benefit the least advantaged, then a sufficiently strong state will be required to accomplish this end. Indeed, something akin to a modern democratic "welfare" state is envisioned. It is this vision of a strong state that sets the stage for Robert Nozick's alternative proposal in *Anarchy, State, and Utopia*.[1]

Justice is not Nozick's dominant concern. His intent is to argue for a limited role for the state. He wants to show that the minimal state— and *only* the minimal state—is justifiable.[2] Questions of justice arise because distributive justice such as that envisioned by Rawls is often cited as a rationale for the more-than-minimal state. In attempting to show that distributive justice does not provide a rationale for a more-than-minimal state, Nozick offers an intriguing and quite distinctive approach to justice. He calls it an *entitlement* view.

THE ROLE OF THE STATE

To see how this theory develops, we must begin with the legitimacy of the minimal state—and the minimal state *only*. Nozick takes a Kantian view that "individuals are ends and not merely means."[3] Individuals are ends in themselves, possessed of certain "natural" rights. This means that there are *constraints* ("side constraints") on action: no actions are permitted that violate fundamental human rights.[4] Thus, for Nozick, a limited set of near-absolute rights constitutes the foundation of morality.[5] In particular, Nozick looks to John Locke's social contract and its inalienable rights to life, liberty, and property.

Locke's right to life includes the right not to be killed or assaulted. No one may be "sacrificed" for others. One of the constraints on action brought about by the inviolability of human rights is therefore a prohibition on aggression against another.[6]

But such a prohibition raises interesting questions about the role of the state. If the state becomes the exacter of justice, then it seems to violate this constraint on aggression.[7] This is the anarchist's challenge: the anarchist argues that *any* state violates individual rights. Against this charge, Nozick argues that a minimal state would come into existence by an "invisible hand" process that does not violate individual rights.[8]

In essence, the argument looks something like this: In a Lockean state of nature, the natural law would not provide for all contingencies where human rights conflict: "private and personal enforcement of one's rights . . . leads to feuds. . . . And there is no firm way to *settle* such a dispute."[9] Self-interested and rational persons would therefore form protective agencies to help adjudicate conflicting claims and to make sure that their claims were protected.[10] One such protective agency will tend to become dominant in a territory.

This dominant agency is not yet a state because it does not claim monopoly on who may legitimately use force to settle disputes, nor does it protect all within its territory.[11] However, once the transition is made to include both these elements, then we arrive at the minimal state.[12] How, then, does a dominant protective agency move to acquire a monopoly over force and protect all within its territory?

When a protective agency is dominant but does not have a monopoly over a territory, problems arise between it and "independent" agencies within the territory. How are border crossings to be adjudicated? Nozick's argument here takes the form of procedural concerns about border crossings between those under the care of a dominant protective agency and the independents who are not under its care but nonetheless inhabit its territory.[13]

In such circumstances, a dominant agency would be tempted either to prohibit all border crossings or to permit all border crossings as long as the person was adequately compensated.[14] But neither of these responses will do.

Permitting all border crossings as long as the person is compensated is not an acceptable alternative for several reasons. First, it puts the "buyer" (or border crosser) in charge: nothing is safe from confiscation as long as compensation is paid. This raises anxiety. Moreover, some injuries may not be compensable (e.g., death). Thus, to permit all border crossings as long as there is compensation would simply raise too many fears.[15]

Then it seems that the dominant protective agency would attempt to enforce a total ban on all border crossings. But such a ban is not realistic, for it, too, will raise many fears and uncertainties. It is not always possible to avoid crossing a border and not always possible to negotiate consent beforehand. Thus, some border crossings must be permitted, even where there is no consent.[16]

But once again, this possibility raises the issue of compensation. Remembering that we begin from a position of individual rights—and particularly rights to freedom of action and rights against aggression—the key ingredient in Nozick's theory becomes a *principle of compensation*.

Nozick suggests there are two places where compensation must be given. One is where an unconsented crossing is permitted. In this case, the person whose boundaries are transgressed without consent is to be compensated for his loss.

However, the second case where compensation is required is equally, if not more, important. It is where a ban is instituted, and border crossings are prohibited simply because they *might* be harmful to someone. In this case, one's liberty (to cross boundaries) has been infringed. The person whose action is forbidden because it might be dangerous to others, but where it has not been proven to be so, is to be compensated for the loss of freedom to act.[17]

Thus, both permitting and prohibiting border crossings can give rise to situations requiring compensation. This is a procedural principle for Nozick. To this principle of compensation for loss of freedom, Nozick adds one more procedural consideration: one does not have a right to do something unless one knows certain facts. Specifically, one cannot punish a transgressor unless one is sure the person *is* a transgressor.[18]

But now consider the following dilemma for dominant protective agencies. What should the dominant protective agency in a territory do if it deems the procedures for enforcing rights used by independents in the territory not to be sufficiently reliable? Putting together the principle of compensation and the procedural requirement for knowledge, we arrive at an answer. On grounds that the independent agency does not have a right to punish unless its knowledge is adequate, the dominant agency can legitimately prohibit an independent agency from such punishment or enforcement of borders.

But then the dominant agency has restricted the independents' freedom simply because of a *chance* that its insufficient knowledge will result in harm to others. The principle of compensation therefore requires that the dominant agency compensate the independents for the disadvantages they suffer because of this restriction.[19] The least expensive way to compensate them is to provide protective services to them.

Thus, we arrive at the dominant protective agency protecting all in its territory and claiming a monopoly in that territory on the legitimate use of force.[20] These were the two conditions necessary for the minimal state, and thus we have arrived at the minimal state.

This minimal state arises through the natural process of the formation of a dominant protective agency coupled with principles of compensation and adequate knowledge. Hence, the minimal state arises through an invisible hand process resting on minimal principles and containing no immoral maneuvers. It is therefore legitimate, contrary to the anarchist's claim.

Moreover, Nozick argues that this minimal state is not only defensible but exciting. Nozick rejects the idea that there is a single way of life that would constitute utopia for everyone. Since people are so different, a single utopian vision would be absurd. The minimal state leaves people with the liberty to form utopian communities within the overall framework without having their rights violated: "Treating us with respect by respecting our rights, it allows us . . . to choose our life and to realize our ends . . . aided by the voluntary cooperation of other individuals possessing the same dignity."[21] The minimal state therefore provides a framework for utopia.[22]

We have arrived, then, at the justification for the minimal state. Such a state does not violate anyone's rights since it arises by an invisible hand process coupled with a fundamental moral principle of compensation for loss of freedom. But it remains to establish that only the minimal state is justifiable. Here is where Nozick develops his understanding of justice.

DISTRIBUTIVE JUSTICE

At first glance, Nozick's minimal state appears to be redistributive. It redistributes goods by compelling some people to pay for the protection of others. This suggests that perhaps the grounds have been laid for a broader approach to distributive justice: "If some redistribution is legitimate in order to protect everyone, why is redistribution not legitimate for other attractive and desirable purposes as well?"[23]

However, Nozick argues that the minimal state is *not* redistributive. Its actions are justified not by principles of redistribution of goods but only by the principle of compensation (coupled with the invisible hand process).[24] Thus, no grounds have been established by which the state may take from some persons in order to *assist* others. As yet, the door has not been opened to considerations of redistribution of goods on grounds of justice. The minimal state arises through the operation of negative rights of nonintervention and related principles of compensation and knowledge; it does not arise through nor imply any positive rights of citizens to be supported by the state.

But is a more extensive state justified in order to provide such support or to achieve distributive justice? Both Rawls and the utilitarians would legitimize a more-than-minimal state in order to ensure that goods are distributed justly—either to protect the least advantaged or to ensure the greatest overall good. Is such a more-than-minimal state entailed by considerations of justice?

Nozick's answer to this question is a resounding no. The pattern of distribution of goods in society, argues Nozick, is not the result of some central agency that distributes everything. Rather, it is the result of myriads of individual exchanges, gifts, and decisions.[25] Lacking such a central distributive or allocative agency, there can be no question of distributive justice. Instead, we merely have patterns of individual holdings. Hence, the question is posed more accurately as one of "justice in holdings."[26]

When are a person's holdings just? Nozick's answer takes the form of one basic principle: *whatever arises from a just situation by just steps is just.*[27] Picture any original set of holdings or distribution of goods that seems just (e.g., an equal distribution of goods to each person). Then permit people to make choices about exchanging those goods and about giving to each other from their share.

For example, suppose everyone wants to see Taylor Swift sing, and they are each willing to give her one dollar for the pleasure of watching her in concert.[28] Each exchange of one dollar to Swift is itself fair. After some time, however, holdings will no longer be equal: Swift will be far richer than everyone else. Yet this discrepancy in holdings is just, says Nozick, since the holdings arise by fair means from an initially just situation. Any attempt to redistribute goods according to some end goal or pattern (e.g., Rawls's difference principle) must therefore intrude on these free decisions made by people.[29]

Justice in holdings, then, is comprised of the justice of the original acquisition and the justice of the transfers made.[30] This system might be referred to as the principle "from each as they choose; to each as they are chosen."[31] Nozick calls it a *historical* theory because justice is determined by how the distribution came about, not by what the distribution is.[32]

Indeed, Nozick rejects all "patterned" principles of justice that distribute goods in accord with some chosen "end-state" (e.g., equality of holdings, bettering the position of the least advantaged) or along dimensions suggested by formulae such as "to each according to need" or "to each according to merit." Such principles look only at *what* the final distribution is and ignore the *manner* by which the distribution came into effect.

In contrast to such patterned principles, says Nozick, "*historical principles* of justice hold that past circumstances or actions of people can create differential entitlements or differential deservingness to things."[33] Hence, this is an "entitlement" theory. Justice is determined not by the pattern of the final outcome of distribution but by whether "entitlements" are honored.

Since transfers made in an entitlement system are often done for reasons (e.g., I exchange with others because they will benefit me), "strands of patterns will run through it."[34] That is, the actual distribution will look in part as though it were done on the basis of some formula such as "give to each according to their contributions." Yet the overall system is not patterned according to any such formulae but is simply based on the procedural principles of fair acquisition and fair transfer.

Locke's right to property is the key assumption here. One of the few positive rights that Nozick permits as a fundamental human right is the right to acquire and transfer property.[35] Nozick does not elaborate a full theory for fair acquisition and transfer. In general, he seems to support the underlying assumptions of market exchange.

He does accept, however, a "Lockean proviso" on the justice of original acquisition: I am free to acquire by "mixing my labor" with something, *provided* I do not hurt others in the process. Hence, it is not just for me to acquire something that is so limited that my acquisition of it worsens others' condition.[36]

This reasoning about original *acquisition*, suggests Nozick, applies by extension to *transfer* and *purchase*. It would not be just for me to transfer or purchase something so limited that its concentration in the hands of one and its absence to others hurts their situation:[37] "Each owner's title to his holding includes the historical shadow of the Lockean proviso on appropriation."[38] In short, at the root of this system appears to lie a *prohibition against harm* to others deriving from their rights as human beings. One has the right to own goods but not when that ownership harms others.

However, Nozick gives several interesting twists to the "Lockean proviso." For example, instead of remaining firm on the notion that one may not acquire severely limited goods, he argues that one may indeed acquire them as long as one compensates others so that their situation is not worsened.[39] He argues that a scientist has the right to horde a new compound that she has invented. While there may be some who need the compound in order to live, creating the compound did not *worsen* their state from what it was before. Thus, the scientist is not under any obligation to give or sell the compound and may exchange it at any price the market will bear.[40]

The notion of what it means to "harm" or "worsen" someone's situation is therefore very central to this theory. Nozick acknowledges that a full theory of justice in holdings needs both a baseline for determining what it means to "harm" others or to make them worse off and also a theory of property rights.[41]

This approach to justice puts individual liberty and choice in a primary position over any claims for equality of holdings. Indeed, one of Nozick's strongest criticisms of "patterned principles," such as Rawls's difference principle, is that they inevitably involve violations of freedom of choice. Since they force arrangements that redistribute the goods that people have chosen to give or exchange, they violate the fundamental Kantian principle of respect for people's autonomy of choice.[42]

One of the interesting implications of this approach is Nozick's understanding of taxes. Taxes, he declares, are equivalent to forced labor.[43] Paying taxes is like being forced to work n hours for someone else. Hence, patterned principles of distributive justice that require taxation (e.g., in order to benefit the least advantaged) are "appropriating" or "seizing" people's labor.[44] To seize another's labor is to use that other as a means, not respecting them as an end in themselves. Taxes violate Kantian "side constraints" and are not morally permissible.

The net result of this reasoning is that no justification can be offered for a more-than-minimal state on grounds that it is necessary to ensure distributive justice. Justice is not "distributive" but depends on just acquisition and transfer of holdings. Freedom of choice is violated by any state or system that imposes patterns of redistribution or attempts to achieve any end state of allocation of goods: "If the set of holdings is properly generated, there is no argument for a more extensive state based upon distributive justice."[45]

REVIEW

In short, Nozick begins with a minimal state based on a minimal set of fundamental rights: rights against injury by others, rights to freedom of choice and action, and rights to own private property. The state has legitimacy only to ensure protection of these rights and compensation for their violations. Where Rawls sees the necessity for societal principles to ensure just distribution, Nozick rejects any role for the state in distributive justice. Justice is limited to the "commutative" sphere of individual exchanges.

Hence, justice for Nozick consists in a fair exchange. Justice makes no substantive claims but consists only of procedural requirements for fairness in exchange. One cannot argue that justice requires any particular distribution of goods. Any distribution of goods that results from free choice and exchange is just as long as the beginning point and the exchange itself are fair.

Significantly, justice does not consist in promoting the greatest good of the greatest number or in protecting the least advantaged. Neither society as a whole nor any individual or group can make claims against the state for a distribution of goods other than that which arises from free exchanges among individuals. It may be *unfortunate* that some are wealthier than others, but it is not *unjust*, provided the rules for free choice in exchange have not been violated.

CRITIQUE

The implications of Nozick's theory are startling. Not only does it imply, as he suggests, that taxes are a form of forced labor, but it also sets no "utility floor" or bottom to the plight of those worst off; it requires no limits on the disparity between rich and poor, and it provides no protections against a decline in overall welfare.[46] Thus, clearly, it already stands in tension with utilitarian concerns for maximizing welfare and with Rawlsian concerns for protecting those who are disadvantaged. As one critic puts it, "So long as rights are not violated it matters not for [Nozick's] morality . . . how a social system actually works, how individuals fare under it . . . or what misery or inequalities it produces."[47] But this does not necessarily make it wrong.

Indeed, Nozick would argue that both the utilitarians and Rawls have misunderstood the nature of justice. Though Rawls claims to offer a pure procedural justice, Nozick charges that, in fact, Rawls winds up with an end-state approach. Nozick's own historical view, in contrast, does give a pure procedural justice—whatever the end result is, it is just, as long as it arose from procedures that are themselves just. As for the utilitarians, they clearly permit the possibility that one person's rights are to be sacrificed for the good of others. This is a violation of Kantian principles of respect for persons.[48]

Does Nozick, then, offer a more defensible liberal approach to justice? We shall not deal here with those who would argue that any theory of justice must include at least a principle of need or of desert in addition to Nozick's principle of free choice.[49] Rather, we will focus on criticisms raised about his central claims: the historical nature of principles of justice, the centrality of liberty, and the Lockean proviso on the justice of holdings.

According to James Fishkin, Nozick's approach is nothing more than "protecting 'capitalist acts between consenting adults.'"[50] That is, Nozick begins with assumptions, drawn from Locke, about the right to own private property and to exchange it within certain boundaries of free and knowledgeable consent. Nozick admits his belief that "the free operation of a market system will not actually run afoul of the Lockean proviso."[51]

But these assumptions raise several questions. First, why should property rights have such an "absolute, permanent, exclusive, inheritable and unmodifiable" character?[52] The right to own property is not a negative right against interference but a positive right. Nozick offers no arguments for limiting the range of positive rights to those of acquisition and transfer of property. He assumes the legitimacy of private ownership as part of Locke's "state of nature," but neither Nozick nor Locke ever justifies it.

Moreover, property rights entail limitations on freedom. Liberals, suggests G. A. Cohen, "see the freedom which is intrinsic to capitalism, but they do not notice the unfreedom which necessarily accompanies it."[53] There are two "freedoms" that might be associated with property: the freedom to own it and the freedom to use it: "Freedom to buy and sell belongs to capitalism's inmost nature. Other freedoms do not."[54] Thus, argues Cohen, my freedom to *own* property is always accompanied by limitations on others' freedom to *use* that property. Hence, private property distributes freedom *and* unfreedom.[55] My positive right to own property, therefore, is bought only at the price of interference with others' freedom to use it.

But surely Nozick would argue that such interference is justified. The nonowner remains free from "unjustified" interference. This is what Cohen calls the *moralized* definition of liberty. But once we permit such moralized definitions that distinguish between justified and unjustified interference with liberty, we have undermined the grounds for arguments against taxation and social services. To be sure, such things may limit my liberty, but they may do so only in a "justified" way.[56]

In short, one must distinguish types of interference with liberty. H. L. A. Hart concurs. Indeed, he suggests that much of Nozick's argument rests on the use of value-laden metaphors (e.g., calling taxation "forced labor," as though there was no difference between restrictions on income and restrictions on physical freedom). Taking account of the gravity of restrictions on different liberties and their importance for the conduct of a meaningful life, argues Hart, will undermine Nozick's claim that all restrictions on liberty violate the separateness of persons.[57]

Moreover, a number of critics raise questions about Nozick's central claims regarding justice in exchange and transfer. His theory depends on the notion that market exchanges, as long as they are genuinely "free" and do not violate fair procedure, result in just outcomes. Nozick assumes that if distribution D1 is fair and we move from D1 to distribution D2 through a process of free choice, then D2 is also fair. But is this necessarily the case?

Here, we might begin by noting that Nozick provides no historical data regarding market systems and their operations. He claims that market systems do not violate the Lockean proviso. But liberation theologians point to the growing gap between rich and poor to suggest that market systems do indeed make some worse off than they were before.[58] Nozick acknowledges the need for principles of rectification of injustice but does not deal with their actual operation in society.

Many critics suggest that Nozick ignores important aspects of market mechanisms and social cohesion. Bruce Ackerman argues that Nozick's basic rights, such as ownership of property, are absolute only in an ideal world and not in the real world we inhabit: "Nozick's position is dialogically indefensible in a world deeply scarred by illegitimate domination."[59]

Michael Walzer also argues that market exchange is problematic as a basis for justice. He proposes that each social good being distributed occupies its own "sphere"; market exchange is acceptable as the basis for justice within certain spheres but not in all. There are "blocked exchanges"—things that money cannot and should not be able to buy, such as human life. The problem, however, is that "money is insidious, and market relations are expansive."[60] Thus money, far from being the "neutral" medium through which fair exchanges can be worked out, is in practice a dominant good: "money seeps across all boundaries—this is the primary form of illegal immigration."[61]

What both of these authors point to is the fact that in the real world, under circumstances of domination and exploitation, exchange is never as just or neutral as it needs to be in order to support Nozick's theory. This point is well elaborated by Jon Gunnemann.[62] Gunnemann accepts that market economies are characterized by exchange. Therefore, the justice of a market economy is characterized by justice in exchange—commutative justice, not distributive justice per se. Nozick is correct, therefore, insofar as he points to the importance of exchanges and to commutative instead of (or in addition to) distributive justice.

However, Nozick has failed to take sufficiently seriously the implications of commutative justice. Following Adam Smith, suggests Gunnemann, the root notion in commutative justice is avoidance of harm. Nozick appears to acknowledge this but does not draw out its implications for the market arena. Harm is avoided by guaranteeing the equivalence of exchange. This requires shared social meanings and equal competence to evaluate the items to be exchanged.

Shared social meaning and equal competence to evaluate the worth of exchanges require a face-to-face encounter and a shared cultural experience. Indeed, Adam Smith thought that exchanges were unjust when they involved the extraordinary profits that are gained by distance, secrecy, or other distortions of mutual knowledgeability. Such face-to-face encounters are typical of some market societies, claims Gunnemann, but not of modern capitalistic market systems.

Nozick writes as though we operate in a simple market economy characterized by face-to-face encounters. However, our economy is not characterized by face-to-face encounters but by capitalist systems that depend on accumulation of capital and great distance between seller and purchaser. Nozick's example of paying to see a star perform is therefore "deceptive," suggests Gunnemann. No one who purchased tickets for a Taylor Swift concert has any *direct* dealings with Swift. Tickets are sold by a large agency. Media attention hypes the event. Without the trappings of capitalist market systems, it is very unlikely that Swift would develop the kind of fame that makes everyone want to watch her sing or that she could indeed become much richer than others.

In short, modern capitalist market societies are not characterized by the circumstances that make for fair exchange and not-harming but rather exactly by the reverse. Any theory of justice in exchange must take these factors seriously, as Nozick fails to do.

For instance, free and knowledgeable exchange requires access to information. As Bruce Ackerman suggests, this raises serious questions about the justice of new technologies, which are generally rather expensive. Ackerman concludes that "laissez-faire will systematically give some people special transactional advantages to exploit ignorance."[63] Walzer concurs: "A radically laissez-faire economy would be like a totalitarian state, invading every other sphere, dominating every other distributive process."[64] Many years ago, Emil Brunner pointed out that "exchange, if left to itself, generates phenomena which destroy free exchange, among others economic monopolies."[65]

John Langan also notes that Nozick ignores the large public inputs into the productive process that make private decisions inappropriate as a base for justice in production and exchange.[66] Individuals do not simply create and exchange goods: "All property is acquired under conditions which the acquirer has not himself created."[67] Nozick ignores the extent to which all transactions are protected and promoted by the community—and hence, the extent to which the community has a "partial right to private property which it claims, for instance, in the form of taxes."[68] Taxes are not forced labor but rather a recognition of the community's contribution to and proper share of the earnings of the individual.

In sum, these critics claim that Nozick's proposal for just holdings arising from freedom of choice is not realistic. Nozick ignores some of the complexities of modern society that make his simple norms of commutative exchange inadequate.

Moreover, Nozick draws many of his examples from the private—indeed, from the intimate—sphere. For example, to argue that those who are not chosen have no reason for complaint, he uses the choice of a marriage partner as an example.[69] The example seems suspect at best since the arena of romantic love is not one in which we usually think issues of distributive justice apply. Minimally, Walzer would say that Nozick is inappropriately using norms from one distributive sphere to apply to another.[70] Fishkin charges that the extension of assumptions from one arena to the other requires a more elaborate theory of the benchmarks for assessing harm in each.[71]

This raises yet another question for Nozick: his understanding of human community and human nature. Hart proposes that "meaningful life" requires not simply protection of liberty but access to the resources and opportunities needed to exercise that liberty.[72] William A. Galston attacks Nozick's approach to the researcher who synthesizes a new drug. Nozick claims that the researcher has no obligations to others to distribute the drug since he has not made their situation worse off than it was before. Galston proposes, however, that Nozick misunderstands the fundamental point of the Lockean proviso: it is intended to ensure that no one is prevented from fulfilling basic needs as a result of another's actions. Hence, since the researcher prevents others from fulfilling basic needs—needs for life itself—he is "as culpable as the person who appropriates the last water hole and refuses to share it."[73]

Similarly, Langan charges that while Nozick correctly captures the importance of claims based on specific actions and agreements, he "ignores the possibility of our being bound by ties of natural duty."[74] This is another way of saying that Nozick appears to have a truncated notion of human community. Here Walzer offers a strong critique: he proposes that human society does not arise, as Nozick would have it, merely out of the need for mutual protection. Rather, government arises out of cultural endeavors: "Individuals . . . will necessarily seek out other individuals for the sake of collective provision. They need too much from one another—not only material goods, which might be provided through a system of free exchange, but material goods that have, so to speak, a moral and cultural shape."[75] By limiting the origins of the state to the need for defense alone, Nozick already limits his notions of human nature and therefore of the possibilities for justice.

Finally, perhaps the most striking criticism comes from Susan Moller Okin. If people acquire ownership by mixing their labor with raw materials, then the clear implication is that all children are "owned" by their mothers, who mixed their labor with the raw materials of sperm and egg: "Since he so firmly upholds . . . the principle that persons are fully entitled to whatever results from their natural talents and capacities, he would seem to have no way of avoiding the conclusion that . . . women own the children they produce."[76]

ASSESSMENT

It appears, then, that there are serious problems with this approach to justice in its present form. Nozick himself has pointed to some of the work that would be needed in order to complete the theory: a theory of harms and an understanding of private property. In addition, his critics suggest there are serious underlying issues to be considered, including the adequacy of his notion of human nature and the norms for simple exchange in a complex capitalist society.

Nonetheless, Nozick's libertarian challenge will leave an important legacy for those concerned with justice. First, his stress on the *historical* nature of justice is important. Justice does have to do with entitlements as well as with end states. The utilitarian concern for overall good and the Rawlsian concern for the plight of the least advantaged may be necessary components of a theory of justice, but any such theory must also account for the claims and entitlements created by human activity.

As an ideal, his theory surely captures something that is important to justice. If an original distribution is fair, and if all subsequent exchanges are fair, then there is at least a *prima facie* case for thinking that the final distribution is itself fair. Whether there are other mitigating factors must, of course, be considered. Nonetheless, many of the cries of injustice raised today focus on the unfairness either of an original distribution of goods or of exchanges made—treaties with Indigenous tribes unjustly broken, lands unjustly appropriated from Japanese Americans during World War II, and others. The focus of these cries of injustice on issues of acquisition and exchange gives force to Nozick's basic notion of justice in holdings through fair exchange.

Another important contribution of Nozick's theory is to point us squarely to the problem of liberty and its incompatibility with equality. As Fishkin notes, contemporary liberals tend to uphold three values that exist in uneasy tension: merit, equality of life chances, and the autonomy of the family. It is not clear that these values are compatible: Liberty exercised by the family (e.g., through decisions about inheritance) always threatens to make life chances unequal and hence to undermine fair opportunity and other procedural underpinnings of liberal theory.[77] If liberty is the primary value, then equality may have to be sacrificed. If equality is upheld, there will be violations of liberty. These trade-offs are clearly perceived by Nozick.

And yet Nozick's limiting of claims or entitlements to negative rights against intervention does not fulfill what many take to be the demands of justice. Most of those who see claims as central to justice include within those claims not only negative entitlements based on free choice but also entitlements based on need, desert, and other elements seemingly ignored by Nozick's theory.[78]

It is to one such approach that we turn next. The communitarian approach will shift our debate in significant ways, including a recognition that different social goods require different distributive reasoning (e.g., we should not distribute elite college admission and donor kidneys using the same criterion). More fundamentally, however, communitarianism will seek to recover the value of the common good for considerations of justice.

NOTES

1 Robert Nozick, *Anarchy, State, and Utopia* (New York: Basic Books, 1974), 153.
2 Nozick, *Anarchy, State, and Utopia*, 52–53.
3 Nozick, *Anarchy, State, and Utopia*, 31. Indeed, he puts it even more strongly in the preface: "Individuals have rights and there are things no person or group may do to them" (ix).
4 Nozick, *Anarchy, State, and Utopia*, 28–29.
5 H. L. A. Hart, "Between Utility and Rights," in *The Idea of Freedom: Essays in Honour of Isaiah Berlin*, ed. Alan Ryan (Oxford: Oxford University Press, 1979), 81.
6 Nozick, *Anarchy, State, and Utopia*, 33: "This root idea, namely, that there are different individuals with separate lives and so no one may be sacrificed for others ... leads to a libertarian side constraint that prohibits aggression against another."
7 Nozick, *Anarchy, State, and Utopia*, 51.
8 An "invisible hand explanation" shows that something that appears to have been produced by intentional design was in fact brought about by a process that did not have that design in mind (Nozick, *Anarchy, State, and Utopia*, 19–20).
9 Nozick, *Anarchy, State, and Utopia*, 11.
10 Nozick, *Anarchy, State, and Utopia*, 13.
11 Nozick, *Anarchy, State, and Utopia*, 22–23.
12 To show that the state is legitimate, says Nozick, one must show (1) that an "ultraminimal" state arises out of the system of protective agencies, (2) that it is transformed into a minimal state, and (3) that each of these moves is morally legitimate (Nozick, *Anarchy, State, and Utopia*, 52).
13 Nozick, *Anarchy, State, and Utopia*, 56.
14 Nozick, *Anarchy, State, and Utopia*, 59.
15 Nozick, *Anarchy, State, and Utopia*, 63–70.
16 Nozick, *Anarchy, State, and Utopia*, 71.
17 Nozick, *Anarchy, State, and Utopia*, 81.
18 What we may do is limited not only by the rights of others but also by moral considerations about the person acting (some component of knowledge is important) [Nozick, *Anarchy, State, and Utopia*, 106–107].

19 "It is morally required to [protect all] by the principle of compensation, which requires those who act in self-protection in order to increase their own security to compensate those they prohibit from doing risky acts which might actually have turned out to be harmless" (Nozick, *Anarchy, State, and Utopia*, 114).

20 Nozick, *Anarchy, State, and Utopia*, 110–111.

21 Nozick, *Anarchy, State, and Utopia*, 334.

22 Nozick, *Anarchy, State, and Utopia*, 333.

23 Nozick, *Anarchy, State, and Utopia*, 27.

24 Nozick, *Anarchy, State, and Utopia*, 118–119.

25 Nozick, *Anarchy, State, and Utopia*, 149.

26 Nozick is not the only one to stress justice in holdings. Although a critic of Nozick on many counts, William Galston asserts that justice has to do with "rightful possession." This is close to Nozick's definition of justice, whatever other differences there may be between the two theorists. See William A. Galston, *Justice and the Human Good* (Chicago: University of Chicago Press, 1980), 105.

27 Nozick, *Anarchy, State, and Utopia*, 150.

28 Nozick, *Anarchy, State, and Utopia*, 161–162. Nozick uses Wilt Chamberlain as his example.

29 Nozick, *Anarchy, State, and Utopia*, 163: "No end-state principle or distributional patterned principle of justice can be continuously realized without continuous interference with people's lives."

30 Nozick, *Anarchy, State, and Utopia*, 150–152. In addition, there will need to be a principle for rectification of injustice in case either the original holdings or the transfer are not just.

31 Nozick, *Anarchy, State, and Utopia*, 160. Indeed, Nozick claims (168) that most theories of justice consider only the recipients of goods and not the rights of the givers of goods. In this regard, it is interesting to recall one of the examples Mill offers for the inadequacy of justice to solve difficult issues of distribution. In considering whether remuneration should be given for talent and contribution or for effort (doing the best one can), Mill declares that "the one looks to what it is just that the individual should receive, the other to what it is just that the community should give" (John Stuart Mill, *Utilitarianism* [New York: Bobbs-Merrill, 1957], 71).

32 Nozick, *Anarchy, State, and Utopia*, 153.

33 Nozick, *Anarchy, State, and Utopia*, 155.

34 Nozick, *Anarchy, State, and Utopia*, 157.

35 Hart, "Between Utility and Rights," 81.

36 Nozick, *Anarchy, State, and Utopia*, 175.

37 Nozick, *Anarchy, State, and Utopia*, 178–179. However, Nozick limits the "hurt" here to the damage done because others can no longer "use" the thing; their inability to acquire it themselves is a permissible hurt, in his view.

38 Nozick, *Anarchy, State, and Utopia*, 180.

39 Nozick, *Anarchy, State, and Utopia*, 178.

40 Nozick, *Anarchy, State, and Utopia*, 181.

41 Nozick, *Anarchy, State, and Utopia*, 177–178.

42 Nozick, *Anarchy, State, and Utopia*, 167. Nozick does allow one possible role for such patterned principles. He suggests (231) that a principle such as Rawls's difference principle might serve as a "rough rule of thumb" for approximating the principle of rectification in places where acquisition and transfer have not been fair.

43 Nozick, *Anarchy, State, and Utopia*, 169.

44 Nozick, *Anarchy, State, and Utopia*, 172. The value-laden nature of Nozick's language here and elsewhere in the book should be noted.

45 Nozick, *Anarchy, State, and Utopia*, 230.

46 See James S. Fishkin, *Justice, Equal Opportunity, and the Family* (New Haven, CT: Yale University Press, 1983), 13.

47 Hart, "Between Utility and Rights," 81.

48 In a well-known passage, Nozick says, "Individually, we each sometimes choose to undergo some pain or sacrifice for a greater benefit or to avoid a greater harm. . . . Why not, *similarly*, hold that some persons have to bear some costs that benefit other persons more, for the sake of the overall social good. But there is no *social entity*. . . . There are only individual people. . . . Using one of these people for the benefit of others, uses him and benefits the others. Nothing more" (*Anarchy, State, and Utopia*, 130).

49 Cf. Galston, *Justice and the Human Good*, and Michael Walzer, *Spheres of Justice: A Defense of Pluralism and Equality* (New York: Basic Books, 1983).

50 Fishkin, *Justice*, 135.

51 Nozick, *Anarchy, State, and Utopia*, 182.

52 Hart, "Between Utility and Rights," 85.

53 G. A. Cohen, "Capitalism, Freedom and the Proletariat," in Ryan, *The Idea of Freedom*, 10–11.

54 Cohen, "Capitalism, Freedom and the Proletariat," 15.

55 Cohen, "Capitalism, Freedom and the Proletariat," 15.

56 Cohen, "Capitalism, Freedom and the Proletariat," 13.

57 Hart, "Between Utility and Rights," 85.

58 Gustavo Gutierrez, *A Theology of Liberation* (Maryknoll, NY: Orbis, 1973), 89; see also Penny Lernoux, "The Long Path to Puebla," in *Puebla and Beyond*, ed. John Eagleson and Philip Sharper (Maryknoll, NY: Orbis, 1979).

59 Bruce A. Ackerman, *Social Justice in the Liberal State* (New Haven, CT: Yale University Press, 1980), 186. Ackerman's own proposal for a liberal approach depends on notions of "neutral dialogue" in which rights are not preexistent but emerge out of a carefully constrained dialog. The primary constraint is that no one is permitted to claim superiority over others.

60 Walzer, *Spheres of Justice*, 119. We will examine Walzer's spheres in more detail in chapter 4.

61 Walzer, *Spheres of Justice*, 22.
62 Jon P. Gunnemann, "Capitalism and Commutative Justice," *Annual of the Society of Christian Ethics* 5 (1985): 101–122. Note that Gunnerman responds directly to Nozick's use of Wilt Chamberlain. The shift to Taylor Swift here is for consistency with our earlier example.
63 Ackerman, *Social Justice*, 188. Ackerman uses access to television and computers as his example, but the concern has become no less salient as the technology has advanced. In their recent reports on the ethics of the emerging field of artificial intelligence, both UNESCO and the European Commission saw fit to name "access to AI" as a fundamental right if that technology is left completely to the free market. See UNESCO, "Recommendation on the Ethics of Artificial Intelligence," November 23, 2021, https://unesdoc.unesco.org/ark:/48223/pf0000381137; High-Level Expert Group on AI, "Ethics Guidelines for Trustworthy AI," Shaping Europe's Digital Future, European Commission, April 8, 2019, https://digital-strategy.ec.europa.eu/en/library/ethics-guidelines-trustworthy-ai.
64 Walzer, *Spheres of Justice*, 119.
65 Emil Brunner, *Justice and the Social Order* (London: Lutterworth, 1945), 161.
66 John P. Langan, "Rawls, Nozick, and the Search for Social Justice," *Theological Studies* 38 (1977): 357.
67 Brunner, *Justice*, 134.
68 Brunner, *Justice*, 134.
69 Nozick, *Anarchy, State, and Utopia*, 237.
70 At another point, Nozick uses the example of grading to show there are entitlements (199). Walzer clearly distinguishes norms for justice in the assignment or grades or prizes from norms for justice in the economic arena.
71 Fishkin, *Justice*, 136, n. 36.
72 Hart, "Between Utility and Rights," 85. The argument here is reminiscent of Daniels's challenge to Rawls that liberty without "worth of liberty" is not liberty at all. See Norman Daniels, "Equal Liberty and Unequal Worth of Liberty," in *Reading Rawls*, ed. Norman Daniels (New York: Basic Books, n.d.).
73 Galston, *Justice and the Human Good*, 230. Indeed, Galston and others would argue that *need* is a fundamental claim precisely because of the close connection between need and harm (199).
74 Langan, "Rawls," 357.
75 Walzer, *Spheres of Justice*, 74.
76 Susan Moller Okin, *Justice, Gender, and the Family* (New York: Basic Books, 1989), 83.

77 Fishkin, *Justice*, 4–6, 159. Fishkin (83) therefore proposes that we have a "trilemma"––a three-legged stool whose legs cannot stand together. He calls contemporary liberalism an "incoherent ideal" for public policy.
78 See, for example, Nicholas Rescher's careful distinction between claims and entitlements, and his arguments for need and desert in *Distributive Justice* (New York: Bobbs-Merrill, 1966).

CHAPTER FOUR

A Communitarian Rebuttal

Michael Sandel

In the first three chapters of this book, Nozick, Rawls, and Mill have offered us the philosophical justification for three familiar perspectives in the modern social and political landscape. In examining these first three theories together, we can see two common elements. First, we find an attempt to build society around one central philosophical ideal. Nozick's theory of justice grounds the libertarian view that justice is a matter of maximizing individual *liberty*. Rawls's theory prioritizes *fairness*. Mill focuses on a goal of maximizing happiness and minimizing suffering, or, in a word, increasing overall *utility*. In each of the first three cases, we occasionally see secondary principles and goals for society, but, ultimately, each framework places these principles and goals in service of the primary principle of the theory (e.g., Rawls and Mill both appeal to liberty as necessary but ultimately place liberty in service of fairness or utility, respectively). The second common element we find among each of these accounts of a just society is a tremendous emphasis being placed on the individual. Nozick emphasizes the priority of *individual* liberty and is wary that collective power, in the form of a government, might be wielded unjustly by individuals in office. Rawls's thought experiment begins with those principles that *an individual* would choose behind a veil of ignorance and proceeds to protect a system of equal individual liberties, fair distribution of goods to individuals (including protecting the individual in the minimum position), and the opening of offices of power to free competition among individuals. Utilitarianism's focus on the greatest good for the greatest number may seem to be the only theory examined thus far that prioritizes the collective. But even here, there is little appeal to the *common* good in Mill's writings; the collective is only understood as the aggregate sum of *individual* pleasures and pains.

In the 1980s, several philosophers began to push back on both of these tendencies in philosophy of the time. Among these, Alasdair MacIntyre, Michael Walzer, Charles Taylor, and Michael Sandel are often labeled together as the leading communitarian philosophers.[1] These philosophers shared a trenchant critique of the current state of American and European public philosophy as placing too great an emphasis on the individual—and especially individual liberty to choose one's values and ends—at the cost of the value of community and to the loss of a concept of the common good. However, when it comes to offering a vision of the alternative social philosophy, each of these philosophers has his own vision, and they only somewhat overlap. In this chapter, we have used Michael Sandel as our primary communitarian interlocutor and leaned on others when their work supports Sandel's approach but is more extensive on a particular topic. Sandel's communitarian theory of justice is noted by three elements: it is teleological, narrative, and oriented toward the common good.

A TELEOLOGICAL METHODOLOGY

In *Liberalism and the Limits of Justice*, Sandel offers a full-throated critique of Rawls's deontological conception of justice. Sandel does not reject the importance of principles, rules, rights, or duties in achieving justice, but he does question whether "rights can be identified and justified in a way that does not presuppose any particular conception of the good life."[2] We have seen this question already. In chapter 2, we noted that critics of Rawls (including Sandel) question the implications of Rawls's veil of ignorance thought experiment. Can one make moral choices behind the veil without knowledge of what one will *value* in the real world?[3]

For communitarians, justice cannot be abstracted in this way. Deontologies begin with the question "where does justice come from?" They seek to offer an abstract, procedural response to this question. For communitarians, the first question is, instead, "what is justice *for*?" We cannot abstract this question from lived experience. Rather, we must descend into the context of the case.

Here many communitarians appeal to the ancient Greek philosopher Aristotle. For Aristotle, the observation of human experience in the world around us reveals that all things have a *telos*, or purpose. The *telos* of a human being is to achieve *eudaimonia*. *Eudaimonia* is often translated into English as *happiness*, but it is better understood as the fulfillment of a life well lived. Thus, what is right cannot be prior to what is good (i.e., it is value judgments about what is good and worthy that determine what is right). Rules, rights, duties, and principles can be named to identify necessary protections in a particular context, but for communitarians, these are all subsequent to our conceptions of the good life: "Rights depend for their justification on the moral importance of the ends they serve."[4]

In short, communitarianism uses a teleological methodology. Utilitarianism is also a teleology: the *telos* for Bentham is maximal pleasure and minimal pain; Mill expanded this somewhat by including other possible measures of happiness. However, by restricting the *telos* of utilitarianism to pleasure or happiness alone, utilitarians significantly limit much of what many would consider necessary aspects of the good life. A distinguishing mark of communitarian teleology is the necessity of the community to live a complete life. For utilitarians, the value of any relationship, and indeed the value of community itself, was dependent on the pleasure it could bring to the individual. Communitarians recognize that elements such as camaraderie, friendship, trust, loyalty, and empathy are all valued independently from individual pleasure or pain and cannot exist apart from community. Conversely, community also implies social *responsibilities* that cannot be ignored in our discussions of justice: "obligations of solidarity or membership may claim us for reasons unrelated to [personal] choice—reasons bound up in the narratives by which we interpret our lives and the communities we inhabit."[5]

THE NECESSITY OF NARRATIVE

In addition to being teleological, communitarianism is a narrative method: "Man is in his actions and practice, as well as in his fictions, essentially a story telling animal. . . . There is no way to give an understanding of any society, including our own, except through the stock of stories which constitute its initial dramatic resources. Mythology, in its original sense, is at the heart of things . . . the telling of stories has a key part in educating us into the virtues."[6]

Children are taught right from wrong through the telling of myths and parables. These stories resonate through us and through our communities and provide our sense of meaning and value. We can all share in an understanding "about wicked stepmothers, lost children, good but misguided kings, wolves that suckle twin boys, youngest sons who receive no inheritance but must make their way in the world and eldest sons who waste their inheritance on riotous living and go into exile to live with the swine" and it is through such sharing of communal narratives that children "learn or mislearn . . . what the ways of the world are."[7]

One of the markers of communitarian thought is allowance of different moral reasoning to apply in different contexts: "The principles of justice themselves are pluralistic in form; . . . different social goods ought to be distributed for different reasons, in accordance with different procedures, by different agents; [and] these differences derive from different understandings of the social goods themselves—an inevitable product of historical and cultural particularism."[8]

Implicit to this thesis is a distinction between goods-in-themselves and social goods. Social goods are not intrinsically valuable but, rather, derive their value from the society in which they operate. For example, the twenty-dollar bill in my pocket holds hardly any value outside of the value we collectively agree a piece of paper with Andrew Jackson on it is worth.

But Walzer goes further and contends that "all the goods with which distributive justice is concerned are social goods."[9] A screwdriver, a Harvard education, and the position of third base for the New York Yankees all derive their value from the community in which they exist. A screwdriver only works because it is compatible with a social norm of screwheads; the value of a Harvard education is determined, in large part, by the social capital of an Ivy League degree; and the position of Yankee third baseman is a function on the number of fans that player can bring to the stadium each year. If Walzer is correct, then by extension, the just movement of social goods through society is contingent on the meaning that a given community ascribes to a social good.

Within the community, it is our shared narratives that give coherence to communitarian arguments[10]—that is to say, which path will make sense for living the good life. The good life is a richer and deeper understanding of the human *telos* than mere pleasure or even happiness, but this richness and depth cannot be summed into a singular concept: "Morality is thick from the beginning, culturally integrated, fully resonant, and reveals itself thinly only on special occasions, when moral language is turned to specific purposes."[11] Principles are useful for specific purposes, but to grasp the whole of morality, we need to tell stories. More specifically, to understand a thick conception of justice, we need to tell stories about the purpose of community.

THE VIRTUES OF COMMUNITY

"A public philosophy is an elusive thing," writes Sandel, "for it is constantly before our eyes. It forms the often unreflective background to our political discourse and pursuits. In ordinary times, the public philosophy can easily escape the notice of those who live by it."[12] It is difficult to analyze the stories that shape our communities and us because to do so requires us to distance ourselves from the very stories that provide our identity. Communitarians often gain this distance by attempting to view the moral life through the lens of the not-so-distant past. Sandel contends that society today is failing to fulfill its *telos* because, over the past few decades, Western industrialized societies, and especially

America, took a turn in public philosophy toward what he terms "moral individualism."[13]

In our contemporary world, individualistic concepts abound. Today, we take for granted that society includes individual rights, liberties, and freedoms. We hold individuals accountable for their personal responsibilities, risks, liabilities, and, when necessary, criminal prosecution. We own personal property, earn personal income, and pay personal income tax. Even when we do think about the collective, we do so through the lens of the individual. Economic market forces are the aggregate of personal purchasing decisions. Business corporations are owned in individual shares and operated by individuals in specific roles and positions. Representative democracies move the power of government, ultimately, to the people but do so by electing individuals to individual offices through a system of one person, one vote.

This rampant individualism pervades and shapes other elements of our society as well. In the pursuit of personal rewards, does public service have a place? In an economy ruled by market forces, are there limits to what can be bought and sold? In a meritocratic system, is inequality a concern? In an individualistic society, what has become of the common good? In our protection of individual rights, is there any virtue in the community? As atomized individuals, are we answerable for the sins of our parents and grandparents? Or conversely, are we responsible for raising our kids and grandkids?

Behind these public assumptions, Sandel identifies a pervasive "doctrine of moral individualism," that is shared across utilitarianism, Rawlsian liberalism, and libertarianism: "The doctrine of moral individualism does not assume that people are selfish. It is rather a claim about what it means to be free. For the moral individualist, to be free is to be subject only to obligations I voluntarily incur; whatever I owe others, I owe by virtue of some act of consent—a choice or promise or an agreement that I have made, be it tacit or explicit."[14]

Libertarians consider the freedom to choose one's own ends to be the fundamental principle of society and humanity and seek to protect freedom as such with a negative rights regime. For Rawls, by contrast, the greatest threat to individual freedom is not the oppressive power of the state but the coercive power of our more powerful neighbor in an unequal society. Thus, a welfare state of positive rights and privileges must be established to maintain the equity necessary for individuals to choose their own ends. Despite such differences, Sandel recognizes that both of these deontological theories reduce freedom to "the capacity of persons to choose their values and ends."[15] Utilitarianism does not begin with a notion of freedom as intrinsically worthy of protection. Nevertheless, Mill does recognize that the utilitarian conception of justice requires that individuals are able to express and seek what makes them most happy. Thus, for Mill, individual liberty is protected for the sake of the *telos*, but the result is the same: the freedom to choose one's values and ends.

This "liberal freedom" operates as if each individual exists on an island of their own design and only engages with other islands by voluntary choice. But under such a view, "we can't make sense of a range of moral and political obligations that we commonly recognize, even prize. These include obligations of solidarity and loyalty, historic memory, and religious faith—moral claims that arise from the communities and traditions that shape our identity."[16]

Sandel juxtaposes moral individualism and liberal freedom against "civic republicanism," the public philosophy that preceded and was gradually replaced by moral individualism. In eighteenth- and nineteenth-century America and Europe, the locus was not the individual but the community. For civic republicans, freedom cannot be separated from the common good. Sandel notes that for the American founding fathers, "No phrase except 'liberty' was invoked more than 'the public good,' which for them meant more than the sum of individual interests. The point of politics was not to broker competing interests but to transcend them and to seek the good of the community as a whole. More than a break with England, independence would be a source of moral regeneration; it would stave off corruption and renew the moral spirit that suited Americans to republican government."[17]

In the first century and a half of American independence, freedom was not about personal choice but self-rule, and, more importantly, self-rule was not understood through our contemporary individualistic lens. For a community to rule itself involved citizens deliberating as a community: "Central to the republican theory is that liberty depends on sharing in self-government. . . . It means deliberating with fellow citizens about the common good and helping to shape the destiny of the political community. But to deliberate well about the common good requires more than the capacity to choose one's ends and to respect others' rights to do the same. It requires a knowledge of public affairs and also a sense of belonging, a concern for the whole, a moral bond with the community whose fate is at stake."[18]

In so far as freedom concerns the individual, it is not about personal choice but the development of the moral and civic virtues necessary to sustain the community: "To share in self-rule therefore requires that citizens possess, or come to acquire, certain qualities of character, or civic virtues. But this means that republican politics cannot be neutral toward the values and ends its citizens espouse. The republican conception of freedom, unlike the liberal conception, requires a formative politics, a politics that cultivates in citizens the qualities of character self-government requires."[19]

Here we return to the distinction between the deontological question "where does freedom come from?" and its teleological counter, "what is freedom for?" For communitarians, it is important to begin with the understanding that freedom is *for* the formation of the individual and the promotion of the common good.

THE DOMINATION OF MARKETS AND MERIT

In the communitarian scheme, social goods ought to be distributed according to the social meaning of the good itself. For Walzer, this means that each social good should be contained within its own social sphere, and those who come to possess an inequity—or even a monopoly—of a particular social good should not be able to parlay that possession into gaining social goods in another sphere. A politician should not be able to enrich themselves by way of their office, the child of a famous actor should not have an advantage in college admissions, and wealth should not be able to buy different treatment in the criminal justice system. Injustice is not the monopolization of a particular social good. Rather, injustice arises when monopoly becomes domination: "I call a good dominant if the individuals who have it, because they have it, can command a wide range of other goods. . . . Dominance describes a way of using social goods that isn't limited by their intrinsic meanings or that shapes those meanings in its own image."[20]

Walzer points to three distributive principles that cover most cases. Social goods can be distributed by free exchange, need, or desert. The first two are self-explanatory. Free exchange we have already explored in abundance in chapter 3. Unlike libertarianism, though, Walzer's scheme would limit this logic to only certain goods. Paying to watch Taylor Swift sing is an example where free exchange seems to make sense. Free exchange applied to kidney donations or political office, however, strikes us as unjust. Distribution of kidneys seems better suited for a logic of need. But notice again that the identification of a need is con-textual and imputed from the social understanding of the good and the need. Who needs the kidney more, the elderly patient who will die soon without it or the youthful patient who could survive for months, even years, on dialysis but for whom the kidney will presumably be useful for many more years? At the same time, some social goods clearly can-not be distributed according to need: allocation of luxury automobiles can hardly utilize such logic because no one *needs* a luxury automobile.

Desert is the criterion that cuts the widest swath: who *deserves* to play third base for the Yankees, or to be governor of Mississippi, or to gain entrance into Stanford University? Measuring "desert" for any of these offices cannot be reduced to a single criterion. Rather, merit or desert is complex and not easily rendered into precise formulae. Nor is desert limited to offices: Who deserves what salary for their contributions? And who deserves what sentence for their crimes? Communitarian-ism does not ease this complexity, but it does shift the question in an important way. Sandel recalls the argument that Aristotle makes in *Nicomachean Ethics* regarding who deserves the best flutes in a society: "Many orchestras conduct auditions behind a screen, so that the quality of the music can be judged without bias or distraction. Less familiar is Aristotle's reason. The most obvious reason for giving the best flute to the best flute players is that doing so will produce the best music, making listeners better off. But this is not Aristotle's reason. He thinks the best flutes should go to the best flute players because that is what flutes are *for*—to be played well."[21]

In this example, we can see the application of a nonconsequentialist (i.e., it is not about making listeners happy) teleology, where the *telos*, and by extension the logic of distribution, is implicit in the good itself. Desert is not about the outcomes, for the public at large (the listeners) or the flutist who does or does not receive the flute; it is about the *fit* of quality flute to quality flute player. Knowing and communicating such complex and nuanced understandings, once again, cannot be rendered in thin principles or formulae. Distribution according to desert or fit requires understanding the meaning ascribed to a good, and meaning is ascribed in thick narratives.

It is not clear that free exchange, need, and merit cover all possible distributive logics. Other mechanisms we morally accept for the distribution of social goods include queuing (i.e., first come, first served[22]), pooling (e.g., all members of a congressional district are represented by the same congressperson, all employees of the same company are pooled for medical insurance), equal distributions (e.g., for most democratic elections, every citizen gets exactly one vote in our democracy), or random distributions (e.g., lotteries for limited seats in a particular school). Still, it is clear that navigating the complexity of a system of different logical spheres deriving from an array of social goods requires a road map. For communitarians, however, there is not, nor should we aspire to draw, one map that will suit all communities. Justice does not yield "an ideal map or a master plan, but rather a map and a plan appropriate to the people for whom it is drawn."[23] The community-specific moral road map, once again, is fulfilled by the narratives of the community.

Market Triumphalism

Sandel has written extensively on two instances of increasing domination in our contemporary society. The first is the problem of "market triumphalism"—the ever-expanding role that money and markets play in the life of our communities and the distribution of our social goods.[24] Market triumphalism presents our societies with two problems. First, it moves social goods that were previously distributed by need or merit to be instead subject to market forces. It puts a price on social goods that otherwise should never have been measured in such ways. For Sandel, this is a corruption of the social good: "We often associate corruption with ill-gotten gains. But corruption refers to more than bribes and illicit payments. To corrupt a good or a social practice is to degrade it, to treat it according to a lower mode of valuation than is appropriate to it."[25]

More insidiously, though, market triumphalism has also come to dominate our narratives about what society is and is for: "Without quite realizing it, without ever deciding to do so, we drifted from *having* a market economy to *being* a market society. The difference is this: A market economy is a tool—a valuable and effective tool—for organizing productive activity. A market society is a way of life in which market values seep into every aspect of human endeavor. It's a place where social relations are made over in the image of the market."[26]

Like moral individualism, market triumphalism is grounded in a particular concept of the individual and that individual's freedom. For libertarians, "letting people engage in voluntary exchanges respects their freedom; laws that interfere with the free market violate individual liberty." Utilitarians argue that free markets will also promote the general welfare: "when two people make a deal, both gain. As long as their deal makes them better off without hurting anyone, it must increase overall utility."[27]

Communitarians question both of these claims. Markets are never as free as they might seem, and the value we place on goods is tied up into communal narratives and communal practices. Sandel points to the example of lobbyists paying people to stand in line to attend congressional hearings that were otherwise open to the public on a first-come-first-served basis. First, he offers the market narrative for the practice: "From an economic view, allowing free access to congressional hearings 'underprices' the good, giving rise to queues. The line-standing industry remedies this inefficiency by establishing a market price."

But, for Sandel, this values the good of representative government the wrong way. Sandel offers an alternative story: "Suppose, striving mightily to reduce the national debt, Congress decided to charge admission to its hearings—$1,000, say, for a front-row seat at the Appropriations Committee. Many people would object, not only on the grounds that the admission fee is unfair to those unable to afford it but also on the grounds that charging the public to attend a congressional hearing is a kind of corruption . . . to corrupt a good or a social practice is to degrade it, to treat it according to a lower mode of valuation than is appropriate to it."[28]

In this example, we see both the communitarian method and the communitarian commitments at work. The juxtaposition of the two narratives allows us to wrestle with the logic we think appropriate for this social good. For communitarians, who are committed to the preservation of the community and the structures of open and free representative democracy that sustains it, the choice is clear.

The Tyranny of Merit

In those places where markets have not come to be dominant, desert or merit has. Once again, for certain goods, merit is appropriate: "In filling jobs, merit matters for at least two reasons. One is efficiency. I will be better off if my plumber is capable rather than incompetent. The other is fairness. It would be wrong to discriminate against the most qualified applicant based on racial or religious or sexist prejudice."[29] But the meritocracy is larger than any one decision about plumbing or surgery. When merit becomes a sorting mechanism for an entire society, the principle of merit can take a "tyrannical" turn.

The problem is twofold. First, our measures of merit and desert are often inaccurate. Thus, we often use proxies to stand in for merit. Perhaps the most pervasive proxy used in contemporary society is admission into an elite university. Getting into an elite university opens doors to obtaining the most lucrative jobs and the most powerful positions in industry and government, but entrance to such universities is correlated with existing familial wealth more than any other factor.[30]

Second, this inaccuracy of merit is compounded when meritocracy grants additional weight to "success" or "failure" on the assumption that one's lot in life is deserved: "The dark side of the meritocratic ideal is embedded in its most alluring promise, the promise of mastery and self-making."[31] Once again, we see the doctrine of moral individualism shaping the lens through which we understand our basic social structures. Historically, we can recognize in the narratives of most cultures the existence of an "ethic of fortune," which "sees that the cosmos does not necessarily match merit with reward. It leaves room for mystery, tragedy, and humility."[32] Contemporary American society has moved more and more, however, toward an "ethic of mastery," which puts individual choice, once again, at the center of the social order: "The more we view ourselves as self-made and self-sufficient, the less likely we are to care for the fate of those less fortunate than ourselves. If my success is my own doing, their failure must be their fault." This narrative is "corrosive to commonality." It prevents gratitude, humility, and empathy for the other, and without such virtues, it becomes harder to seek the common good.

REVIEW

Communitarianism utilizes a teleological methodology that places conceptions of the good prior to any application of rules, rights, or duties. Unlike utilitarianism, though, the *telos* of human existence for communitarianism is not merely mounting up joys and happiness but attaining a more holistic fulfillment in one's values and conception of the good life. Communitarians recognize that the complexity of the moral life—especially one that is lived in community—must rely on multiple and varied logics of justice. The key is not to find the one logic on which all others depend but instead to find the *fit* between a given social good and the distribution logic that defines it and then to hold to that fit and not allow the distribution of one social good to exert dominance on another social good (e.g., market triumphalism, the tyranny of merit).

This multifaceted approach to questions of justice is complex but not unknowable. Nor is it groundless. Key to communitarian justice is the act of narrative storytelling, which thickens the conceptions of the good life and helps them to cohere. But storytelling, by its nature, cannot be an individual practice. This is one of many reasons communitarianism opposes moral individualism, which places the locus of moral wisdom in the individual's personal knowledge, ability, and will. Justice cannot be reduced to the sum of individual choices. The values that inform our thick conceptions of justice and the good life are communal.

Communitarians acknowledge that human experience is necessarily a communal experience. We are not islands connected only by willing choice and agreement. We are born into communities, educated in communities (beginning with the first community, our family), live in communities, work and play in communities, tell stories in communities, and, most importantly, believe in communities. Out of that communal experience also emerges communal claims: "Obligations of solidarity or membership may claim us for reasons unrelated to a choice—reasons bound up in the narratives by which we interpret our lives and the communities we inhabit."[33] Justice is not just the aggregate of effects on individuals. The *telos* of communitarian justice is the common good—a measure of the flourishing of the community itself, which, in turn, allows the individual to live their best life.

CRITIQUE

By allowing the local community, rather than an objective principle or formula, to set the values of social goods and their corresponding logic of just distribution, critics argue communitarianism subjects itself to the norms of that community. At worst, this makes communitarianism a form of cultural relativism or a quick slide down a slippery slope to the same. It means that questions of moral consequence can turn with changing social norms. Does communitarianism hold any commitments by which we could judge the practices of societies to be morally unjustified?

Here we have to take a slightly wider look at the communitarian label itself. Each of the four primary communitarians has, in their own way, taken issue with the label of "communitarianism." Sandel identifies two ways of understanding the term *communitarian*:

> One way of linking justice with conceptions of the good holds that principles of justice derive their moral force from values commonly espoused or widely shared in a particular community or tradition. This way of linking justice and the good is communitarian in the sense that the values of the community define what counts as just or unjust.
>
> A second way of linking justice with conceptions of the good holds that principles of justice depend for their justification on the moral worth or intrinsic good of the ends they serve. On this view, the case for recognizing a right depends on showing that it honors or advances some important human good.

The cultural relativism inherent in the first kind of communitarianism is problematic in that it offers no means to judge a culturally accepted practice as immoral. For example, many societies have traditions that oppress women. Most feminists seek a way to make some value judgments that apply across cultures in order to eliminate the worst injustices.[34]

However, Sandel claims the second sense of *communitarianism* and believes that it avoids the charge of relativism: if communitarian justice is understood as a teleological method in which the common good is the *telos* of community, then different societies may value different goods in different ways, and may even choose to distribute goods in different ways, but the appeal to a *telos* of community prevents the slippery slide down to relativism.

Walzer approaches the problem of making judgments across cultures in his exploration of the "thinness" and "thickness" of moral claims: "Moral terms have minimal and maximal meanings; we can standardly give thin and thick accounts of them, and the two accounts are appropriate to different contexts, serve different purposes. It is not the case, however, that people carry around two moralities in their head, two understandings of justice, for example. . . . Rather, minimalist meanings are embedded in the maximalist morality, expressed in the same idiom, sharing the same (historical/cultural/religious/political) orientation."[35]

Walzer points to the example of demonstrators holding signs of "justice" during the 1991 Velvet Revolution in Prague. The sign-holders had their maximal interpretation of what was meant by *justice*. Simultaneously, Walzer, while watching the events on television, had his own maximal interpretation of what that word means that was necessarily different from the Czech demonstrators. Nevertheless, a thin concept of justice was shared by the Czech demonstrators and the American academic thousands of miles away: "When I saw the picture, I knew immediately what the signs meant—and so did everyone else who saw the same picture. Not only that: I recognized and acknowledged the values that the marchers were defending—and so did (almost) everyone else."[36]

Communitarianism allows differing communities to have their own thick narratives about the value of a social good and what constitutes just distribution of that good. At the same time, thin conceptualizations of the same social good can and do transcend particular cultures. Ultimately, though, there is a difference between thick conceptions of justice that are rendered thinly for the purposes of shared understanding, and communication and conceptions of justice that are purposefully abstracted from cultural and other contexts in order to provide a thin principle or formula that is meant to stand on its own.

To understand this, let us draw on a claim Aristotle makes that *there are persons for whom slavery is the better or just condition*. For most readers of this book, this claim strikes us as absurd. But does it sound absurd because liberty is an absolute right? Or does it sound absurd because most readers of this book are steeped in the narratives of enlightenment liberalism and a twenty-first-century American culture for which *slavery* is an inherently dirty word? Communitarians would argue the latter. In fact, it is a regular practice in contemporary society for one person to be placed under the complete authority of another person. Children are the first example. Parents are given sole discretion to make all choices for their child—including the assignment of household chores but also choices of lifetime consequence such as where the child will live, go to school, and so on. Only in very particular contexts of abuse or neglect is this authority limited in any meaningful way. Liberty is also curtailed for those who are incarcerated for crimes, and while we acknowledge the significant injustices of the American penal system, few would suggest that the worst killers and rapists should be let free. In neither of these cases do we call these persons *slaves*; we call them *minors* or *criminals*.

The language matters because much value and moral meaning are imbued in the thick conceptions we have of the labels *child*, *criminal*, and *slave*. To abstract from this thick conception and simply claim a thinly abstracted right to "liberty" fails to capture the different meanings and values we place on different liberties for different people in different contexts. We need the narratives to give meaning—as well as limits—to the principles.

Of course, this cuts both ways. While thick cultural and linguistic contexts help to provide boundaries against unacceptable practices like slavery, they can also be used to maintain widely accepted but still morally problematic practices like misogyny and racism, unless Sandel's *telos* of "community" includes some careful restrictions. Feminists and others might still have a problem with who decides what is an important human good.

Moreover, as much as libertarianism, utilitarianism, and Rawlsian liberalism are guilty of neglecting much of the cultural and narrative "thickness" that undergirds their claims, the communitarians we examine here are also steeped in a legacy of Enlightenment thought that they may not be able to escape. "Communitarianism is the product of developed countries with long traditions of liberalism," writes Chinese philosopher Li Zehou. "It has referential value, but if directly or indiscriminately adopted in other societies it can be quite dangerous."[37] Zehou worries that the thick Western liberalism that undergirds communitarian claims like Sandel's might be able to move thinly from one Western context to another, but if exported unfiltered to a foreign culture such as China's, it would become unmoored from its thick foundations. Attempting communitarian claims, grounded as they are in Aristotle, in a society more rooted in Confucius risks losing any salience in the method at all.

A similar critique is leveled against Sandel by his fellow communitarian Walzer, who claims that "civic republicanism" focuses too much on the state and makes citizenship a "new form of oppression."[38] Walzer argues that citizens are not just part of one community: "I can be, all at once, a Jew, a socialist, . . . an academic political theorist, a New Yorker, . . . [a] citizen of the American republic—and a brother, husband, father, and grandfather."[39] The various communities in which we participate are multiple, various, and layered; each provides its own influence on our identity and our values, but the full thickness of our identity and values is only understood completely through all of the layers: "Of course, some people will make one community central in their lives, relish its intensity, and set themselves apart from (and perhaps against) their fellow citizens. . . . [But] many of us will instead choose to be members of different communities, and the intensity of our commitment will vary across the plurality of our memberships."[40]

When such fissures between communitarians arise, we begin to see another common critique. The common element that binds communitarians together is a shared criticism of the liberal structures that have emerged from the European Enlightenment. Communitarians hold less in common when asked to provide their own theory of justice. As Fareed Zakaria once wrote, "Communitarianism was supposed to be a third way, neither liberal nor conservative, that charted a new course for philosophy and politics. But . . . it has become a collection of meaningless terms, used as new bottles into which the old wine of liberalism and conservatism is poured. Community means one thing if you are a conservative and another if you are a liberal."[41]

We do not need the political references to see the issue. MacIntyre attempts to recall narrative virtue ethics from its medieval and ancient past; Walzer uses a casuistic examination of our present structures to develop his theory of spheres, monopolies, and domination; and Sandel critiques our present ills (e.g., libertarian freedom, a market society, meritocracy) by looking to recent but still familiar alternatives (e.g., civic republicanism, market economics, the common good). For those looking for a methodological alternative to Mill, Rawls, or Nozick, communitarianism collectively fails to deliver.

There are two rebuttals to this claim. First, this critique reveals itself as somewhat unfair when we remind ourselves that the umbrella of communitarianism has always been a label applied from the outside. None of the philosophers examined in this chapter claims themselves to be communitarians. MacIntyre calls himself an Aristotelean and Thomist. Walzer often calls himself a social democrat but, in keeping with his recognition of the multiple communities to which he belongs to, also calls himself by many labels. Sandel claims civic republicanism (though, more recently, he has warmed to the "communitarian" label so long as it carries proper caveats).

Second, and more germane to this chapter, Zakaria's claim seems to miss the central proposition of communitarianism: that the meaning and value of social goods are culturally defined. The problem is not that communitarianism molds itself too easily into other political or philosophical stances. Most methods, when taken loosely, can defend claims on both the political right and political left of contemporary American and European politics. The problem is that this critique of communitarianism believes that community is and has to be one thing. Walzer's description of minimal and maximal meanings of terms allows for a more nuanced understanding of community. The political right and the political left each holds its own thick definitions of community and the common good, but in a shared society, even if political and cultural pluralism exists, there is also still some "overlapping consensus" around the meaning of community and the common good. Sandel is attempting to argue from that shared place, appealing to the consensus through the promotion of common narratives. This is what the communitarian project has been about: identifying the narratives that can thicken and strengthen our commonality and, by extension, our community and the common good.

ASSESSMENT

Just as libertarians are named for their emphasis on liberty and utilitarians for their emphasis on utility, communitarians share an emphasis on the importance of *community* to both defining and achieving justice. This emphasis on community operates on three overlapping levels, and it is worth assessing each in turn, since each adds something unique to our pursuit of an understanding of justice.

First, communitarians recognize that we cannot know justice alone; we experience justice (and injustice) precisely because of our sociality. Liberal philosophies emerging from the Enlightenment focused on individual rights, liberties, and benefits in ways that set up a contemporary society with impoverished understandings of markets, merit, liberty, and, consequently, justice itself. Communitarian thought rebuffs these shifts toward the individual and instead seeks to balance the good of the individual against the virtues of community in our attempts to achieve the good life. That is, the good sought as the end of communitarian justice is a *common* good. This term is meant to exemplify both the common goal of justice—the betterment of society—and also the collective effort necessary to attain justice.

Second, communitarianism begins with a teleological logic that places the good prior to any conceptions of the right. For communitarians, justice does not exist prior to human experience—as an instruction manual for the game of society. Communitarian justice is concurrent with and emerges from our lived experience in society. As a teleology, communitarianism reminds us that justice needs to have a forward-looking perspective and a goal to strive for collectively. Justice that sets the rules from behind a veil of ignorance is static and cannot be specified to the complexities of a lived social life. But justice oriented toward a *telos* encourages movement *toward* something. It is not entirely clear that communitarians can agree on what that "something" actually is. This incoherence has drawn criticism onto the method, but some cohesion can be recovered if we focus, primarily, only on one communitarian's thought. Sandel's critiques of power structures that protect personal liberty to choose one's own ends and values, a market society where everything can be bought and sold, and a tyrannical meritocracy where the few things that cannot be bought and sold are distributed by corrupted measures of merit all reflect a shift in the past century from a set of social norms and narratives that oriented us toward the preservation and promotion of society and the bonds that hold us together to a set of norms and narratives aimed at personal freedom, personal responsibility, and personal rewards.

Third, the appeal here to norms and narratives reminds us that communitarian thought also recognizes the importance of thickly constituted communal values in informing specific local conceptions of the just society. The sets of norms and narratives of civic republicanism are endangered in modern society but still familiar enough to resonate for us because they are part of our recent social history and thus part of the stories we still tell, if only occasionally these days. The need for narrative thickness in our public philosophy is perhaps one of the greatest contributions of communitarianism. In the critique section above, we noted that, globally, communitarianism has drawn critical responses because it is steeped in Western enlightenment narratives. This is equally true of utilitarianism, libertarianism, and Rawlsian liberalism, but unlike these other theories, communitarianism offers a means to explain *why* Western philosophies are being rejected when read in non-Western contexts: we lack a shared concept—even a thin concept—of justice. If this is true, then bridging such cultural gaps requires, first, discovering thin but shared moral claims through open dialogue and, second, thickening the supports of the bridge according to the local culture and narratives that operate on each side of the gulf.

In the end, in drawing our attention to the importance of the community for naming, understanding, and then enacting justice, communitarianism contributes a necessary element—the importance of community—to the conversation we have been having in the first four chapters of this book. Sandel offers one important thread of thought on the changing meanings of concepts such as freedom, markets, and merit within American society over the past century. But to Walzer's point, the American society to which Sandel dedicates his attention is merely one of many overlapping communities to which we belong. In the coming chapters, we will consider other communities in which membership shapes and challenges all our justice commitments. Even in the cases where we are not a member of these communities, it is still important to gain perspective on the thick narratives of those communities with which we share a broader geographic community.

NOTES

1 It should be noted that each of these four thinkers has expressed some pushback on the "communitarian" label. MacIntyre refers to himself as a Thomist, Walzer self-describes as a social democrat, and Taylor and Sandel prefer *civic republicanism* (Alasdair C. MacIntyre, *After Virtue: A Study in Moral Theory*, 2nd ed. [Notre Dame, IN: University of Notre Dame Press, 1984], x; Michael Walzer, *Radical Principles: Reflections of an Unreconstructed Democrat* [New York: Basic Books, 1980], 12–13; Michael J. Sandel, *Democracy's Discontent* [Cambridge: Cambridge University Press, 2007, 4–7]). Nevertheless, since we lack a better term and, in keeping with what has become a well-established label, we will continue to use *communitarian* to describe the commonalities of these thinkers and differences between them and the others in this book. Also, Walzer's and Sandel's use of *democrat* and *republican* in their self-descriptions ought not be confused with the American political parties that bear these names. Both Walzer and Sandel are referring to philosophical, not political, perspectives.

2 Michael J. Sandel, *Liberalism and the Limits of Justice*, 2nd ed. (Cambridge: Cambridge University Press, 2005), loc. 85, Kindle.

3 According to Sandel, for Rawls, "the principles of justice that specify our rights do not depend for their justification on any particular conception of the good life or, as Rawls has put it more recently, on any 'comprehensive' moral or religious conception" (see Sandel, *Liberalism and the Limits of Justice*, loc. 99). Principles are, in Rawls's own phrasing, "purely procedural" and, thus, thought to be impartial. See John Rawls, *A Theory of Justice*, rev. ed. (Cambridge, MA: Belknap Press of Harvard University Press, 1999), §14.

4 Sandel, *Liberalism and the Limits of Justice*, loc. 115.

5 Michael J. Sandel, *Justice: What's the Right Thing to Do?* (New York: Farrar, Straus, and Giroux, 2009), 241.

6 MacIntyre, *After Virtue*, 216.

7 MacIntyre, *After Virtue*, 216. For this reason, communitarian philosophy finds common cause with those historians, social scientists, and others who have sought to better understand the societies and communities in which we live. Classical social observers like Alexis de Tocqueville and Emil Durkheim and contemporary social scientists like Robert Bellah and Robert Putnam all make common appearances in communitarian writings. Relatedly, communitarian philosophers themselves fill their writings with narratives drawn from history and current events, meant to ground the particular argument by tying it to a meaningful story for the reader.

8 Michael Walzer, *Spheres of Justice: A Defense of Pluralism and Equality* (New York: Basic Books, 1983), 6.

9 Walzer, *Spheres of Justice*, 7.

10 "To live life is to enact a narrative quest that aspires to a certain unity or coherence," writes Sandel. "When confronted with competing paths, I try

to figure out which path will make sense of my life as a whole" (Sandel, *Justice*, 221).

11 Michael Walzer, *Thick and Thin: Moral Argument at Home and Abroad* (Notre Dame, IN: University of Notre Dame Press, 1994), 4.

12 Sandel, *Democracy's Discontent*, loc. 313.

13 The various communitarians differ on the timeline. MacIntyre levies his critique as a complete failure of the "Enlightenment project" (see MacIntyre, *After Virtue*, chaps. 1–2). Sandel similarly suggests that the issues are rooted in "a tradition of thought that emphasizes toleration and respect for individual rights and that runs from John Locke, Immanuel Kant, and John Stuart Mill to John Rawls," but he aims his critiques at the second half of the twentieth century (Sandel, *Democracy's Discontent*, loc. 313).

14 Sandel, *Justice*, 213.

15 Sandel, *Democracy's Discontent*, loc. 313.

16 Sandel, *Justice*, 220.

17 Sandel, *Democracy's Discontent*, loc. 441.

18 Sandel, *Democracy's Discontent*, loc. 333.

19 Sandel, *Democracy's Discontent*, loc. 338.

20 Walzer, *Spheres of Justice*, 10–11.

21 Sandel, *Justice*, 188.

22 For a particularly good analysis of queuing, see chapter 1 of Michael J. Sandel, *What Money Can't Buy: The Moral Limits of Markets*, reprint ed. (New York: Farrar, Straus and Giroux, 2013).

23 Walzer, *Spheres of Justice*, 26.

24 Sandel, *What Money Can't Buy*, 7.

25 Sandel, *What Money Can't Buy*, 34.

26 Sandel, *What Money Can't Buy*, 10–11.

27 Sandel, *Justice*, 75.

28 Sandel, *What Money Can't Buy*, 37.

29 Michael J. Sandel, *The Tyranny of Merit: What's Become of the Common Good?* (New York: Farrar, Straus and Giroux, 2020), 33.

30 According to Sandel, "Higher education has become a sorting machine that promises mobility on the basis of merit but entrenches privilege and promotes attitudes toward success corrosive to the commonality democracy requires" (Sandel, *Tyranny of Merit*, 155).

31 Sandel, *The Tyranny of Merit*, 34.

32 Sandel, *What Money Can't Buy*, 43.

33 Sandel, *Justice*, 241.

34 In *No Longer Patient: Feminist Ethics and Health Care* (Philadelphia: Temple University, 1992), chap. 3, Susan Sherwin argues that moral judgments made relative to existing standards in a community will almost always be problematic from a feminist perspective, and she argues that one must look at *how* community standards were developed and whose *power* is encapsulated therein.

35 Walzer, *Thick and Thin*, 2–3.

36 Walzer, *Thick and Thin*, 1.

37 Li Zehou, Paul J. D'Ambrosio, and Robert A. Carleo III, "A Response to Michael Sandel and Other Matters," *Philosophy East and West* 66, no. 4 (2016): 1068–1147.

38 Walzer writes that in civic republicanism, the "republic was an overheated community where citizenship was turned into a new form of oppression. A liberal communitarianism would reduce the heat. It would allow citizens to avoid (some) meetings for the sake of their private happiness. . . . It would combine the zeal of participatory democracy with the coolness of representative democracy, so that those who don't love politics would still have a say in political decisions. Its schools would aim at creating patriots by inclination but not by necessity." Michael Walzer, *The Struggle for a Decent Politics: On Liberal as an Adjective* (New Haven, CT: Yale University Press, 2023), 91.

39 Walzer, *The Struggle for a Decent Politics*, 91–92.

40 Walzer, *The Struggle for a Decent Politics*, 91.

41 Fareed Zakaria, "The ABCs of Communitarianism," *Slate*, July 26, 1996, https://slate.com/news-and-politics/1996/07/the-abcs-of-communitarianism.html.

CHAPTER FIVE

A Catholic Option

Pope Francis

Sandel begins his study of the requirements of justice with several strik-ing case studies. One of those involves the dilemma faced by a special forces team of Navy SEALS on a secret mission in Afghanistan. While searching for a Taliban leader, they came upon a herd of goats and goat keepers. Should they kill the goat herders? If they did not, it was likely that the goat herders would betray the presence of the SEALS to the Tali-ban, and the special forces' mission would be thwarted, and they would all be killed. One of the SEALS argued that they should kill the goat herders, even though they were innocent humans and not part of the Taliban fighting force. "In my soul," says Officer Marcus Luttrell, "I knew he was right. . . . But my trouble is, I have another soul. My Christian soul." Drawing on his Christian conviction that the "innocent" should not be killed, Luttrell cast his vote against killing the innocent goat herders.[1] Does it make a difference to be a Christian when confronting questions of justice? We think so.

However, Christianity is a thick tradition with a rich narrative his-tory, including Gospel stories of the life and death of Jesus, stories from the Hebrew Scriptures, and two thousand years of church history and theology. Any religious tradition that claims a history on the order of millennia is bound to have different interpretations, even schisms. And so, while the next four chapters will focus on justice theories that all arise from Christian tradition, the understandings of justice that emerge are varied. We begin with the tradition of teachings that come from the Roman Catholic teaching magisterium, especially the contributions of Pope Francis.

Catholic social teaching (CST) is the set of letters and other documents that offer the Catholic doctrinal contribution to the topic of justice. Francis has contributed two encyclicals and several other documents to this tradition. We will return to Francis after first unpacking the broader tradition to which he contributes.

CATHOLIC SOCIAL TEACHING

CST began in the wake of the industrial revolution when industrialization and urbanization had upended living and working conditions in industrialized nations. By the 1890s, several concurrent movements examined and responded to these changes.[2] In 1891, Leo XIII penned the encyclical *Rerum Novarum* as a Catholic response to those social and economic conditions. Papal encyclicals are letters written with the highest authority of the office. In recent centuries, encyclicals have often been used to engage the world as a whole in conversation on topics of global importance. Drawing on a fundamental commitment to the concept of human dignity, *Rerum Novarum* offered a critical lens on unfettered capitalism and offered a defense of worker rights, including the right to unionize.

The rapidity of social change did not slow down with the turn of the twentieth century. In 1931, *Quadragesimo Anno* renewed *Rerum Novarum*'s call for the protection of workers amid the Great Depression. In the 1950s and early 1960s, the tradition widened its focus to include global concerns of famine and war and expanded from a focus on worker rights into a defense of basic human rights.

The Second Vatican Council (1962–1965) was a watershed event for the Catholic Church. Three shifts in Catholic moral theology germinated from the council: a shift in focus, a shift in worldview, and a shift in method. The focus shifted from the realm of personal sin and confession to a discipline focused on "a critical understanding of faith for Christian living," thus binding the personal more closely to the social.[3] The council called for a strengthening of the links between Catholic theology and the world.

Prior to the council, the tradition saw the world as a completed project: the laws of creation were immutable and unchanging, history was cyclical, and the world was marked by the "harmony of an objective order." But Vatican II shifted the Church from a "rather static concept of reality into a more dynamic, evolutionary one."[4] The historically conscious worldview that emerged saw history as a process of dynamic change and growth, and humanity as cocreators with God in this dynamic and changing world.[5]

When creation was thought to be static and knowable, justice was merely the deductive application of eternal principles to contemporary problems. A historically conscious worldview, however, requires a shift in method toward one that is empirical and inductive. "This is not to say that deductive reasoning has no place in modern moral theology. It still does. But moral theology today is more likely to begin with historical particulars, the concrete, and the changing."[6]

These three shifts not only mark a moment of discontinuity for CST but also provide a justification for that discontinuity. If the tradition is called to be historically conscious, then of course it will adapt over time to changing questions. While CST is understood to be an articulation of the immutable wisdom of God through the intervention of the Holy Spirit, the documents that comprise CST have been written by different authors, in different decades, and, importantly, responding to different social and economic contexts; they draw current issues, thick with historical and cultural context, into dialectic with eternal and immutable wisdom.[7]

Even as the tradition is charged with reading the signs of the times and continuing to develop Catholic teaching as a result, three basic affirmations seem to unify the tradition: (1) the inviolable dignity of the human person, (2) the essentially social nature of human beings, and (3) the belief that the abundance of nature and of social living is given for all people.[8] While these affirmations do not result in a static and unchanging interpretation of the social situation, they do yield a striking continuity at the level of moral principles and hence of understanding the demands of justice.

Human Dignity and Human Rights

From 1891 through today, the foundation on which social structures must be built is the transcendental worth of persons who are "created in God's image."[9] People are prior to institutions, and institutions exist for the sake of people. Thus, CST has consistently rejected any economic system that denies the rights of workers or treats them without dignity. For example, the tradition has consistently rejected the free contract as the basis for a wage.[10] Instead, CST demands a living wage.[11]

Until the 1960s, human dignity was most clearly expressed as dignity of the worker, but mid-twentieth-century contributions to the tradition began connecting economic justice with issues of participation and political rights as well. Noting that the dignity of persons includes the whole person, not just economic well-being, *Mater et Magistra* argued for social as well as economic development.[12] The dignity of persons requires not only treating them justly in the determination of wages but also according them their full measure of total human rights.[13] An economic system that produces large quantities of goods and distributes them fairly will nonetheless be unjust if its organization and structure are such that "the human dignity of workers is compromised, or their sense of responsibility is weakened, or their freedom of action is removed."[14] By 1971, *Justice in the World* spoke not merely about the injustice of the contract or market system but about an entire "network of domination, oppression and abuses." It was a "myth" that economic development alone will help those who are poor.[15]

The Common Good and Solidarity

As the tradition developed, the notion of individual worth and dignity became increasingly linked to the social nature of human beings. Because human beings are social by their very nature, human dignity will be addressed in social relationships. Justice is not simply a matter of proper distribution of goods (distributive justice) but also of permitting and indeed requiring each person to participate in the communal production of those goods (social justice).

Thus, concrete historical manifestations of social institutions become important for the expression of human dignity, and human dignity is tied up with the common good. *Mater et Magistra* defines the common good as "the sum total of those conditions of social living whereby [people] are enabled more fully and more readily to achieve their own perfection."[16] CST's emphasis on the common good shares three elements with communitarianism's appeal to the same concept. First, the common good serves as "an important counterbalance" to the individualism that liberal conceptions of rights can evoke.[17] Second, it recognizes that the value of the social is not merely the aggregate sum of individual goods (as utilitarianism argues). Finally, it emphasizes that the role of the community is to enable human flourishing.

The tension between individual rights and personal responsibilities on the one hand and common good and structural injustice on the other is fleshed out through the concept of solidarity. *Sollicitudo Rei Socialis* defines solidarity as "a firm and persevering determination to commit oneself to the common good; that is to say to the good of all and of each individual, because we are responsible for all."[18] Solidarity is a personal responsibility to aid in the creation of a society that is oriented toward the common good, which in turn aids individual flourishing. "The exercise of solidarity within each society is valid when its members recognize one another as persons," that is, imbued with human dignity.[19]

The Preferential Option for the Poor and Vulnerable

Commitments to the common good and solidarity take their most concrete form in CST's consistent concern for the plight of those in poverty. For CST, the mere fact of inequality of wealth is a sign of injustice. *Rerum Novarum* declares, "A very few and exceedingly rich . . . have laid a yoke almost of slavery on the unnumbered masses of non-owning workers."[20] *Quadragesimo Anno* asserts that the immense numbers of those poor, on the one hand, and the superabundant riches of the few, on the other, are "an unanswerable argument" that goods are "far from rightly distributed and equitably shared."[21] These concerns culminate in what is today called the "option for the poor": "true relationships of justice and equality," declares *Octogesimo Adveniens*, require "the preferential respect due to the poor."[22]

POPE FRANCIS

When Pope Francis ascended to the Catholic Papacy in 2013, the moment was historic in several senses. A native of Argentina and, at the time, the archbishop of Buenos Aires, Francis was the first pope elected from the Americas and the first pope from the Global South. In fact, Francis was the first non-European pope since the eighth century. Thomas Massaro suggests that it is Pope Francis's personal history witnessing poverty in Argentina that animates the tension between the personal and the structural in his writings: "Without doubt, the skewed pattern of social and economic relations that [Francis] had observed all his life in the distinctive context of Latin America contributed to his keen sensitivity to the human suffering that springs from poverty and marginalization."[23]

In the hands of Pope Francis, the tradition of CST has both maintained and deepened the fundamental commitments outlined above. Francis laments the inequalities that our social structures continue to reproduce, but he extends the lamentation to include the ways in which our modern conditions also diminish our human connections. Consider the following passage from the apostolic exhortation *Evangelii Gaudium*: "Just as the commandment 'Thou shalt not kill' sets a clear limit in order to safeguard the value of human life, today we also have to say 'thou shalt not' to an economy of exclusion and inequality. Such an economy kills. How can it be that it is not a news item when an elderly homeless person dies of exposure, but it is news when the stock market loses two points? This is a case of exclusion. Can we continue to stand by when food is thrown away while people are starving? This is a case of inequality."[24]

This passage typifies the way in which Francis holds personal choices and structural forces together in a new, deeper tension than we have seen in the tradition before. The personal command "*Thou* shalt not kill," typically understood with the singular pronoun (i.e., *I* should not pull the trigger), is recast as an entire "economy that kills" (i.e., we have *all* pulled the trigger when a person dies of exposure). Conversely, exclusion is not typically a choice that can be made by one person—it takes an *ingroup* to outcast—and yet Francis does not resign the problem to society as a whole. We are *each* responsible for homelessness and hunger.

For Francis, there exists a vicious cycle between a lack of personal human connection (and, by extension, empathy for the suffering other) and the impersonal social structures that dominate our society (and diminish our human relationships). In response, a major theme of his social teachings is a call to attend to our relationships. We will organize this section around three relationships in particular: our relationship with the ends of economic production (i.e., technology), our relationship with our fellow humans, and our relationship with creation.

The Technocratic Paradigm

In *Rerum Novarum*, Leo XII responded to the ills wrought by the *industrial* revolution. A century and a quarter later, Francis is troubled by the consequences of the *digital* revolution. However, where Leo XIII says very little about the actual technology of the industrial age, Francis is distressed by the ways in which our interactions with technology have eclipsed our other relationships. Francis is not anti-technology; he embraces the ability to conceive and create as an expression of our humanity: "The Church never ceases to encourage the progress of science and technology placed at the service of the dignity of the person, for an 'integral and integrating' human development."[25] But he is critical of the *relationship* we have with technology today and what that relationship does to human flourishing.

Technology should be a tool we use to achieve other, intrinsically valuable, ends: better health, better communication, stronger human relationships, more time for leisure and enjoyment, more space for prayer and worship, and so on. Instead, technology has become an end unto itself: "Technology tends to absorb everything into its ironclad logic, and those who are surrounded with technology know full well that it moves forward in the final analysis neither for profit nor for the well-being of the human race."[26] We desire new products not because they are useful but because they are new. We want the smartphone with the fastest processor, even though the marginal difference from the phone in our pocket is imperceptible. We replace our washing machine, refrigerator, or toothbrush with one that is smart, even if we never use these features in real life. And most recently, every product seems to tout the integration of artificial intelligence regardless of whether that integration improves the product's utility.

In our pursuit of technology, we also seek progress as if it were an intrinsic good and without asking questions about the benefits or costs of our pursuits. Francis declares, "Our immense technological development has not been accompanied by a development in human responsibility, values and conscience. Each age tends to have only a meager awareness of its own limitations. It is possible that we do not grasp the gravity of the challenges now before us."[27] We have power, but in Francis's view, we have not learned to use that power well. Indeed, Francis laments that "the economy accepts every advance in technology with a view to profit, without concern for its potentially negative impact on human beings. Finance overwhelms the real economy. . . . [Corporations show] no interest in more balanced levels of production, a better distribution of wealth, concern for the environment and the rights of future generations . . . maximizing profits is enough."[28]

As we take those things that should be valued instrumentally and give them intrinsic value, we also do the converse. From the outset of Catholic social teaching, human life and dignity have been raised as intrinsically valued and inviolable. Today, as in the time of *Rerum Novarum*, "human beings are themselves considered consumer goods to be used and discarded. We have created a 'throw-away' culture which is now spreading."[29] We treat human beings as human resources and creation as natural resources to be consumed as necessary for the sake of technology, progress, disruption, and profit themselves.

For Francis, none of these social shifts is independent. Rather, they are all part of a single "technocratic paradigm" that is deeply embedded in the structures and culture of the modern digital world. The result is "a reductionism which affects every aspect of human and social life." Thus, "we have to accept that technological products are not neutral, for they create a framework which ends up conditioning lifestyles and shaping social possibilities along the lines dictated by the interests of certain powerful groups. Decisions which may seem purely instrumental are in reality decisions about the kind of society we want to build."[30]

The technocratic paradigm sets our values and shapes our decisions. It determines everything—how engineers design, how marketers market, and how users use products. It even shapes our choices for the discarding and disposal of that same technology. Francis names the technocratic paradigm as the source of many of the injustices that plague our communities in the twenty-first century.

From Ecological Discord to Integral Ecology

Popes take on a new name when they ascend to the papacy, and Jorge Mario Bergoglio chose the name Francis in honor of the thirteenth-century friar Saint Francis of Assisi. Saint Francis truly lived *in communion* with the poor of his community and the natural world around him. Born into a rich family, after receiving a Divine calling, Saint Francis famously and publicly renounced his wealth and titles, stripped himself naked in the street, and went to live in austerity on the outskirts of Assisi, among the poorest in the community. Saint Francis was also known to have a particular connection to animals and recognized the natural world as a mirror on the beauty of God. Pope Francis, in choosing the name of Saint Francis, sought to reflect this attention for both the poor and creation onto the Church and the world.

Laudato Si' is the first papal encyclical dedicated to addressing ecological concerns.[31] In keeping with the post-Vatican II commitment to drawing contemporary issues into conversation with Catholic commitments, Francis organizes *Laudato Si'* against the account of creation in the first chapter of Genesis: "The earth was here before us and it has been given to us. . . . Nowadays we must forcefully reject the notion that our being created in God's image and given dominion over the earth justifies absolute domination over other creatures. The biblical texts are to be read in their context, with an appropriate hermeneutic, recognizing that they tell us to 'till and keep' the garden of the world."[32]

For Francis, if God expressed intent in the act of creation, then that intention demands respect: "This responsibility for God's earth means that human beings, endowed with intelligence, must respect the laws of nature and the delicate equilibria existing between the creatures of this world."[33]

However, we do not respect creation or its laws. We use the laws of science to make creation into a resource to be used and thrown away, disregarding the moral expectations that natural law would have us recognize. *Laudato Si'* is where Francis first identifies the technocratic paradigm that affects our pursuit of human flourishing at every level, from the interpersonal to the international.

Francis declares that "the technological paradigm has become so dominant that it would be difficult to do without its resources. . . . It has become countercultural to choose a lifestyle whose goals are even partly independent of technology, of its costs and its power to globalize and make us all the same."[34] What we must do is define a new paradigm. Francis asks us to recall the command to "till and keep" creation. This is not technocratic domination over creation but an appeal to moral stewardship of an "integral ecology," in which we do not separate humanity from creation but recognize that anything that affects, degrades, and dominates the natural world also affects, degrades, and dominates humanity as well. Here he recalls Saint Francis: "Francis helps us to see that an integral ecology calls for openness to categories which transcend the language of mathematics and biology, and takes us to the heart of what it is to be human. . . . His response to the world around him was so much more than intellectual appreciation or economic calculus, for to him each and every creature was a sister united to him by bonds of affection. That is why he felt called to care for all that exists."[35] Following Saint Francis requires we recognize that we share creation with all living beings and that our ecological fate is bound together.

From Social Discord to Social Fraternity

Pope Francis introduces important elements of his thought on the proper ordering of society in earlier works, but it is not until his third encyclical, *Fratelli Tutti*, that he fully articulates his vision for social justice. *Fratelli Tutti* was written with specific attention to the division and discord that the technocratic paradigm has wrought on our social relationships. As he did in *Laudato Si'*, Francis begins by invoking his familiar image of a throwaway culture, but in *Fratelli Tutti*, he turns his attention to the ways in which we discard our fellow humans. Francis includes a wide array of social disunities under the same umbrella, from global pandemics, migrant and refugee crises, terrorism, and war on the international level to bigotry, hate, aggression, subjugation, alienation, and the destruction of self-esteem on the interpersonal level. While this grouping may seem disjointed, Francis believes each of these cases is an example of a fundamental break in the bonds that hold society together.

As he did with the creation story in *Laudato Si'*, Francis builds this encyclical around a biblical story—the parable of the Good Samaritan in the Gospel of Luke: "Jesus tells the story of a man assaulted by thieves and lying injured on the wayside. Several persons passed him by, but failed to stop. These were people holding important social positions, yet lacking in real concern for the common good. . . . Only one person stopped, approached the man and cared for him personally, even spending his own money to provide for his needs. . . . Without even knowing the injured man, he saw him as deserving of his time and attention." For Francis, the parable offers a metaphor for our social divisions today. It "evokes the interior struggle that each of us experiences as we gradually come to know ourselves through our relationships with our brothers and sisters." Indeed, "sooner or later, we will all encounter a person who is suffering. Today there are more and more of them. The decision to include or exclude those lying wounded along the roadside can serve as a criterion for judging every economic, political, social and religious project."[36]

The Samaritan's actions in the face of suffering are exemplary, but for Francis, it is the *posture* of the Samaritan toward his fellow human that is most worthy of note. The Samaritan saw humanity prior to the divisions of Samaritan and Jews, he saw suffering prior to his other responsibilities, and he saw the other prior to himself. Francis defines this posture as "social friendship" or "fraternity," and for Francis, it is a necessary ingredient for a just society.

In making his case, Francis draws this posture of fraternity, exemplified in Scripture but familiar to all, into conversation with secular moral commitments of liberty, equality, and individualism. Against rights regimes built on libertarianism and Rawlsian liberalism, Francis argues that liberty or fairness/equality cannot be fully realized without first developing fraternity. Genuine community does not come from "a climate of respect for individual liberties, or even of a certain administratively guaranteed equality. Fraternity necessarily calls for something greater, which in turn enhances freedom and equality."[37] When fraternity is not "consciously cultivated," liberty becomes "nothing more than a condition for living as we will, completely free to choose to whom or what we will belong, or simply to possess or exploit. This shallow understanding has little to do with the richness of a liberty directed above all to love."[38] Similarly, equality is not achieved "by an abstract proclamation that 'all men and women are equal.' Instead, it is the result of the conscious and careful cultivation of fraternity."[39]

For Francis, the opposite of fraternity is humans interacting at the shallowest of levels, for the sake of material benefit only, disregarding the value of genuine human bond. In this same breath, Francis also rejects individualism: "Individualism does not make us more free, more equal, more fraternal. . . . Radical individualism is a virus that is extremely difficult to eliminate, for it is clever. It makes us believe that everything consists in giving free rein to our own ambitions, as if by pursuing ever greater ambitions and creating safety nets we would somehow be serving the common good."[40]

Instead of individualism, Francis calls for the universalization of fraternity across society. We must reject individualist culture, a culture of walls, a throwaway culture, and a technocratic paradigm in favor of a "culture of encounter": "To speak of a 'culture of encounter' means that we . . . should be passionate about meeting others, seeking points of contact, building bridges, planning a project that includes everyone. This becomes an aspiration and a style of life."[41]

A Road Map for Justice?

In the end, Francis is reading the signs of our times and recognizing that "the sense of belonging to a single human family is fading, and the dream of working together for justice and peace seems an outdated utopia. What reigns instead is a cool, comfortable, and globalized indifference, born of deep disillusionment concealed behind a deceptive illusion: thinking that we are all-powerful, while . . . [lacking] a shared roadmap." In response, Francis calls for a "rebirth of a universal aspiration to fraternity" between all men and women:[42] "Unless we recover the shared passion to create a community of belonging and solidarity worthy of our time, our energy and our resources, the global illusion that misled us will collapse and leave many in the grip of anguish and emptiness."[43] But in doing so, Francis also develops the tradition of Catholic social thought in notable ways.

First, Francis is not satisfied with rendering morality in terms of moral principles alone. Catholic social teaching has always held that we are inherently social creatures, but Francis calls for a strengthening of our *relationships* with the fellow humans who make up our societies, the creatures who comprise our integral ecology, and the God who created us all.

Relatedly, Catholic social teaching has persistently held the importance of human dignity as central to its teachings. In early CST, this manifested most directly through the protection of worker rights. Later, the central tool for the protection of dignity shifted to human rights. For Francis, rights remain an important minimal condition of justice, but in calling for fraternity, he argues that association is not enough. To truly achieve justice, we need the recognition of ourselves in the other—human or ecological—that bears the consequences of our choices and actions.

Finally, Francis's call for fraternity also deepens the meaning of the CST principles of solidarity and the preferential option for the poor and vulnerable. It is not enough to recognize our neighbor's suffering. It is not enough to protest alongside our suffering neighbor (as contemporary interpretations of solidarity are often expressed). It is not enough to enshrine preference for those who are poor and vulnerable into liberal laws and policies. While these actions are sometimes necessary, fraternity reminds us that they are insufficient. In the model of Saint Francis of Assisi, as well as the good Samaritan, we must make our neighbor's suffering our own and walk with them, even carrying them through the suffering. In this way, we are in solidarity with and give true preference for our neighbor by *encountering* them and sharing in their "joys and hopes, griefs and anxieties."[44]

REVIEW

Justice, in the Catholic view, is not determined by assessing the fairness of the exchanges involved historically. Nor is it determined by principles of autonomous choice or calculations of the greatest overall good. Discrepancies in wealth indicate a situation in which some fail to remember that the goods of the earth are given for use by all; such a situation is unjust because it violates both the social nature of human beings and the purposes for which God gives the riches of the earth.

Because CST advocates certain rights of the individual that are prior to the interests of the state and that cannot be abrogated by the state, it appears similar to Nozick. But where Nozick's rights are primarily negative rights against interference, Catholic tradition has always upheld positive rights to welfare and a living wage. Thus, taking a perspective that advocates individual rights does not yield the same understanding of economic justice. The contributions Francis makes to the tradition go further still, focusing on relationship, empathy, and encounter—categories that find no equivalent in any of the philosophical theories examined here.[45]

Because protections of the worst off loom large for Francis and CST, this tradition shares much with Rawls. But the grounding for protection of those disadvantaged is quite different. For Rawls, protection of those least advantaged is the result of a self-interested calculation under "fair" conditions; for Francis and CST, it is the result of acknowledging the fundamental human dignity of every person, regardless of their utility on a cost-benefit calculation. CST also recognizes more explicitly than Rawls that economic differences will result in political inequalities. And once again, Francis's emphasis on recognizing the other through encounter (including encounter with nonhuman creatures) pushes CST further away from the rational calculations of Rawls (or utilitarianism).

Finally, Francis's appeals to the common good may align with communitarianism. This case is further supported by the fact that Francis operates within the living, narrative tradition of CST that responds to the signs of the times and, since Vatican II, has sought to embrace a historically conscious worldview. Communitarians assert, and Catholic social teaching affirms in practice, that while thin, shared principles are necessary for building an overlapping consensus, the thick traditions that undergird those principles must not be discounted. For his part, Francis's location within millennia of religious narrative and over 130 years of developing theory around social justice provide him a rich teleological set of narratives.

CRITIQUE

Any critique of Francis must begin with the treatment the tradition gives to voices and perspectives of women. For a tradition that claims to give preference to those who are poor and vulnerable, there seems to be a blind spot to the degradation and vulnerability of women in modern society. The accusation of paternalism can be levied against the entire Catholic social tradition, of course, but the critique is particularly notable for Francis because one cannot explain away the patriarchal language as simply the product of an earlier time. Sometimes, Francis seems to double down on the use of patriarchal language and the privileging of male voices. The most prominent example is the definitive male gender in the title of *Fratelli Tutti*—literally *all brothers*—and its primary principle, fraternity. Lisa Sowle Cahill does note that "defenders maintained that 'fraternity' is meant inclusively. . . [and] is qualified early and often by the explanatory addition of 'brothers and sisters.'"[46] It is also often paired with the gender-neutral synonym *social friendship*, apparently as a response to critiques of earlier drafts of the document. Still, this defense will not satisfy many feminists.

Laudato Si' also suffers from the pitfalls of gendered language, with the gendered use of a feminine earth and a masculine Creator God throughout the document. Here again, nuanced readings reveal a more complicated picture. As Emily Reimer-Barry writes,

> Pope Francis argues that the abuse of the feminine (earth) is a problem, and it is a problem because humans adopted a patriarchal mindset—"we have come to see ourselves as her lords and masters." . . . The dominion model empowers men over women, humans over animals and the natural world. Pope Francis is challenging this model explicitly, as have ecofeminists for years. It becomes confusing only because Laudato Si' contains both these rebukes of patriarchy together with descriptions of Mother Earth as fragile, weak, and in need of protection, while God is Father, Lord, and All-Powerful Master of All.[47]

Others are more critical. Even if deeper analysis may reveal nuanced intentions, leaning into gendered language allows readers of these documents, especially those steeped in a long history of patriarchal intention from the Church, to avoid the nuanced reading and sustain the more morally problematic consequences of a patriarchal tradition. As Phyllis Zagano argues, "Yes, of course educated people can understand that the Holy Father would never eliminate women from thought or action. But many in the Vatican might be only too happy to. . . . No one seems to be telling the Holy Father that the title itself endangers women around the world. . . . The risks and dangers, not to mention the repeated abuses, disrespect and contempt of women, continue unabated throughout the world."[48]

Moreover, including gender-neutral terms is not the same as including women themselves. Susan Rakoczy points out that only two women are mentioned by name in *Laudato Si'*, and neither is given much more than passing attention.[49] And throughout *Fratelli Tutti*, "women are largely absent," writes Meghan Clark. "Despite the pope saying he's been inspired by 'brothers and sisters' it is only three men Francis lists: Martin Luther King Jr., Desmond Tutu, and Mahatma Gandhi."[50] In the end, Francis does seem to be genuinely attempting to move a tradition that has been historically steeped in patriarchy toward a more inclusive future, but the tradition still has a ways to go. Is it fair, as Cahill contends, to say that these gestures "represent an evolving commitment by the teaching Church and by Pope Francis himself"?[51]

Francis's contributions have also drawn criticism from advocates of the free market system. His trenchant evaluation of our "throwaway culture" and "technocratic paradigm" are new contributions to a tradition that has always been critical of unfettered markets. However, previous popes were often careful to toe a line between unrestrained capitalism and socialism. Early documents offered a strong defense of private property, and with the rise of the Cold War, later documents explicitly rejected the compatibility of Christianity and state-controlled socialism.[52] Francis, by contrast, never mentions socialism in either of these encyclicals and, leaning more deeply into the preferential option for the poor, asserts that "the right to private property can only be considered a secondary natural right, derived from the principle of the universal destination of created goods."[53] Robert Sirico pushes back that Francis's critique is misplaced and that the free market is the best mechanism to achieve the goal of feeding the world's hungry: "The pope speaks of the 'cold logic of the market' which he associates with a greedy focus on 'mere economic profit' and the reduction of 'food to a commodity.' One presumes by 'cold logic' the pope is raising the concern that the market lacks a personal, subjective intimacy. This is true, but only to the extent that a market, when unobstructed by various interventions, furnishes vital information related to things like supply and demand. Without ruthlessly accurate data, the entire capacity of providing for people's needs would be mis-calibrated and people would starve."[54]

CST has also long been criticized for putting too much power in the hands of governments. Francis's contributions may appeal too much to global institutions to solve the world's problems from the top-down: "Much of Pope Francis' preaching fails to appreciate crucial aspects of the Church's rich and considered jurisprudence on the proper role of the State in the economy. In doing so, it diminishes this tradition and sows confusion."[55]

Such critiques of Francis and CST recall earlier chapters in this book on the difference between libertarian and Rawlsian approaches to economic distributions. In light of this, it is worth noting that the criticisms above rarely come from trained economists. By contrast, economist Jeffrey Sachs has praised Francis for aiming "at nothing less than re-establishing a moral foundation for our local, national, and global economic dealings by . . . invoking universal themes that are shared by many major religions, as well as by agnostics and atheists."[56]

These appeals are often paired with critical comments that Francis, an Argentinian, is too deeply connected to Latin American liberation theology with its Marxist leanings. We will examine liberation theology in chapter 7, but for now, it is enough to recognize that liberation theology's influences on CST did not begin with Francis. For example, the notion of a "preferential option for the poor" gained its initial prominence through the work of liberation theologians, including Gustavo Gutiérrez, before being introduced into CST in *Sollicitudo Rei Socialis* in 1987.[57] Nevertheless, if the primary concern in identifying a creep toward liberation theology is a fear that it will encourage Marxist class revolution, such fears should be put to rest by Francis's consistent call to "fraternity" (not class war) as well as his repeated rebukes of any type of war (including revolution) in the twenty-first century.[58]

Critics who accuse Francis of shifting the tradition toward liberation theology are met by others who suggest that the Catholic Church has not lived up to its own commitments. For example, it is hard to claim worker rights are central when Catholic universities, hospitals, and other organizations work against the formation of unions.[59] It is hard to claim solidarity and a preferential option for the poor when Francis's signature appeals to "fraternity" are held next to the "diatribe on gender theory" in *Dignitas Infinita*, a document issued under his leadership by the Dicastery for the Doctrine of the Faith.[60]

ASSESSMENT

Catholic social thought does not rely on a simple set of principles or a simple formula to get to justice. Rather, it is, as communitarians suggest is necessary, a thick tradition of narratives that together begin to describe what justice should look like. When those narratives stretch across several thousands of years and around the entire globe, it can be helpful to have a set of formal writings that organize the ways in which ancient scriptural sources and present-day reasoning apply to contemporary issues. This is what the tradition-within-a-tradition of CST does for the Catholic faithful and, as recent popes hope, the ongoing global conversation. As a narrative tradition, CST does not seek to resolve every tension that emerges. In many cases, it embraces those tensions: CST is understood to be both universal and contextual, immutable and reflecting the signs of the times, and a statement of Catholic doctrine as well as a rational appeal to a global audience. None of these pairings is mutually exclusive. Universal truths can apply specifically and contextually. Immutable truths are often articulated in limited and imperfect ways. And starting at different places does not mean we cannot arrive at the same destination, but it will sometimes mean we have to take different routes. Nevertheless, the tensions do remain and remind us that, ultimately, Catholic social teaching is a living and adaptable tradition of thought.

As we move from the two-millennia history of the Catholic Church to the 130-year history of CST to those specific contributions of Pope Francis's papacy, we become more specific in our attention. The signs of the times in the first quarter of the twenty-first century have pointed to two extremely consequential issues: the way in which we have treated the natural world and the way in which we are treating each other, all in the name of profit and so-called progress. Francis responds to each of these concerns, respectively, but in doing so he offers a message that is both internally consistent and a logical extension of the broader CST to which he contributes. He leaves us with new terms and concepts—throwaway culture, technocratic paradigm, integral ecology, and fraternity—but remains committed to old themes of fundamental human dignity, pursuit of the common good, and protection of those who are poor and vulnerable. Each of these themes has some salience with the philosophies we have already examined and the Protestant theologies yet to come.

NOTES

1 Michael J. Sandel, *Justice: What's the Right Thing to Do?* (New York: Farrar, Straus, and Giroux, 2009), 24–27. Ultimately, Luttrell regretted his decision as the farmers did indeed notify the Taliban of the SEAL presence, and all but Luttrell were killed. However, the dilemma Luttrell faced and his reflection on it do suggest that Christian values and principles can make a huge difference when asking about right action or the demands of justice.

2 The American Federation of Labor, the largest union in the United States today, was established in 1888 to defend workers' rights. The US government formed the Department of Labor in 1888. In academia, the discipline of sociology was emerging as the formal study of social forces and structures. See Ellen Terrell, "Research Guides: This Month in Business History: Formation of the American Federation of Labor," Research guide, accessed June 6, 2024, https://guides.loc.gov/this-month-in-business-history/december/american -federation-of-labor; Randall Collins, *Four Sociological Traditions* (New York: Oxford University Press, 1994), chap. 1.

3 Richard M. Gula, *Reason Informed by Faith: Foundations of Catholic Morality* (Mahwah, NJ: Paulist Press, 1989), 28.

4 Vatican Council II, *Gaudium et Spes* (Rome: Vatican Library, 1965), §5, https://www.vatican.va/archive/hist_councils/ii_vatican_council /documents/vat-ii_const_19651207_gaudium-et-spes_en.html.

5 Gula, *Reason Informed by Faith*, 31.

6 Gula, *Reason Informed by Faith*, 37. One cannot help but see methodological similarities between this turn in Catholic teaching and the shift in public philosophy that Sandel and the communitarians were advocating in the previous chapter. While the methodological claims are similar, the "thick" foundations of the two theories are derived from very different sources.

7 A note on papal infallibility is necessary here. Catholic doctrine distinguishes between infallible and noninfallible teachings: "Infallible teaching on the basis of the gift of the Holy Spirit claims to be free from error even though the teaching may not be perfect. Noninfallible teaching does not claim to be free from error even though it enjoys the assistance of the Holy Spirit" (Charles E. Curran, *The Catholic Moral Tradition Today*, [Washington, DC: Georgetown University Press, 1999], 200). In order to be an infallible teaching, the document must be an *ex cathedra* pronouncement of faith and morals. Importantly, none of the documents considered to be part of the Catholic social tradition were issued *ex cathedra*, and thus CST has the authority of Divine wisdom but is not considered to be perfect or infallible.

8 Charles E. Curran attributes these three affirmations to the Catholic ethicist John A. Ryan. See Curran, *American Catholic Social Ethics: Twentieth Century Approaches* (Notre Dame, IN: University of Notre Dame Press, 1982), 61. However, Ryan was a man of his tradition, and these three statements

serve as a summary of the basic affirmations underlying papal and conciliar documents during this period.

9 David Hollenbach says, "The thread that ties all these documents together is their common concern for the protection of the dignity of the human person" (*Claims in Conflict: Retrieving and Renewing the Catholic Human Rights Tradition* [New York: Paulist Press, 1979], 42).

10 Leo XIII, *Rerum Novarum* (Rome: Vatican Library, 1891), https://w2 .vatican.va/content/leo-xiii/en/encyclicals/documents/hf_l-xiii_enc_15051891 _rerum-novarum.html, §63. *Populorum Progressio* spelled out the reasoning: "if the positions of the contracting parties are too unequal, the consent of the parties does not suffice to guarantee the justice of their contract" (Paul VI, *Populorum Progressio* [Rome: Vatican Library, 1967], https://www.vatican.va/content/paul-vi/en/encyclicals/documents/hf _p-vi_enc_26031967_populorum.html, §§58–59.). The sentiment was echoed in *Mater et Magistra*, declaring that workers must receive a wage "sufficient to lead a life worthy of man" (John XXII, *Mater et Magistra* [Rome: Vatican Library, 1961], http://w2.vatican.va/content/john-xxiii/en/encyclicals/documents/hf _j-xxiii_enc_15051961_mater.html, §71).

11 The phrase *living wage* is commonly used in secular writing and government documentation today but can be originally attributed to the early-twentieth-century Catholic ethicist John A. Ryan (*A Living Wage: Its Ethical and Economic Aspects* [London: MacMillan, 1912]). While Ryan gave it a name, the concept was already present in *Rerum Novarum*.

12 John XXIII, *Mater et Magistra*, §73. He called it a "strict demand of social justice."

13 A rather complete listing of rights is provided by Pope John XXIII in John XXIII, *Pacem in Terris* (Rome: Vatican Library, 1963), §§11–27, https://www.vatican.va/content/john-xxiii/en/encyclicals/documents/hf _j-xxiii_enc_11041963_pacem.html. "The right to take an active part in public affairs and to contribute one's part to the common good" is explicitly mentioned (§26).

14 John XXIII, *Mater et Magistra*, §83.

15 World Synod of Catholic Bishops, *Justice in the World* (1971), §§3, 16, https://www.cctwincities.org/wp-content/uploads/2015/10/Justicia-in -Mundo.pdf.

16 John XXIII, *Mater et Magistra*, §65.

17 Thomas Massaro, *Living Justice: Catholic Social Teaching in Action*, 4th classroom ed. (Lanham, MD: Rowman & Littlefield, 2024), 89.

18 John Paul II, *Sollicitudo Rei Socialis* (Rome: Vatican Library, 1987), §37, http://w2.vatican.va/content/john-paul-ii/en/encyclicals/documents/hf _jp-ii_enc_30121987_sollicitudo-rei-socialis.html.

19 John Paul II, *Sollicitudo Rei Socialis*, §39.

20 Leo XIII, *Rerum Novarum*, §§5, 6.

21 Pius XI, *Quadragesimo Anno* (Rome: Vatican Library, 1931), part II, sec. 3, https://w2.vatican.va/content/pius-xi/en/encyclicals/documents/hf_p-xi _enc_19310515_quadragesimo-anno.html.

22 Paul VI, *Octogesima Adveniens* (Rome: Vatican Library, 1971), §23, https://www.vatican.va/content/paul-vi/en/apost_letters/documents/hf _p-vi_apl_19710514_octogesima-adveniens.html. See also Donal Dorr, *Option for the Poor: A Hundred Years of Vatican Social Teaching* (Maryknoll, NY: Orbis, 1983). Dorr argues, however, that the very explicit meaning of this phrase, which has emerged with liberation theology, has not always been present in Catholic tradition.

23 Thomas Massaro, *Mercy in Action: The Social Teachings of Pope Francis* (Lanham, MD: Rowman & Littlefield, 2018), 31.

24 Francis, *Evangelii Gaudium* (Rome: Vatican Library, 2013), §53, https://www .vatican.va/content/francesco/en/apost_exhortations/documents/papa -francesco_esortazione-ap_20131124_evangelii-gaudium.html. *Evangelii Gaudium* was issued a mere eight months into Francis's papacy and is considered a "manifesto" for what Francis hoped to accomplish during his papacy. See Naomi O'Leary, "Pope Attacks 'Tyranny' of Markets in Manifesto for Papacy," Reuters, November 26, 2013, https://www .reuters.com/article/us-pope-document-idUSBRE9AP0EQ20131126/.

25 Francis, "Address of His Holiness Pope Francis to the Members of the Pontifical Academy for Life," February 20, 2023, https://www.vatican.va/content /francesco/en/speeches/2023/february/documents/20230220-pav.html.

26 Francis, *Laudato Si'* (Rome: Vatican Library, 2015), §108, https://www .vatican.va/content/francesco/en/encyclicals/documents/papa-francesco _20150524_enciclica-laudato-si.html.

27 Francis, *Laudato Si'*, §105.

28 Francis, *Laudato Si'*, §109.

29 Francis, *Evangelii Gaudium*, §53. See also Francis, *Laudato Si'*, §§20–22.

30 Francis, *Laudato Si'*, §107.

31 As of this writing, Francis has issued three encyclicals. *Laudato Si'* is his second encyclical. The first encyclical credited to Francis, *Lumen Fidei*, was actually mostly drafted by Francis's predecessor, Benedict XVI. More importantly for this book, it is not generally considered a social teaching and offers little on questions of justice, so it will not play a significant role here.

32 Francis, *Laudato Si'*, §67.

33 Francis, *Laudato Si'*, §68.

34 Francis, *Laudato Si'*, §108.

35 Francis, *Laudato Si'*, §11.

36 Francis, *Fratelli Tutti* (Rome: Vatican Library, 2020), §63, §69, https://www .vatican.va/content/francesco/en/encyclicals/documents/papa-francesco _20201003_enciclica-fratelli-tutti.html.

37 Francis, *Fratelli Tutti*, §103.

38 Francis, *Fratelli Tutti*, §§103–104.

39 Francis, *Fratelli Tutti*, §§103–104.

40 Francis, *Fratelli Tutti*, §105.

41 Francis, *Fratelli Tutti*, §216.

42 Francis, *Fratelli Tutti*, §8.

43 Francis, *Fratelli Tutti*, §36.

44 Vatican Council II, *Gaudium et Spes*, §1.

45 Robert P. Barnidge, "Against the Catholic Grain: Pope Francis Trumpets Socialism over Capitalism," *Forbes*, sec. Opinion, March 11, 2016, https://www.forbes.com/sites/realspin/2016/03/11/against-the-catholic-grain-pope-francis-trumpets-socialism-over-capitalism/.

46 Lisa Sowle Cahill, "Social Friendship Includes Women, but Social Change Must Engage Women," *Berkeley Forum* (blog), October 26, 2020, https://berkleycenter.georgetown.edu/responses/social-friendship-includes-women-but-social-change-must-engage-women.

47 Emily Reimer-Barry, "On Naming God: Gendered God-Talk in Laudato Si,'" *Catholic Moral Theology* (blog), June 30, 2015, https://catholicmoraltheology.com/on-naming-god-gendered-god-talk-in-laudato-si/.

48 Phyllis Zagano, "'Fratelli Tutti' Does Not Include Women, and Neither Does 'Fraternity,'" *National Catholic Reporter*, September 21, 2020, https://www.ncronline.org/opinion/just-catholic/fratelli-tutti-does-not-include-women-and-neither-does-fraternity.

49 Susan Rakoczy, "Is Pope Francis an Ecofeminist?," *openDemocracy* (blog), October 20, 2015, https://www.opendemocracy.net/en/transformation/is-pope-francis-ecofeminist/; Reimer-Barry, "On Naming God."

50 Megan Clark, "'Fratelli Tutti' Shares Practical Wisdom, but Lacks Insights of Women," *National Catholic Reporter*, October 5, 2020, https://www.ncronline.org/opinion/guest-voices/fratelli-tutti-shares-practical-wisdom-lacks-insights-women.

51 Cahill, "Social Friendship Includes Women."

52 See Leo XIII, *Rerum Novarum*, §§ 15, 22, 32; Pius XI, *Quadragesimo Anno*, §§44–68, 111–124; John XXIII, *Mater et Magistra*, §30–34; John Paul II, *Centesimus Annus* (Rome: Vatican Library, 1991), §§10–14, http://w2.vatican.va/content/john-paul-ii/en/encyclicals/documents/hf_jp-ii_enc_01051991_centesimus-annus.html.

53 Francis, *Fratelli Tutti*, §120.

54 Robert Sirico, "Pope Francis Makes an Enemy of the Poor's Best Friend—the Free Market," *Fox News*, October 24, 2021, https://www.foxnews.com/opinion/sirico-pope-francis-free-market-economics.

55 Barnidge, "Against the Catholic Grain."

56 Jeffery D. Sachs, "Market Reformer: An Economist Considers Pope Francis' Critique of Capitalism," *America*, March 14, 2014, 19, https://www.americamagazine.org/issue/market-reformer.

57 John Paul II, *Sollicitudo Rei Socialis*, §42.

58 See Francis, *Message for the Celebration of the Fifteenth World Day of Peace— Nonviolence: A Style of Politics for Peace* (Rome: Vatican Library, 2017), https://www.vatican.va/content/francesco/en/messages/peace/documents /papa-francesco_20161208_messaggio-l-giornata-mondiale-pace-2017 .html.

59 See Debra Erickson, "Adjunct Unionization on Catholic Campuses: Solidarity, Theology, and Mission," *Journal of Moral Theology* 8, special issue, no. 1 (2019): 26–50; Kerry Danner, "Saying No to an Economy That Kills: How Apathy towards Contingent Faculty Undermines Mission and Exploits Vocation at Catholic Universities and Colleges," *Journal of Moral Theology* 8, special issue, no. 1 (2019): 51–74.

60 James F. Keenan, "Dignitas Infinita Falters When It Doesn't Practice What It Preaches," *Outreach*, April 19, 2024, https://outreach .faith/2024/04/james-f-keenan-s-j-dignitas-infinita-falters-when-it-doesnt -practice-what-it-preaches/; see also "Declaration of the Dicastery for the Doctrine of the Faith 'Dignitas Infinita' on Human Dignity," accessed June 15, 2024, https://press.vatican.va/content/salastampa /en/bollettino/pubblico/2024/04/08/240408c.html.

CHAPTER SIX

A Protestant Stance

Reinhold Niebuhr

Throughout much of the twentieth century, American Protestant Christianity was being pushed and prodded by the prodigious works of Reinhold Niebuhr. While Niebuhr's own thought underwent considerable change,[1] a core understanding of justice permeates his long career and provides a significant Protestant alternative to the Catholic view.[2]

Niebuhr respected his Catholic peers but thought that they, like their liberal counterparts in the philosophical world, were not sufficiently realistic about the necessity for struggle in history. Hence, his own "Christian realism" attempts to take seriously the limits of political and social possibilities. In rather stark contrast to Francis's recent call for fraternity, Niebuhr saw the social order as endemically conflictual.

LOVE AND SIN

Like Francis, Niebuhr's view is rooted in Christian tradition—in this case, in prophetic Protestant tradition. For Niebuhr, prophetic religion combines an utmost seriousness about history with a transcendent norm. It never permits us to ignore history or seek escape from it, yet it does not find its ultimate goals or standards within history. Therein lies the special gift of prophetic religion.

In Christianity, Jesus is the "perfect fruit of prophetic religion": he is both in history and points beyond history.[3] Jesus represents seriousness about history (incarnation) and yet a normative realm beyond history (the kingdom of God). From Jesus, we get the supreme ethical command: love. His ethical ideal is one of complete obedience to God's will.[4] This is perfect love, which Jesus both embodies and commands.

For Niebuhr, therefore, Christian ethics begins with love. Love is, first, a derivation of faith. At the same time, love is a "natural" requirement for humans. Individuals can realize themselves only in community, or "brotherhood." The kingdom of God indicates our fulfillment in a world of perfect harmony. Love, therefore, is the primary law of human nature and the highest principle of Christian ethics.[5]

What is love? Niebuhr distinguishes "mutual" love from "self-sacrificial" love.[6] Mutual love is not simply a calculating reciprocity; it springs from concern for the other. But it is never free from prudential concern for oneself as well. It is therefore never the purest form of love. Self-sacrificial love requires a selfless identification with the needs of the other.[7] It is characterized by "disinterestedness," meaning a lack of self-interest and a concern only for the life and well-being of the other.[8] Its ideal is perfect harmony, its purest expression self-sacrifice.[9] Hence, for Christians, the cross is the symbol of this ultimate perfection.[10]

If such selflessness were a simple possibility in history, there would be no need for justice since all would coexist in a perfect harmony of love.[11] Unfortunately, claims Niebuhr, there is no such possibility: "The love commandment stands in juxtaposition to the fact of sin."[12] It is the attempt to be "realistic" about sin that grounds Niebuhr's approach to social ethics. Where Catholic tradition stresses the creation of humans in God's image, Niebuhr stresses another part of the creation story: the fact that humans are "fallen" sinners.

Sin, for Niebuhr, has two dimensions. The religious dimension of sin is idolatry: "The sin of man is that he seeks to make himself God."[13] We are creatures, but we are constantly tempted to forget that fact and attempt to be God. A common form of this sin of idolatry is identifying our interests with the general interests or thinking that our perception of truth is *the* truth.[14]

But sin also has a moral dimension: "The ego which falsely makes itself the center of existence in its pride and will-to-power inevitably subordinates other life to its will."[15] If perfect love is the sacrifice of self, sin is the assertion of self against others: "Sin is always trying to be strong at the expense of someone else."[16] The moral dimension of sin, therefore, is *injustice*—an unwillingness to value the claims of the other or see one's own claims as equal but not superior to the other's.[17] The key injustice is exploitation: "exploiting, enslaving, or taking advantage of other life."[18]

In the face of these "historical realities" of self-interest and exploitation, sacrificial love is not an adequate social ethic. Its ethical ideal of disinterestedness "is too rigorous and perfect to lend itself to application in the economic and political problems of our day."[19] Niebuhr's constant theme is that a profound faith must appreciate "the recalcitrance of sin on every level."[20] He rails against those who underestimate the power of sin in individual life and especially in collective life. Even for the individual, a life of selfless giving is impossible.

But when we move from the individual to the collective level, the impossibility of disinterestedness is compounded. For here, the one who would act out of self-sacrifice is sacrificing not only their own interests but the interests of others. Thus, self-sacrifice becomes "unjust betrayal" of the other.[21] Groups, therefore, must never be expected to behave altruistically: "Groups have never been unselfish in the slightest degree."[22] This is particularly true of nations: "No nation in history has ever been known to be purely unselfish in its actions."[23] It is also true of classes.[24]

For Niebuhr, love remains an "impossible possibility"—relevant as the ultimate standard by which actions may be judged but not possible for immediate implementation in the social world. Economic and political affairs must therefore be governed by what Niebuhr calls the "nicely calculated less and more" of justice.[25]

JUSTICE

Justice is, for Niebuhr, a multifaceted term: he uses it rather loosely to cover a plethora of functions.[26] He speaks of the "spirit of justice,"[27] of "rules" and "structures" of justice,[28] of calculating rights,[29] and, most often, of balancing forces or competing interests.[30] He declares that "justice that is only justice is less than justice."[31] To understand these diverse uses of the term and the seeming contradictions involved, one must understand the tension between love and justice in Niebuhr's thought.

Perfect justice would be a state of "brotherhood" in which there is no conflict of interests.[32] But such a state is no more possible in the world of sin than is a state of perfect love. Indeed, perfect justice would be love. But since love cannot be fully realized, neither can perfect justice. To be "realistic," justice must assume the continued power of self-interest.[33] In history, we live always within the realm of "imperfect" or "relative" justice.[34] It is the inevitability of these relative distinctions in history that is so often ignored by Christian thinkers, says Niebuhr.[35] Relative justice involves the calculation of competing interests, the specification of duties and rights, and the balancing of life forces.

Such relative justice therefore has a somewhat paradoxical relationship to love. On the one hand, rules of justice extend our obligations toward dealing with complex, continuing, and socially recognized obligations that go far beyond the immediate boundaries of what we would naturally feel for others.[36] In doing so, such rules serve the "spirit of brotherhood," or love. In this sense, then, the rules of justice support love and must not be excluded from the domain of love. Complex relations require justice.

Yet, because justice is always imperfect, it is always capable of improvement. Any historical manifestation or rule of justice could always more closely approximate the ideal of love.[37] Justice is the best *possible* harmony within the conditions created by sin, but it is not the best *imaginable* harmony. Indeed, the laws and rules of justice themselves will always reflect the partiality of human perspectives: they are not "unconditionally" just.[38]

Hence, all historical enactments of justice stand under the judgment of love. Love requires justice for the complex realities of the sinful social world. Yet love also transcends, fulfills, negates, and judges justice. It transcends justice because it goes beyond, exceeding the demands of justice.[39] It fulfills justice because it never implies less than justice: where life affirms life, justice is done.[40] It negates and judges justice because every historical justice is imperfect and stands under the judgment of more perfect possibilities of community.[41]

This explains the paradoxical statement that "justice that is only justice is less than justice." The minimal justice of equal rights before the law, for example, is indeed justice. But it never fulfills the total spirit of the willing affirmation of life with life that is required for "perfect justice" or love. In the real world, love and justice exist in uneasy tension.

Niebuhr's ethical stance is therefore dualistic, affirming the necessity for norms of both justice and love, neither of which is sufficient in itself.

But what, then, are the requirements of justice? Niebuhr elaborates on these in terms of rules or laws (the more theoretical side of justice) and in terms of structures.

RULES OF JUSTICE

Because every historical justice is less than love and is therefore capable of improvement, there are, for Niebuhr, no universal or absolute standards of justice.[42] Indeed, Niebuhr suggests that any attempt to codify justice—for example, into a listing of rights—always develops into injustice because "the perspective of the strong dictates the conceptions of justice by which the total community operates."[43]

But this does not imply a relativism that acknowledges no standards at all. For Niebuhr, there are generally valid principles that inform and judge historical choices. The two most important of these are freedom and equality.[44]

Freedom is the essence of human nature and therefore always stands as a crucial value. But unfettered freedom in the economic sphere too often means that those who are poor are priced out of the market.[45] Thus, freedom cannot stand alone as a social principle: it must always be "relegated" to justice, community, and equality.[46]

Equality emerges as Niebuhr's highest standard of justice: "A religion which holds love to be the final law of life stultifies itself if it does not support equal justice as a political and economic approximation of the ideal of love."[47] Equality is the "regulative principle" of justice, a "principle of criticism under which every scheme of justice stands."[48] Equal justice is the best approximation of brotherhood—or love—under the conditions of sin.[49] Equal justice is therefore "the most rational possible social goal."[50] The rule of equality includes concerns for both process (e.g., impartiality in the calculation of needs) and equality as a substantive goal (e.g., equal civil rights).[51]

Even equality, however, can be modified. Indeed, in historical societies, differences of need and social function make inequality a necessity.[52] In addition, "imaginative justice" goes beyond simple equality to note the needs of the neighbor.[53] And equal justice will itself issue into a kind of "option for the poor": "A social conflict which aims at greater equality has a moral justification which must be denied to efforts which aim at the perpetuation of privilege. . . . The oppressed have a higher moral right to challenge their oppressors than these have to maintain their rule by force."[54]

STRUCTURES OF JUSTICE

But how is justice to be established? It is obvious from Niebuhr's elaboration of freedom and equality that *reason* has a role to play in bringing about justice. It is "constitutive" in the rules of justice.[55] Its canons of consistency will lead us to condemn special privileges that cannot be justified.[56] It enables us to judge things from a more inclusive perspective.[57] It helps provide a penetrating analysis of factors in the social situation.[58] Moreover, it can destroy illusions.[59]

But reason alone cannot bring about justice. First, reason itself is not free from the influence of human passions and interests. Reason, too, is "fallen."[60] All rational estimates of rights and interests are contingent and finite, "tainted" by passion and self-interest.[61] Thus, "even the most rational" of people will propose corrupted definitions of justice.[62] *Our truth is never* the *truth.*[63]

Indeed, Niebuhr suggests that the development of rationality has actually injured the search for social justice by "imparting universal pretensions" to partial social interests.[64] The privileged classes are particularly guilty of this form of sin; they do not realize how much their presumed rational calculations are affected by their economic interests.[65] Thus, Niebuhr gives a kind of "epistemological privilege" to the oppressed, suggesting that "those who benefit from social injustice are naturally less capable of understanding its real character than those who suffer from it."[66]

It is partly because of the distortions of reason that there can be no universal "rational" standards of justice. It is also for this reason that neutrality in social struggle is impossible and that efforts to remain neutral really have the effect of working to the advantage of entrenched interests.[67]

Second, reason alone is not adequate to establish justice because justice involves the totality of human life, which includes both reason and passion. The realist knows, claims Niebuhr, that "history is not a simple rational process but a vital one."[68] Justice in history therefore requires not merely rules and principles but the balancing of competing forces, the taming and ordering of human "vitalities."[69]

This is to say that justice requires the use of power or coercion to establish order: "Justice is achieved only as some kind of decent equilibrium of power is established."[70] Niebuhr is perhaps best known for his constant stress on the balance of power: "Any justice that the world has ever achieved rests upon some balance between the various interests."[71] This, he declares, is a "clear lesson of history."[72]

This also means that, for Niebuhr, *power* yields injustice. Niebuhr speaks frequently of the injustice of power: "It may be taken as axiomatic that great disproportions of power lead to injustice."[73] Justice in social systems, therefore, is not simply a matter of how goods are distributed but is also a question of the proper ordering and balancing of power. The struggle for justice is a struggle to increase the power of the victims of injustice.[74]

POLITICAL AND ECONOMIC IMPLICATIONS

Since justice requires a balance of power, the centers of power are crucial to the historical enactment of justice. Two such centers loom large for Niebuhr: the political and the economic.

In response to the threat of fascism, much of Niebuhr's energies went to arguing for and supporting forms of strong democratic government.[75]

The "structures of justice" needed for balancing vitalities in society require both a strong organizing power, or government, and a balance of powers.[76] Too little organizing power results in anarchy; too much becomes tyranny.[77] Government must always be understood as both necessary and oppressive.[78]

But governments are not the only important centers of power. Niebuhr's concern for social justice took root during his pastorate in a church in Detroit; it was the struggles of the workers during hard economic times that set the agenda for his lifelong passion.[79] In contemporary society, argues Niebuhr, centers of power are largely economic.[80] In his early years, Niebuhr saw political power as so dependent on economic power that "a just political order is not possible without the reconstruction of the property system."[81] While he later modified this seemingly trenchant Marxism, he never lost his concern about the power of the economic sphere. The diffusion of political power in democracy makes for justice, he declared, yet the political power of the individual does not eliminate "flagrant forms of economic injustice" in capitalist democratic countries.[82]

Thus, economic justice is a prime concern for Niebuhr. Both liberalism and Marxism, Niebuhr charges, fail to understand property as a form of power.[83] Because property is power, "inequalities in possession have always made for an unjust distribution of the common social fund."[84] Niebuhr therefore is a staunch critic of contemporary capitalism, which he finds "a particularly grievous form of social injustice":[85] "Modern capitalism breeds injustice because of the disproportions of economic power that it tolerates and upon which it is based."[86]

Since justice requires a balance of power, Niebuhr asserts early on what Catholic tradition also affirms: economic justice requires political participation and the use of power.[87] But, for Niebuhr, political participation will be won only by the conflict of force with force. Sinful people will never voluntarily give up their power and self-interest. Justice requires coercion.

Therefore, Niebuhr refused to deny the possibility of revolution or other violent approaches to the establishment of justice. The balance of power that represents justice always involves a tension: tension is covert conflict, and covert conflict can become overt.[88] While Niebuhr often argued on *pragmatic* grounds against violence, he found no absolute arguments against it *in principle*: "Once we have made the fateful concession of ethics to politics, and accepted coercion as a necessary instrument of social cohesion, we can make no absolute distinctions between nonviolent and violent types of coercion."[89] Hence, "the fight for justice will always be a fight."[90]

To those who would say, "*If only* we loved each other, violence would not be necessary," Niebuhr would retort that they underestimate that *if*.[91] To those who advocate nonviolence as the "Christian" way, he would retort that they fail to observe the ways in which they *are already* involved in violence: "The whole of society is constantly involved in both coercion and violence."[92] For Niebuhr, government especially is a source of injustice and violence: in preserving "peace," it always does so by enforcing certain injustices.[93] Niebuhr rails against modern "robber states" that deny to the poor the very privileges that they have seized for themselves.[94]

In brief, Niebuhr's understanding of justice might be summed up in the phrase *love compromising with sin*. Justice is derivative from love yet distinct from it. The demands of justice are, in the end, the demands of love.[95] Perfect love is a harmony in which human wills are not in conflict. Justice approximates that harmony through norms of equality and liberty. Yet there can be no absolute rules of justice since any approximation always stands under the possibility of correction. Justice requires constant attention to the distortions in our perspectives. It also requires the use of coercion to achieve a balance of power.

For Niebuhr, the Protestant affirmation of justification by faith alone does not make efforts for justice irrelevant. Rather, it means that "we will not regard the pressures and counterpressures, the tensions, the overt and covert conflicts by which justice is achieved and maintained, as normative in the absolute sense; but neither will we ease our conscience by seeking to escape involvement in them."[96]

REVIEW

Niebuhr's approach to justice differs from all those considered above because of his emphasis on sin. For Niebuhr, sin and conflict among people are persistent and enduring aspects of human life. Hence, utilitarians would be "unrealistic" in assuming a harmony between individual interests and the greater good. Rawls's dependence on reason also fails because reason itself is tainted by sin and thus cannot alone yield valid principles of justice. Nozick's trust in the "free" exchanges of market systems ignores the fact that humans will always seek unfair advantage in exchange, so that resulting divisions of goods are unjust. In a world permeated by sin, no single principle or approach can yield eternally valid principles of justice. Sandel and Francis would probably be judged too irenic in their reliance on a vision of the common good since "brotherhood" is an ideal that will not be realized in history.

Instead, justice must be characterized first by a balance of power. The ideal is harmony of self with self; justice approximates this ideal by balancing powers so that those who are weak are protected against those who are strong. Such a balance is not only a relative harmony but it is also a necessary and just harmony. Even Rawls's first principle of equal liberty would probably not satisfy Niebuhr since it does not ensure a balance of power between classes.

But a balance of power is not itself the ideal. Thus, every historical enactment of justice, for Niebuhr, also involves injustice. Justice is never finished or achieved. Every relative justice is a relative injustice as well. One can never rest satisfied that justice has been done simply because the greatest good has been done, or those who are disadvantaged are better off than they were before, or exchanges are fair, or living wages are granted. Each of these creates a part of justice but also holds within it a perversion of justice. All structures and arrangements of justice are temporary and partial. They always await the better balance, the closer approximation of the harmony of love that is perfect justice.

CRITIQUE

Niebuhr's works have been subjected to long scrutiny. Almost every aspect of his work has been criticized—his theology, his Christology, his factual interpretations of history. And almost every criticism by one party has brought defense of Niebuhr by another. Only those issues immediately relevant to understanding his theory of justice will be addressed here.

Let us begin with the most inclusive criticism: the charge that Niebuhr *has* no theory of justice. Emil Brunner puts it pointedly: "Reinhold Niebuhr has never worked out a clear concept of justice whereby the difference between the demands of justice and those of the supreme ethical norm of love might be understood."[97]

Gordon Harland defends Niebuhr at this point. He argues that failure to define a term does not mean that one lacks a clearly articulated concept of it. *Justice* is not defined by Niebuhr, he suggests, because it is a relational term—it has no meaning independent of love.[98] Niebuhr says much the same in responding to his critics: "Justice is an application of the law of love. The rules . . . are applications of the law of love and do not have independence from it."[99]

Nonetheless, there is merit in Brunner's charge. Though it is clear that love and justice exist in relationship for Niebuhr, it is not always clear what this means. Niebuhr tries to walk a tightrope between philosophical and theological definitions of justice. On the one hand, he appears to adopt some philosophical concepts of justice—for example, in his advocacy of equality and freedom as basic requirements. But not only are these terms never well defined by Niebuhr, they also carry unexamined liberal freight in a theology otherwise critical of liberalism.[100]

On the other hand, the identification of perfect justice with the theological norm of love also raises problems. If the demands of justice are, in the end, the demands of love, then it would seem that the principles of love and justice should be compatible in substance: whatever justice requires should be what love requires. Niebuhr seems to imply this when he says that love can exceed justice but never abrogate justice.[101]

But if justice admits the claims of the self, while love requires the sacrifice of the self's interests, it is difficult to see how they can always be substantively identical. It seems that self-interest is legitimate for one and not for the other. This means that, at least in relationships involving the self, love and justice cannot require the same thing. One critic charges that Niebuhr's ethics leaves the Christian caught between two worlds with two ultimate norms, "distraught and divided in all ethical decisions."[102]

Niebuhr would no doubt reject this assessment. In a sinful world, love *must* compromise with sin. In a sinful world, self-interest always enters, and justice—the fair promotion of interests—is therefore always needed. Love is ethically purer than justice but not more valuable socially.[103] Love is not a direct norm for action in the social world. Rather, it functions as a reminder of the ideal of complete harmony and of the need to keep seeking a more perfect resolution to the conflict. Moreover, in a sinful world where all life does not affirm all other life, the sacrifice of the self's interests is the truest expression of seeking after harmony. Thus, love is appropriate in every negotiation for justice as a leavening force to restrain the exercise of self-interest.[104] Though justice and love are not identical, they are complementary.

Still, the relationship between love and justice would be clearer if Niebuhr spelled out the requirements of justice in more detail. He does not specify procedures or rules for determining how interests are to be weighed and how to determine what is "due" in justice. This failure begs vital questions, charges Kenneth Thompson: "What, for instance, does the norm *justice* . . . mean in practical terms?"[105] Does Niebuhr's "realistic"—and ultimately pragmatic—approach amount to nothing more than his own idiosyncratic reading of what is "right" in each situation? Even Niebuhr's use of middle axioms such as equality and balance of power does not prevent his ethic from being a "more or less intuitive approach to ethical issues," Dennis McCann suggests.[106]

Other critics defend Niebuhr at this point. Gene Outka grants that the rules of justice are not well elaborated in the theological literature of Niebuhr's generation. He nonetheless notes the validity of Niebuhr's point that all specific rules will not escape the corruptions of ideology and interest. Thus, he says, we must acquiesce to a certain tentativeness in ethics: "Particular situations often demand a highly sensitive, *appropriate* response which may render formally preferable principles and rules unhelpful or even distortive."[107] Harland agrees: "Because justice always exists in a dynamic relation between *agape* and the uniqueness of concrete historical situations one can never say 'exactly' what justice is apart from either *agape* or the situation."[108]

However, McCann charges that this leaves Niebuhr with an ethic that fails to illuminate "difficult tactical questions." Niebuhr's middle axioms have only limited usefulness as guidelines for social ethics: they "remain intuitive precisely where they should be more explicit."[109] There is in Niebuhr little careful elaboration of the extent to which "justice" means "treatment in accord with needs" or "merit" or "productivity" or some other criterion.[110]

These criticisms reflect Niebuhr's relative lack of systematic theory about justice. Niebuhr's role was often that of the gadfly. His language and style reflected that role: his was the "polemical method of overemphasis"[111] or the "technique of demolition."[112] In a world characterized by gross injustices, Niebuhr's approach is the prophetic technique of exaggeration and excoriation rather than the philosophical technique of reasoned argument. Note, for example, the value-laden language he uses in describing materialistic theory as an antidote for the "toxin of the hypocrisies by which modern society hides its brutalities."[113]

Niebuhr's dialectical approach to love and justice therefore functions more as a cautionary device than as a concrete guideline. Justice requires enough organizing power but not too much. Justice requires struggle for equality yet always with the recognition that our understanding of the situation will be wrong. Justice, for Niebuhr, functions more as a principle of prophetic criticism of *any* stance taken than as a precise norm or philosophical category.

Moreover, his theory is dependent on his historical method—what Catholics would call his reading of the signs of the times. His cautions and decisions on specific social issues are therefore a clue to his understanding of justice. For example, constitutional instruments are required in any international order to "guarantee the weaker nations their rights."[114] The fact that "children do starve and old people freeze to death in the poverty of our cities" is taken as a sign of the violence of structures that constitutes injustice.[115] Equal rights in race relations is the "minimal standard" of justice.[116] The principle of a "living wage" is affirmed, provided it is "generously interpreted" (i.e., coupled with old age insurance and unemployment insurance).[117] Justice requires "equal opportunity of development."[118] The Marxist dictum "to each according to need" stands as an ideal, albeit unworkable.[119] Justifiable inequalities are limited by what is necessary for differentiated social functions.[120]

In fact, some of his criticisms are quite pointed. The idea that the profits of industry are a reward for the sacrifices made by owners may have had merit in the early days of capitalism, he declares, but does not hold in a day when concentrations of capital mean that few "sacrifices" in luxury are made by investors.[121] The issue has become not simply "fair distribution" of property but whether the right of property is legitimate at all.[122] The success of free enterprise in the United States has been due to certain natural and historical factors (e.g., wealth of resources) that make it not a good model for other places.[123] As always in Niebuhr, it is "history" that teaches us and provides ethical insight.

Then it becomes important to ask whether Niebuhr reads history correctly. Here, Herbert Edwards charges that Niebuhr was very much a "white man of his times." In dealing with racial justice, for example, Niebuhr too easily adopted the view of White Southerners and urged patience for Blacks. Though equality was his moral ideal of justice, that ideal was subject to compromise with the "realities" of a situation read through the eyes of a White power structure that saw Black efforts for justice as divisive.[124] In *The Cross and the Lynching Tree*, James Cone acknowledges his own debt to Niebuhr and also acknowledges that Niebuhr spoke out against racism more than other contemporary White theologians. Nonetheless, Cone levels a sharp critique in noting that Niebuhr never condemned the horrible lynchings that were common during Niebuhr's tenure as America's most influential public theologian.[125]

Similarly, M. M. Thomas argues that Niebuhr misread the political and moral dynamics of the non-Western world and therefore came to stress issues of political justice in disregard of other questions of justice.[126] Feminists have also criticized Niebuhr for ignoring the particular injustices faced by women. Where sin for men may be represented by the will to power over others, some feminists argue that sin for women has more often been a too-ready self-effacement.[127]

Some commentators would charge that Niebuhr's reading of history is too affected by his own theological presuppositions. Many have taken him to task for overemphasizing sin and failing to lift up human potentialities for good. Here, Outka is bold in his critique. Niebuhr, he says, "makes the situation of incompatible interests the paradigm of moral reflection within 'historical society.' But this is a mistake. For the interests of [people] are by and large more complementary than conflicting."[128]

Since Niebuhr's understanding of justice is based directly on his assessment of the centrality and persistence of sin in human life, this criticism matters for assessing Niebuhr's approach to justice. If sin is less pervasive than Niebuhr assumes, there would be more possibilities for the direct application of the norm of love to social issues or for the closer approximation of justice to the ideals of "brotherhood" and harmony.

Other critics, however, support Niebuhr on this point. John Bennett asserts that "nothing has happened to refute the realistic analysis of the stubbornness of evil in society."[129] Indeed, one critic suggests that, far from being too pessimistic, Niebuhr is too optimistic about human potential.[130]

Related to the question of whether Niebuhr overestimates sin is the question of whether he underestimates the role of love or reason in social ethics. That is, does Niebuhr underestimate religious and rational sources for social ethics?

Here, the critique of John Howard Yoder is probably most important.[131] Yoder views Niebuhr as providing the "classic" statement of an approach to ethics that makes Jesus irrelevant.[132] In his view, Niebuhr's approach to love and justice amounts to a "concession that Jesus is really on the other side from one's own."[133] That is, if Jesus's ethic is a pure ethic of love, but such an ethic cannot be applied in the world, then whatever ethic we do apply—such as justice—is clearly in contradiction to Jesus. For Yoder, therefore, Niebuhr's ethic would not be Christian. Yoder argues for the direct relevance of the norm of love to the social arena. Far from arguing that we need separate or distinct norms of justice to deal with political issues, Yoder suggests that Jesus gives us a "political" ethic in the application of the cross to the political arena.[134]

Niebuhr would no doubt have respected Yoder's pacifism as an expression of the ideal of love. But he would perhaps have charged that such pacifism ignores the "violence" that is being done all the time precisely in political structures: no one can avow an ethic of pure love "from the vantage point of privilege and security."[135] Moreover, Yoder may not appreciate the extent to which Christians remain sinners and cannot know the will of God in the social arena.[136]

However, this suggested retort raises additional problems for Niebuhr's own theory of justice. If all knowledge is corrupted by one's own social location and historical age, then surely Niebuhr claims too much finality for his own interpretations of Scripture and for their social implications. Henry Nelson Wieman charges that Niebuhr "corrects the Bible according to his own convictions."[137] E. A. Burtt simply accuses him of reflecting "the limited standpoint of Protestant Christianity."[138]

For instance, Niebuhr's identification of Jesus's ethic with an ethic of pure "love" and "disinterestedness" is anathema to other Christians. Frederick Herzog charges that in separating a "religious" ethic of love from a "rational" ethic of justice, "God in Christ is completely removed from the immediate claims of justice."[139] Similarly, Franklin I. Gamwell argues that if personal fulfillment means self-sacrificial love, which cannot be realized in history, then Niebuhr has ultimately moved out of the realm of history and thereby undermines his own professed interest in it.[140]

Although it was always Niebuhr's intention to expose the limitations and fallacies from any perspective, he may have failed to see some of his own. McCann suggests that Niebuhr and his followers in Christian realism failed to sustain the paradox of his own vision. Niebuhr's advocacy of democracy as the best form of government led him to support developmentalism in what was then called the Third World.[141] His view of human nature was based on aggressive personalities and their form of sin: will to power. This may not be the form of sin most expressed by oppressed peoples.[142]

ASSESSMENT

What is Niebuhr's contribution to a theory of justice? The legacy of Reinhold Niebuhr in the field of ethics is a strong one. Ronald Stone declares that "the best starting place for the serious student of social ethics is Reinhold Niebuhr's thought."[143] James Gustafson considers *The Nature and Destiny of Man* "the most important American contribution to Protestant theological ethics in the first half of [the twentieth] century."[144] Abraham Heschel goes even further in his praise: "In boldness of penetration, depth of insight, fullness of vision and comprehensiveness, Reinhold Niebuhr's system excels everything which the whole of American theology has hitherto produced."[145]

However, these comments are directed at Niebuhr's work overall—his theology, his social ethics, his interpretations of American religious behavior. That he was a significant political voice during much of the twentieth century is not in question. But what are the contributions of his theory of justice?

Here, Niebuhr's greatest weaknesses may also be his greatest strengths. Critics appear to find fault with Niebuhr at two fundamental points where justice is concerned: his lack of a clear definition and rules for justice and his (over-) emphasis on sin and the necessity for struggle and balance of power. Yet it is precisely these two points that provide a significant contribution to any theory of justice.

Niebuhr begins with the injustices of history and the recognition that we live in a sinful world. As one critic puts it, Niebuhr "asked the right questions."[146] He takes seriously the historical realities of conflict as well as cooperation. He is the "unveiler par excellence of human sin in its blatant and subtle forms."[147] While Sandel and Francis are also motivated by injustices in the world, they focus on the vision of a common good. In contrast, Niebuhr's strength lies in his stress on the realities of conflicting interests. If justice has to do with competing claims, as David Hume and most of his followers have thought, then a theory of justice must take competition seriously. This Niebuhr does.

Particularly important in this regard is his perception of the distortions built into rational explanation and justification. Critics of Rawls noted that his attempt to find a "neutral rationality" on which a theory of justice could be based ultimately fails because his own definition of the original position carries value assumptions and biases within it. Niebuhr would have predicted this. He cautioned against all attempts to trust too much in our own rationality or our own perceptions.

To be sure, in his suspicion of human rationality and his consciousness of the ubiquity of sin, Niebuhr leaves an ethical system without clear rules and definitions. But this very fact, noted by critics as a weakness, may also be a strength. Niebuhr's paradoxical approach to justice and its complicated relationship to love are unsatisfying for those who seek clear definitions and proposals. Yet it may come closer to truth than efforts to find a single criterion for justice, whether the greatest good for the greatest number, the position of the least advantaged, or the fairness of exchange.

Niebuhr leaves no one with an easy conscience that justice has been achieved simply because those who are poor are now a bit better off than they were before, because industrial systems are more efficient, or because exchanges have been handled fairly. Niebuhr gives no criteria by which we can be assured that justice has been done. Indeed, we can never be so assured precisely because every historical enactment of justice is also an enactment of injustice. Niebuhr's overriding goal was always to caution against the pride that attends any security about our political programs. Humility about our programs and achievements and openness to consider alternatives that might be more just would have salutary effects in some powerful circles.

Yet, this very tendency to distrust any human efforts or programs raises, as we have seen, a crucial question: How does one know? If all reason is suspect, then whence comes knowledge? It is this question that becomes the probing ground of liberation theology, to which we turn in the next chapter. Ronald Stone suggests that Niebuhr's thought "needed the influence of being brought closer to the passionate fires of revolution in the Third World."[148] Those passionate fires—both in the "Third World" and in the United States—suggest a different understanding of justice.

NOTES

1 See Ronald H. Stone, *Reinhold Niebuhr: Prophet to Politicians* (Nashville: Abingdon Press, 1972); also John C. Bennett, "Reinhold Niebuhr's Social

Ethics," in *Reinhold Niebuhr: His Religious, Social, and Political Thought*, ed. Charles W. Kegley and Robert W. Bretall (New York: Macmillan, 1956). However, there is a core to Niebuhr's ethics. We agree with Bennett in locating that core in the "middle" of Niebuhr's writings—those of the 1930s and 1940s. In view of Niebuhr's later refusal to support "any position" taken in his early work *An Interpretation of Christian Ethics* (New York: The Seabury Press, 1979; first published 1935) (see *Reinhold Niebuhr*, ed. Kegley and Bretall, 434–435), we have made use of that volume here only when statements in it are substantially supported by Niebuhr's other writings.

2 That Niebuhr's approach remains influential is demonstrated by the fact that former president Barack Obama identified Niebuhr many times as a major influence on his political thinking. See R. Ward Holder and Peter B. Josephson, "Obama's Niebuhr Problem," *Church History* 82, no. 3 (September 2013): 678–687.

3 Niebuhr, *An Interpretation of Christian Ethics*, 22.

4 Reinhold Niebuhr, *The Nature and Destiny of Man*, 2 vols. (1943; repr., New York: Scribner, 1964), 2: *Human Destiny*, 73.

5 D. B. Robertson, ed., *Love and Justice: Selections from the Shorter Writings of Reinhold Niebuhr* (Gloucester, MA: Peter Smith, 1976), 25; Niebuhr, *Nature and Destiny*, 2:244; Reinhold Niebuhr, *The Children of Light and the Children of Darkness* (London: Nisbet, 1945), 11.

6 Niebuhr, *Nature and Destiny*, 2, chap. 3.

7 Niebuhr, *An Interpretation of Christian Ethics*, 100: "The complete identification of life with life which the law of love demands."

8 Robertson, *Love and Justice*, 31.

9 Gene Outka, *Agape: An Ethical Analysis* (New Haven, CT: Yale University Press, 1972), 169. However, Franklin I. Gamwell, "Reinhold Niebuhr's Theistic Ethic," in *The Legacy of Reinhold Niebuhr*, ed. Nathan A. Scott (Chicago: University of Chicago Press, 1975), 68, suggests that these two are not synonymous, as Niebuhr implied. In Gamwell's view, "perfect harmony" can include an affirmation of the interests of the self, which is excluded by "self-sacrifice."

10 Niebuhr, *Nature and Destiny*, 2:72.

11 Robertson, *Love and Justice*, 27.

12 Niebuhr, *An Interpretation of Christian Ethics*, 39; cf. Robertson, *Love and Justice*, 27.

13 Niebuhr, *Nature and Destiny*, 1: *Human Nature*, 179; see also 140.

14 Reinhold Niebuhr, *Moral Man and Immoral Society* (New York: Scribner, 1932, 1960), 117.

15 Niebuhr, *Nature and Destiny*, 1:179. These two forms of sin are never separate, however. Those who wish to justify injustice always claim a kind of superiority for themselves that amounts to idolatry (166).

16 Robertson, *Love and Justice*, 164; cf. Niebuhr, *Nature and Destiny*, 2:252.

17 Cf. Niebuhr's statement that "in ... distributive justice the self regards itself as an equal but not as a specially privileged member" (*Christian Realism and Political Problems* [New York: Scribner, 1953], 160).

18 Robertson, *Love and Justice*, 282; cf. Niebuhr. *An Interpretation of Christian Ethics*, 90.

19 Robertson, *Love and Justice*, 30; cf. Niebuhr, *Nature and Destiny*, 2:72: "A love which 'seeketh not its own' is not able to maintain itself in historical society." It should be noted here that Niebuhr understands Jesus to have had primarily a personal ethic in which actions are motivated purely by obedience to God and in disregard of social consequences (Robertson, *Love and Justice*, 30–31).

20 Robertson, *Love and Justice*, 212.

21 Niebuhr, *Nature and Destiny*, 2:88; cf. Niebuhr, *Moral Man*, 267.

22 Robertson, *Love and Justice*, 243.

23 Niebuhr, *Moral Man*, 75; cf. 84: "The selfishness of nations is proverbial." Niebuhr notes that loyalty to the nation is a high form of individual altruism but that it becomes transmuted into patriotism, which is national egoism. Thus, "the unselfishness of individuals makes for the selfishness of nations" (*Moral Man*, 91).

24 Cf. Niebuhr, *Moral Man*, 213.

25 Niebuhr, *An Interpretation of Christian Ethics*, 62; *Moral Man*, 68; *Nature and Destiny*, 1:295.

26 John Bennett calls Niebuhr's view of love and justice "extraordinarily many-sided" ("Reinhold Niebuhr's Social Ethics," 58). M. M. Thomas ("A Third World View of Christian Realism," *Christianity and Crisis* 46, no. 1 [1986]: 8) says that it is characterized by "almost unscrupulous fluctuations."

27 Robertson, *Love and Justice*, 25.

28 Niebuhr, *Nature and Destiny*, 2:247.

29 Niebuhr, *Nature and Destiny*, 2:252.

30 E.g., Robertson, *Love and Justice*, 207: "Some balance of power is the basis of whatever justice is achieved in human relations." Cf. 300: "Every historic form of justice has been attained by some equilibrium of power."

31 Robertson, *Love and Justice*, 32; cf. Niebuhr, *Moral Man*, 258.

32 Robertson, *Love and Justice*, 49.

33 Robertson, *Love and Justice*, 28.

34 Robertson, *Love and Justice*, 162: "Maintaining a relative justice in an evil world."

35 Niebuhr, *Nature and Destiny*, 2:280.

36 Niebuhr, *Nature and Destiny*, 2:248.

37 Niebuhr, *An Interpretation of Christian Ethics*, 66–67, suggests that there is an "ascending scale" of moral possibilities that more closely approximate love as societies move from the minimum of rights to life and property toward recognition of a fuller set of rights beyond those that are legally enforced.

38 Niebuhr, *Nature and Destiny*, 2:252. Indeed, here Niebuhr says that Marxism is correct in seeing that rules of justice are "primarily rationalizations of the interests of the dominant elements of a society."

39 Niebuhr, *An Interpretation of Christian Ethics*, 112; *Nature and Destiny*, 1:295.

40 Niebuhr, *An Interpretation of Christian Ethics*, 90, 128; *Nature and Destiny*, 1:295.

41 Niebuhr, *An Interpretation of Christian Ethics*, 85: *Nature and Destiny*, 1:285, 2:246.

42 Niebuhr constantly stresses that there are "higher possibilities of justice in every historic situation" (*Nature and Destiny*, 2:284; see also *Children of Light*, 53). Niebuhr eschews consistency and argues that it is "impossible to fix upon a single moral absolute" in historic situations of justice (*An Interpretation of Christian Ethics*, 121).

43 Robertson, *Love and Justice*, 32.

44 Niebuhr, *Nature and Destiny*, 2:254. Indeed, he calls these part of the "absolute natural law" (*Nature and Destiny*, 2:280).

45 Robertson, *Love and Justice*, 87.

46 Robertson, *Love and Justice*, 95. Gordon Harland (*The Thought of Reinhold Niebuhr* [New York: Oxford University Press, 1960], 55) suggests that Niebuhr increasingly emphasized liberty over the years.

47 Niebuhr, *An Interpretation of Christian Ethics*, 80.

48 Niebuhr, *An Interpretation of Christian Ethics*, 65–66: cf. 121.

49 Niebuhr, *Nature and Destiny*, 2:254; see also *An Interpretation of Christian Ethics*, 65: "In the ideal of equality there is an echo of the law of love, 'Thou shalt love thy neighbor *as thyself*.'"

50 Niebuhr, *Moral Man*, 171.

51 Cf. Bennett, "Reinhold Niebuhr's Social Ethics," 58–59.

52 Niebuhr, *Children of Light*, 55: *Nature and Destiny*, 2:255. Bennett, "Reinhold Niebuhr's Social Ethics," 59, suggests that Niebuhr accepted more inequalities in his later years.

53 Niebuhr, *An Interpretation of Christian Ethics*, 66.

54 Niebuhr, *Moral Man*, 234. Roger L. Shinn, "Realism, Radicalism, and Eschatology in Reinhold Niebuhr: A Reassessment," in Scott, *The Legacy of Reinhold Niebuhr*, 94, notes that although Niebuhr did not think the oppressed were immune from sin, he did see them as in a better position than the powerful to unmask the frauds of society.

55 Niebuhr, *Nature and Destiny*, 2:248.

56 Niebuhr, *An Interpretation of Christian Ethics*, 125.

57 Niebuhr, *Moral Man*, 30–31.

58 Niebuhr, *Moral Man*, 32; cf. Niebuhr, *An Interpretation of Christian Ethics*, 100.

59 Niebuhr, *Moral Man*, 237.

60 Niebuhr, *An Interpretation of Christian Ethics*, 79–80; Robertson, *Love and Justice*, 47; Niebuhr, *Nature and Destiny*, 1:284.

61 Niebuhr, *Nature and Destiny*, 2:252.

62 Robertson, *Love and Justice*, 48.

63 Niebuhr, *Nature and Destiny*, 2:214.

64 Niebuhr, *An Interpretation of Christian Ethics*, 137.

65 Niebuhr, *Moral Man*, xiv. Later, he declares, "Special privileges make all men dishonest. The purest conscience and the clearest mind is prostituted by the desire to prove them morally justified." Niebuhr, *Moral Man*, 162.

66 Niebuhr, *Moral Man*, 80.

67 Robertson, *Love and Justice*, 254.

68 Robertson, *Love and Justice*, 207.

69 Niebuhr, *Nature and Destiny*, 2:257.

70 Robertson, *Love and Justice*, 52. In Niebuhr's view, two things are necessary for the establishment of social justice: (1) a balance of powers and (2) a central organizing power. Each of these can become distorted and contradict the law of love--the first by dissolving into anarchy, the second by becoming tyranny (*Nature and Destiny*, 2:257–258).

71 Robertson, *Love and Justice*, 173.

72 Robertson, *Love and Justice*, 36.

73 Robertson, *Love and Justice*, 199; Niebuhr, *Nature and Destiny*, 2:262; cf. *Nature and Destiny*, 1:223; Robertson, *Love and Justice*, 173.

74 Bennett, "Reinhold Niebuhr's Social Ethics," 60.

75 Langdon Gilkey, "Reinhold Niebuhr's Theology of History," in Scott, *The Legacy of Reinhold Niebuhr*, 36.

76 Niebuhr, *Nature and Destiny*, 2:257.

77 Niebuhr, *Nature and Destiny*, 2:257–258.

78 Niebuhr, *Nature and Destiny*, 2:269; Niebuhr speaks of "both the vice and the necessity of government" (Niebuhr, *Nature and Destiny*, 278).

79 Cf. Stone, *Reinhold Niebuhr*, 27; also Richard Kroner, "The Historical Roots of Niebuhr's Thought," in Kegley and Bretall, *Reinhold Niebuhr*, 30; also Emil Brunner, "Some Remarks on Reinhold Niebuhr's World as a Christian Thinker," in Kegley and Bretall, *Reinhold Niebuhr*.

80 Niebuhr, *An Interpretation of Christian Ethics*, 113; cf. Niebuhr, *Moral Man*, 163. Niebuhr's own beginnings as a pastor in Detroit shaped his sense of the centrality of economic issues; see Stone, *Reinhold Niebuhr*, 27.

81 Niebuhr, *An Interpretation of Christian Ethics*, 113. Niebuhr claimed (*Moral Man*, 149) that Marx grasped the essence of capitalist democracy when he said that "the oppressed are allowed, once every few years, to decide which particular representatives of the oppressing classes are to represent and repress them in politics." See also *Moral Man*, 210, where he declares that economic power is more basic than political power.

82 Niebuhr, *Nature and Destiny*, 2:262–263.

83 Niebuhr, *Children of Light*, 76.

84 Niebuhr, *An Interpretation of Christian Ethics*, 113. Niebuhr's language of "common social fund" brings to mind Sandel's emphasis on the common good.

85 Robertson, *Love and Justice*, 46. It should be noted that Niebuhr recognized the difference between modern capitalism and the capitalism of Adam Smith's theory. A dogma intended to guarantee the economic freedom of the individual became the "ideology" of vast corporate structures and was used to prevent proper control of their power (*Children of Light*, 25).

86 Robertson, *Love and Justice*, 257: cf. Niebuhr, *An Interpretation of Christian Ethics*, 90. In early stages, Niebuhr was frankly Marxian in his economic analysis. However, he always argued that Marxists were wrong to think that the socialization of property alone would bring about justice.

87 Robertson, *Love and Justice*, 92–93.

88 Robertson, *Love and Justice*, 276; cf. 261 and 53.

89 Niebuhr, *Moral Man*, 179. Niebuhr had been a pacifist in his early years but became disillusioned with pacifists after World War I.

90 Robertson, *Love and Justice*, 38.

91 "It is because men are sinners that justice can be achieved only by a certain degree of coercion on the one hand, and by a resistance to coercion and tyranny on the other hand" (Reinhold Niebuhr, *Christianity and Power Politics* [New York: Scribner, 1946], 14).

92 Niebuhr, *Moral Man*, 192: cf. *An Interpretation of Christian Ethics*, 114, where Niebuhr accuses the middle-class church of disavowing "violence" when it is composed of people "who have enough economic and other forms of covert power to be able to dispense with the more overt forms of violence." See also Robertson, *Love and Justice*, 255, where he accuses pacifist Quakers of not realizing "to what degree they are the beneficiaries of an essentially violent system."

93 Niebuhr, *Nature and Destiny*, 2:275; governments are particularly condemned because they "oppressed the poor" (*Nature and Destiny*, 2:269).

94 Robertson, *Love and Justice*, 167.

95 Cf. Harland, *Thought of Reinhold Niebuhr*, 35.

96 Niebuhr, *Nature and Destiny*, 2:284.

97 Brunner, "Some Remarks," 30.

98 Harland, *Thought of Reinhold Niebuhr*, 23.

99 Reinhold Niebuhr, "Reply to Interpretation and Criticism," in Kegley and Bretall, *Reinhold Niebuhr*, 435. For a contemporary Protestant ethicist who argues much the same in developing a theory of justice, see Stephen Charles Mott, *Biblical Ethics and Social Change* (New York: Oxford University Press, 1982).

100 Cf. Daniel Day Williams, "Niebuhr and Liberalism," in Kegley and Bretall, *Reinhold Niebuhr*, 203.

101 See Outka, *Agape*, 80.

102 Williams, "Niebuhr and Liberalism," 210. The suggestion of Dennis P. McCann in *Christian Realism and Liberation Theology: Practical Theologies in Creative Conflict* (Maryknoll, NY: Orbis, 1981, 91) that Niebuhr offers essentially a dispositional ethic might be helpful here. If love and justice do not function as norms for Niebuhr but rather as dispositions, then it is possible to reduce any presumed conflicts since they no longer represent "requirements" in the social world.

103 Niebuhr, *Moral Man*, 57.

104 We are drawing here on several aspects of Outka's analysis (cf. Outka. *Agape*, 80, 169).

105 Kenneth Thompson, "The Political Philosophy of Reinhold Niebuhr," in Kegley and Bretall, *Reinhold Niebuhr*, 173.

106 McCann, *Christian Realism*, 124.

107 Outka, *Agape*, 120.

108 Harland, *Thought of Reinhold Niebuhr*, 28.

109 McCann, *Christian Realism*, 103; see also 91–92.

110 Harland, *Thought of Reinhold Niebuhr*, 52. Longwood attempts to relate Niebuhr's theory to traditional categories such as need, merit, and rank. He argues that Niebuhr clearly permits some inequalities on the basis of both need and rank. See Merle Longwood, "Niebuhr and a Theory of Justice," *Dialog* 14 (1985): 253–262.

111 Bennett, "Reinhold Niebuhr's Social Ethics," 57.

112 Paul Ramsey, "Love and Law," in Kegley and Bretall, *Reinhold Niebuhr*, 83.

113 Niebuhr, *Moral Man*, 155; one could add endless examples!

114 Robertson, *Love and Justice*, 196.

115 Robertson, *Love and Justice*, 257.

116 Robertson, *Love and Justice*, 146.

117 Robertson, *Love and Justice*, 99–100.

118 Niebuhr, *An Interpretation of Christian Ethics*, 121.

119 Niebuhr, *Moral Man*, 160.

120 Niebuhr, *Moral Man*, 128.

121 Niebuhr, *Moral Man*, 125.

122 Niebuhr, *Children of Light*, 64.

123 Robertson, *Love and Justice*, 95–96.

124 Herbert O. Edwards, "Niebuhr, 'Realism' and Civil Rights in America," *Christianity and Crisis* 46, no. 1 (February 1986): 13–14.

125 James H. Cone, *The Cross and the Lynching Tree* (Maryknoll, NY: Orbis, 2011), chap. 2. Cone charges, we think rightly, that Niebuhr saw the suffering of Black people but lacked the "heart" to feel it as his own. See also Traci C. West, *Disruptive Christian Ethics: When Racism and Women's Lives Matter* (Louisville, KY: Westminster John Knox, 2006), chap. 1.

126 Thomas, "A Third World View of Christian Realism." However, Niebuhr himself said that "economic power is more basic than political power." See *Moral Man*, 210.

127 Cf. Isabel Carter Heyward, *The Redemption of God* (Washington, DC: University Press of America, 1982), 161; the Mudflower Collective (Katie G. Cannon et al.), *God's Fierce Whimsy* (New York: Pilgrim, 1985), 91.

128 Outka, *Agape*, 43. Numerous critics join Outka. John Bennett ("Christian Realism: A Symposium," *Christianity and Crisis* 28 [August 5, 1968]: 176) suggests that Niebuhr may have neglected the extent to which history can be influenced by redemptive events. A similar view is voiced by Cox and Geyer in the same symposium. See also Alexander J. Burnstein, "Niebuhr, Scripture, and Normative Judaism," in Kegley and Bretall, *Reinhold Niebuhr*.

129 Bennett, "Christian Realism," 176. See also Abraham I. Heschel, "A Hebrew Evaluation of Reinhold Niebuhr," in Kegley and Bretall, *Reinhold Niebuhr*, 394–395.

130 Henry Nelson Wieman, "A Religious Naturalist Looks at Reinhold Niebuhr," in Kegley and Bretall, *Reinhold Niebuhr*, 346.

131 For critiques of Niebuhr's understanding and use of reason, see Paul Tillich, "Reinhold Niebuhr's Doctrine of Knowledge," and Wieman, "A Religious Naturalist" in Kegley and Bretall, *Reinhold Niebuhr*. Niebuhr refutes Tillich's interpretation in his "Reply to Interpretation and Criticism," in the same volume. Though Niebuhr is critical of the distortions of reason, his view of its role in social ethics does include some positive aspects, as noted above. This criticism, therefore, seems less important than the question of whether love is directly applicable to the social arena.

132 John Howard Yoder, *The Politics of Jesus* (Grand Rapids, MI: Eerdmans, 1972), 16, n. 7.

133 Yoder, *The Politics*, 111, n. 12.

134 Just as Niebuhr limits the cross to "self-sacrificial love," however, so Yoder appears to limit its significance to nonviolence. Niebuhr argues in numerous places that Jesus's ethic is better understood as "nonresistance" than as nonviolence.

135 Robertson, *Love and Justice*, 39.

136 Yoder's critique was made after Niebuhr's death. However, Stone suggests something along these lines (*Reinhold Niebuhr*, 78–79).

137 Wieman, "A Religious Naturalist," 339.

138 E. A. Burtt, "Some Questions about Niebuhr's Theology," in Kegley and Bretall, *Reinhold Niebuhr*, 363.

139 Frederick Herzog, *Justice Church* (Maryknoll, NY: Orbis, 1981), 109.

140 Gamwell, "Reinhold Niebuhr's Theistic Ethic," 77.

141 McCann, *Christian Realism*, 117.

142 McCann, *Christian Realism*, 127.

143 Stone, *Reinhold Niebuhr*, 240.

144 James Gustafson, *Christian Ethics and the Community* (New York: Pilgrim, 1971), 31.

145 Heschel, "A Hebrew Evaluation," 392.

146 Stone, *Reinhold Niebuhr*, 231.

147 Shinn, "Realism, Radicalism, and Eschatology," 87.
148 Stone, *Reinhold Niebuhr*, 241. Ill health in his last two decades prevented Niebuhr from traveling to the Third World to gain the firsthand experience that was often his impetus in ethics.

CHAPTER SEVEN

A Liberation Challenge

James H. Cone

Like Reinhold Niebuhr, liberation theologians stress the reality of conflict in society. Also, like Niebuhr, they argue strongly that sin should be understood as a *structural* phenomenon, not simply a personal peccadillo. Yet Christian realism and liberation theology came to be understood as opposing camps in the theological world. For all the similarities, a different and quite distinctive view of justice emerges from liberation theology. While for Niebuhr, Christian ethics begins with love, for liberation theologians, the starting place is oppression.

Liberation theology is often associated with Latin American theologians and with Gustavo Gutiérrez in particular.[1] Indeed, Pope Francis's emphasis on poverty may reflect his own Latin American origins and the influence of Latin American liberation theology. But liberation theology was not just a Latin American phenomenon. Though sometimes called by different names (e.g., Han theology in Korea), theologies of struggle and liberation emerged in many places. In this chapter, we begin with a brief background on Latin American liberation theology but then turn our attention to the notable development of liberation theology in the United States in the work of James H. Cone.

A NEW METHOD

"God chose from birth to live the same as the poorest, didn't he? . . . He was born poor and wants us all to be poor. Isn't that so? or rather, he wants us all to be equal."[2] These words spoken by a poor woman in Latin America make an appropriate place to begin an examination of liberation theology, for liberation theology is first and foremost a new way of doing theology that starts with those who are poor and their struggles for liberation. It begins with a new method: "Latin American theology does not start with existing theologies but with the real and concrete totality of what is taking place."[3] It starts with praxis—with passionate and committed involvement in the struggle for liberation.[4] It is a dialectical reflection: reflecting on practice in the light of faith and on faith in the light of practice.[5] Theology is therefore the "second movement," after involvement.

At first glance, this focus on "the real and concrete totality of what is taking place" sounds a lot like the communitarian view of Michael Sandel or even the Christian realism of Reinhold Niebuhr. But there is a difference: in liberation theology, involvement in what is taking place has a clear bias—the perspective of the poor and oppressed: "The theology of liberation is an attempt to understand the faith from within the concrete historical, liberating, and subversive praxis of the poor of this world—the exploited classes, despised ethnic groups, and marginalized cultures."[6] The "poor" are variously defined. The term is used both literally and in an extended meaning that applies not only to those who are materially deprived but also to those who are marginalized in society, lacking full access to and participation in socioeconomic and political processes. The "poor" might include laborers, peasants, the elderly and young, those unemployed, women, those from oppressed ethnic and racial groups, and others.[7] These people have become, in Gutiérrez's words, "nonpersons . . . suffering misery and exploitation, deprived of the most elemental human rights, scarcely aware that they are human beings at all."[8]

Thus, two important circumstances set the stage for liberation theology: first, the realities of poverty and oppression and, second, the commitment of Christians to the struggle for liberation.[9] In the Latin America of Gutiérrez' day, the two elements of oppression and struggle for liberation were sharply defined.[10]

Much of Latin America remains characterized by oppression, repression, and dependence. The realities of oppression—"untenable circumstances of poverty, alienation and exploitation"[11]—are everywhere evident: "It leaps out at you. It is impossible not to see it."[12] Former colonization has simply been replaced by new forms of oppression. Internationalization of capitalism and proliferation of multinational corporations have resulted in a situation in which countries in the Global South (formerly called the *Third World*) have relatively little power or autonomy in any bargaining process. If they refuse to provide desired cheap labor, corporations simply go elsewhere. Military regimes and "national security states" ensure compliance of the masses with this economic agenda. The gap grows between rich and poor.[13] The net effect of colonialism is that Latin America has been "from the beginning and constitutively" dependent.[14] Thus, Enrique Dussel calls colonial domination the "original sin" of the prevailing world economic system.[15]

Based on their involvement in these realities, many Christians and church leaders have denounced the grave social injustices in Latin America.[16] They have also formed *comunidades eclesiales de base* (or base communities)—small grassroots organizations that educate and raise consciousness about social justice.[17] As a result of these activities, Christians in Latin America have suffered persecution.[18] To economic poverty is added political repression. Such persecution merely reinforces the perception of the deep social ills plaguing Latin America.

Thus, liberation theology refuses "to conceal the conflictive nature of society under the cloak of generic, innocent-looking terminology."[19] From their stance of involvement in liberation struggles, Latin American liberation theologians no longer trust European-dominated readings either of the situation or of Scripture. They have developed a "hermeneutic of suspicion."[20] The economic gap between those who are rich and poor in Latin America is not just "unfortunate" but "unjust."

As grounding for such a claim, most Latin American liberation theologians turn explicitly to Marxist analysis with its emphasis on class conflict.[21] Social conflict implies class struggle. In the view of most Latin American liberation theologians, history today is characterized by a division "into oppressors and oppressed, into owners of the means of production and those dispossessed of the fruit of their work, into antagonistic social classes."[22] Hence, "only a class analysis will enable us to see what is really involved in the opposition between oppressed countries and dominant peoples."[23]

Such an analysis implies the need for a paradigm adequate to the situation of dependence. *Development* will not do as it implies no conflict between classes. Gutiérrez excoriates those who fail to perceive that lack of equitable distribution of goods is not simply an "unfortunate" circumstance that will be overcome in time but is "the fault of the system itself."[24] In a situation characterized not by "underdevelopment" but by oppression, "liberation" is the proper paradigm: "The concerns of the so-called Third World countries revolve around the social injustice-justice axis, or, in concrete terms, the oppression-liberation axis."[25]

Recognizing the realities of dependence, oppression, and repression, Christians who have joined the struggle for liberation are calling for new interpretations of Scripture and new bases for Christian ethics. Too often, theology has been a tool justifying oppression.[26] From the praxis perspective, Christians argue that salvation is not simply a spiritual phenomenon; it is a unitary concept that includes social justice as well as spiritual well-being. Liberation implies social revolution, not merely reform.[27] Its goal is the creation of a "new person" in a "new society."[28] Nor is sin to be understood as an individual, internal phenomenon: "Latin American theology does not start . . . with a relationship of the solitary self with another individual self but considers the structure in which the sin of the world conditions our own personal sin."[29]

Thus, for example, liberation theologians seek not the "balance of power" lauded by Niebuhr but a *transfer* of power.[30] And "violence" must be understood differently: the violence of the subjugator is evil, while the violence used by those who seek liberation from oppression is not.[31] No general judgments against violence can be levied but only judgments from within the praxis seeking liberation. Liberation theology is thus contextual in its ethics.

Out of these commitments and reflections emerges a new kind of rationality—"the rationality of a concrete, historical undertaking."[32] This rationality dares to posit the vision of a social revolution that others find "utopian." Gutiérrez charges that these "dominators" of the system simply are not familiar with the scientific rigor and rationality of concrete theology. Praxis gives a perception of aspects of the Christian message that escapes other approaches.[33] Dominant among these is an understanding of the central biblical concern for justice.

JAMES CONE AND THE NORTH AMERICAN CONTEXT

The central concern for justice is also key for James Cone. Writing from the North American context, however, he saw the roots of oppression differently from his Latin American contemporaries. While the United States certainly also experiences a gap between the rich and the poor, it has, in addition, a complicated history of racial prejudice and oppression. Where Latin American liberation theologians focused on economic injustices and class conflict, Cone focused on racism and the injustices associated with White supremacy in the United States. In addition, he rooted his approach in the resilience and importance of Black churches and in a liberationist reading of the Bible.

"I am a *black* theologian," declared Cone.[34] This Blackness is the beginning point of a new approach to theological ethics and to understanding what justice requires. Like other liberation theologians, Cone's theology is grounded in the *experience* of suffering. But in his case, it was the experience of suffering and humiliation in the Black community in the United States during the time of segregation and Jim Crow laws. Cone was deeply influenced by the civil rights and Black power movements in America during the 1960s and 1970s and by the assassination of Martin Luther King Jr. Indeed, Cone's first book, *Black Theology and Black Power*, published in 1969, explicitly identifies the Black power movement as Christ's central message to twentieth-century America.[35] While Cone's later work nuanced some of the most stringent claims from this early book, he never deviated from his central contention that the

God of the Bible is a god of *liberation* and that liberation is therefore the core of justice.

The earliest experience of Blacks in the United States was that of slavery and denial of personhood. While Whites came to America to *escape* tyranny, Cone notes, Blacks were brought here from Africa to *serve* tyrants: "We came as bondsmen, chained in ships."[36] Hence, the early Black experience in North America was "a history of servitude and resistance, of survival in the land of death."[37]

Did the Emancipation Proclamation undo the damage from that long period of slavery? No, argues Cone. Former slaves might have been legally "free," but their economic, social, and political oppression did not cease. Indeed, Jim Crow laws and the constant threat of lynching sometimes made the situation of Black people worse than it was during slavery. Cone grew up during the time of lynching and Jim Crow laws. The lynching tree, he suggests, is "the quintessential symbol of black oppression in America."[38] Suffering, humiliation, and oppression were the lot of most Blacks in America. Cone saw America as a racist society where even the White churches represented White interests, and those interests threatened Black lives.[39]

In *The Cross and the Lynching Tree*, Cone gives powerful expression to the agonies of Black people in a White supremacist society where lynching was widespread and White churches and theologians did nothing to stop it. Dominant White theologian Reinhold Niebuhr opposed racism and spoke about the necessity of balancing power but had no "heart" to understand the plight of people who were without power against the state-sanctioned mob violence of lynching.[40] How could White Americans worship a God who was hanged on a cross and then perpetrate the injustice of hanging Blacks on a lynching tree for any or no reason? Lynching was White America's way of reminding Blacks of their inferiority. Hence, charges Cone, "America is an unjust society, and black people have known that for a long time."[41]

An unjust society is permeated with violence. The violence erupting in inner cities during the time that Cone was writing (e.g., the Watts riots of 1965 and the Detroit riots of 1967) was a reaction to the pain of daily oppression. When pain gets unendurable, writes Cone, violence should be expected.[42] Hence, the Black power movement with its violent edges was not anti-Christian but indeed could be seen as the proper expression of Christian faith. Justice requires "complete emancipation of black people from white oppression by whatever means black people deem necessary."[43] Black people must fight for liberation, taking their freedom "with guns, if need be."[44]

In short, when it comes to ethics, the experience of slavery and other forms of oppression changes everything. There can be no abstract principles regarding right and wrong and certainly no calculations in which some people's pleasures would override others' pains. Right and wrong will be determined by survival needs. For example, while slaves considered it "stealing" and wrong to take something from another slave, taking from the slaveholder was not wrong because it was merely appropriating what rightfully belonged to the slaves.[45] To this day, the only principle to guide thinking and action is "an unqualified commitment to the black community as that community seeks to define its existence in the light of God's liberating work in the world."[46]

The theological basis for Cone's work is the biblical story of God's actions in the world: "The central theme of biblical religion is the justice of God."[47] Here, he joins other liberation theologians in seeing the Exodus event as normative. It shows that God's actions in history are oriented toward the liberation of the oppressed. Jesus is the fulfillment of this liberation. Cone declares flatly, "The essence of the nature of God is to be found in the concept of liberation."[48] God is not about inward religious experiences or pious feelings. God acts in history to liberate those who are oppressed. Freedom and justice are interdependent: to demand freedom from oppression is to demand justice.[49]

We know God when we are involved in the struggle for liberation; therefore, revelation comes in community. If God comes to those who are oppressed, and if Black people are quintessentially those who are oppressed in the United States, then God comes to and through the Black community, and only that community has the tools to see where God is active in history. White theology that ignores Black oppression and liberation is not just wrong; it is also nonbiblical. Oppressors cannot know God.

Using this logic, Cone declares that if God is identified with oppressed people in each historical situation, then in North America, God will be Black because Black people represent those oppressed.[50] God—and God in Jesus—is Black:[51] "The Black Theologian must reject any conception of God which stifles black self-determination by picturing God as a God of all peoples."[52] Cone notes that, in Jesus, God became not just "man" but a particular man: God became an oppressed Jew.[53] In other words, we get to the universal by way of the particular. God *chose* the oppressed, and it is therefore the oppressed to whom God brings the Good News, or gospel. In the United States, Black people are oppressed. Hence, God will be revealed through the Black community. In strident language, Cone declares that "what is wrong with America is . . . its belief that people can be white and human at the same time."[54]

Just as Gutiérrez used the word *poor* to mean both those lacking in material wealth and, in a wider sense, those lacking power, Cone similarly uses *Black* and *White* in two senses—literal and symbolic. First is the obvious association of *Black* or *White* with skin color and the Black or White community. But symbolically, *Black* stands as the concrete expression in American history of those who are severely oppressed: enslaved, sold, lynched, raped, beaten, and killed with impunity. At various points, Cone explicitly includes in his list of oppressed people all those with black, brown, red, or yellow skin tones,[55] but generally, he permits *Black* to stand in for all those oppressed by racism. Thus, on a symbolic level, *Black* means a certain way of thinking and acting in the world. To be Black is not necessarily to have dark skin color but rather to be immersed in and to adopt a cultural stance that reflects the pain and oppression of the Black community.[56]

Obviously, it is most likely that thinking and acting "Black" in the world will come most easily for those who are indeed immersed in the Black community, including the Black church and the folk stories, songs, fiction, and even dancing of the Black community and church. Cone's *source* for ethics, then, is not rational deliberation about principles but rather exploration of the folk tales and music and cultural forms that emanate from the Black community. One early book was a study of Black spirituals and blues. Spirituals expressed the longing for freedom during slavery, while blues expressed the pain of continuing oppression after the Civil War. Thus, a major source for ethics and, hence, for an understanding of what justice requires comes from the experiences of the Black community as expressed in music, preaching, and folk stories. Cone's language reflects and appreciates the *passionate* character of such sources, and he is critical of the "rational" tone taken by most White philosophers and theologians: "Ultimate meaning . . . cannot be expressed in rational and historical language."[57] The meaning of a sermon is not just in the words, for example, but in the delivery—in the timing, in the responsive *amen* of the congregation, and in the rise and fall of the voice. Sources for an adequate theology include, in Cone's view, the Black *experience* of humiliation and suffering; Black *history* of slavery, segregation, and Jim Crow laws; and Black *culture* with its distinctive forms of expression of both pain and joy.[58]

Above all, however, Cone's major source is the Bible understood not as an ancient text but as a living testimony and active spirit in the Black community. The biblical witness tells us that God is a God of liberation.[59] Eurocentric church tradition must therefore come under scrutiny as it mostly ignores the biblical mandate to liberate those oppressed. Cone evaluates and generally excoriates many White Eurocentric theologians. For instance, Martin Luther's stress on "law and order" must be rejected if liberation is the mandate.[60] "White theology has made revelation and redemption into an esoteric word game without much meaning for the world at large," he charges.[61] It was the Black church and the felt presence of Jesus that often gave slaves and their descendants a sense of their worth when the White world did everything in its power to tell them they were nothing: "A person can be lynched in other ways than hanging from a tree."[62] Liberation means not just economic and political justice but a cultural and personal shift that signals the self-determination of the Black community and the overcoming of the sense of being nothing.

The Black man who is "new" in Christ will glorify in being Black.[63] This does not mean that he hates the White man but rather that he loves the White man precisely by refusing to speak of love without justice and power. There is no sentimental "love" in Christianity but a hard-nosed approach to a liberating love that means a redistribution of power in society. Here, there are echoes of Niebuhr's emphasis on power and justice, but there remains a difference in Cone's stress on liberation and liberation *now*. If love is where God is at work that means where people are liberated from oppression. From Cone's perspective, White churches have utterly failed to see this. They contribute to doctrines of White supremacy and to a segregated society. They fail to denounce lynching, the Ku Klux Klan, the rat-infested ghettoes in which Black children are raised. They contribute to the structures of racism that breed violence and produce riots. They have failed to be the church that Christ intended.[64]

By contrast, then, the Black Revolution is the work of Christ.[65] For slaves, the Black church was the home base for revolution. Since that time, Black churches have refused any version of Christianity that is not related to social change, though during the Jim Crow years, Black pastors sometimes preached patience. Doing so may have been a strategic move in some circumstances, a way to keep their churches from being burned and their members from being lynched. But this quiescence gave rise to the work of Martin Luther King Jr. and then to the Black power movement with its recognition that "the fight against injustice is never over until all men, regardless of physical characteristics, are recognized and treated as human beings."[66]

REVIEW

What we get in James Cone is a strikingly new American voice in approaches to justice. While his call to treat all people "as human beings" has some resonance with the long Roman Catholic tradition of stressing human dignity, the social teachings of the Catholic Church lack Cone's strident call for Black liberation. While Reinhold Niebuhr understood that justice would never simply be "given" by oppressors but would require a balancing of forces, he never urged Blacks to use force but instead urged patience as the "realistic" approach. He failed to honor Black movements of resistance. For Cone, justice means liberation from oppression in all its forms: cultural, social, political, and economic. Justice is not about rules for the distribution of goods in society, as Nozick might have it, nor even about a basic structure that "lifts up" the least advantaged, as Rawls might urge. Justice is about freedom and full humanity for all those who are oppressed.

In the first edition of this book, Karen Lebacqz noted that "the cry for liberation and justice is an attack on the entire system or social order, not merely on isolated instances of injustice."[67] This is true for Cone as well as for Latin American liberation theologians. But while Latin American liberation theologians tended to stress capitalism as the system responsible for much oppression of the people, Cone stressed the history of racism and White supremacy in America and its link to economic, social, and political oppression. Oppression and its root causes may differ from one context to another; hence, liberation may require different strategies and tactics and may be oriented toward the dismantling of different systems.

Cone's primary source for understanding the ultimacy of liberation is his reading of the biblical text. The Exodus sets the stage for seeing that God seeks liberation of those who are oppressed. Where Niebuhr made love the primary Christian principle and justice needed to be seen in relation to the ultimate commandment of love, Cone made liberation the primary principle, with love having meaning only where it is coupled with justice, power, and liberation.

All liberation theologies are notable for starting not with *theory* but with the concrete realities of injustice and oppression and with a passionate commitment to the struggle for liberation. Thus, it is not likely that we would find a developed *theory* of justice in any liberation theology. Just so does Cone not provide a "theory" of justice but rather a passionate appeal and command to do justice—to bring about the liberation of those who are oppressed and to undo the whiteness that has plagued the United States in its history and culture. If there is a theory of justice here, it is quite simply that justice means liberation—nothing more and nothing less. This might sound simple, but it is not.

CRITIQUE

Where justice becomes liberation for those oppressed, rules and principles give way: "Right and wrong were determined by survival needs in the context of servitude."[68] In the field of ethics, the rejection of principles facilitates a contextual ethic in which anything goes. Indeed, Cone's suggestion that Blacks must grab freedom "with guns if need be" left him open to the charge that his theological ethics was nothing but an excuse for the Black power movement. While the identification of Christian theology with the Black power movement is most evident in Cone's first book, *Black Theology and Black Power*, there are hints of that identification in his subsequent work. Cone's implicit—and even explicit—support of violence in the struggle for liberation was problematic for many critics. But Cone responded to these criticisms: these are favorite *White* questions, he argues, and his White critics never look at the underlying violence that led to the need for a Black power movement.[69]

Cone's language is not only passionate but sometimes extreme. For instance, he suggests that God gives those who are oppressed "the divine right to break the chains by any means necessary."[70] Again, "what we need is the destruction of whiteness."[71] Or "any interpretation of the gospel in any historical period that fails to see Jesus as the Liberator of the oppressed is heretical."[72] Cone appears to find nothing of value in almost all White theology or thinking, although there is an occasional appreciative nod toward Karl Barth, and he does offer some appreciation of Reinhold Niebuhr. But generally, for Cone, all truth seems to come only from those immersed in the Black community. Indeed, Cone is so critical of White thinking that the two authors of this volume would probably have, in his view, no right to assess or critique his arguments.[73] While there is certainly merit in seeing how social location affects thinking, we hold with those who see scholarship as requiring both passion and careful reasoning.

Indeed, we note that Cone himself exhibits careful scholarship in his assessment and critique of mainstream theology. Ironically, he has been criticized by other Black theologians for doing so. At least one critic of Cone seems to suggest that he did not go far enough in his abandonment and rejection of White theology. His own brother, Cecil W. Cone, charged that James Cone's Black theology remained too tied to the categories and thought structures of Eurocentric academic theology and was not sufficiently rooted in the Black church, no matter what James Cone claimed.[74]

A major issue is how to assess sources of truth. While noting that mainstream Christianity has failed to transform the corruption and inhumanity of the world, Sharon Welch argues that we cannot say something is true just because it comes from an oppressed community.[75] Identifying liberation theology as the "true" expression of Christianity, she suggests, falls right into the universalizing and absolutizing that Cone says are wrong. Yet this seems to be what Cone does. James Ellis makes a similar point in noting that Cone presupposes the righteousness of the oppressed and that criteria for oppressed and oppressor are needed.[76] In *The Black Christ*, Kelly Brown Douglas notes that not everything that comes from the Black community is liberating—for example, much rap music contains violent language toward women.[77] There is oppression *within* the Black community as well as *toward* the Black community, she notes.

In fact, to claim that something is oppressive is to assume some basis for universal judgment.[78] Yet Cone in general wants to avoid principles for universal judgment. He grounds his understanding of liberation in the stories of God in the Bible, though he speaks occasionally of not needing the Bible to know that slavery is wrong. While we might agree with him both in his basic reading of the biblical story of God's work in the world and in his assessment of the evils of slavery, we would urge a better articulation of the basis for universal judgments about oppression. As Lebacqz noted in *Justice in an Unjust World* and as James Ellis notes in his critique of Cone, one can be oppressed but also an oppressor.[79]

Indeed, some of Cone's fellow Black theologians criticized his articulation of Black theology. For example, Preston Williams suggested that Cone's approach would not be very appealing unless one accepted his presuppositions about how to interpret the Bible, how to retrieve Black church tradition, how to understand Black culture, and so on. Williams argued for a more "rational" approach that depended on a careful display of facts rather than the impassioned appeals of Cone.[80] Cone responded to this criticism by suggesting that Williams had simply allowed White theologians to define good thinking and that he would "know better" if he would be more immersed in the Black community.[81] More recently, James Ellis argues that "it is not helpful to lift up blacks as the most oppressed of all of America's oppressed people."[82] Cone's approach tends to create division, he argues. Many Christians will not accept his aggressive stance toward White Americans and his tendency to refuse them any place in God's reign.[83]

Since Cone's theology is biblically based, a key question is whether he reads the Bible correctly. Speaking from an evangelical perspective that assumes the accuracy and sufficiency of the Bible, Thabiti Anyabwile charges that Cone's liberation theology makes God too much an instrument for Black liberation. Any sense of God's transcendence is lost when God is wholly identified with liberation struggles. Where earlier Black theologians and preachers held to a view that God was sovereign and would do things in God's own time, Cone seems to require God to be present now in the particular struggles of the American Black community. For Anyabwile, this represents a "decline" in Black theology.[84] "Jesus never acted in a way that suggested a political liberation for his contemporaries," charges Anyabwile.[85] Hence, Jesus cannot be said to have come to "set the captives free" in any direct political or military sense. Similarly, Dennis P. McCann argues against liberation theology in general that seeking grounds for contemporary political activity in an interpretation of what God did for the ancient Israelites assumes an analogy between current and ancient systems that simply does not hold.[86]

Others have charged that liberation theologies have too narrow a concept of sin. James M. Wall, for example, asserts that a weakness of liberation theology is its "preoccupation with oppressive systems" to the neglect of individual sin and its tenacity in human life.[87] Carl E. Braaten says flatly, "A [true] theology of the cross debunks every ideology that claims that the original sin that infects all humanity will be removed as a result of structural changes in the world."[88] For these critics, liberation theologies either neglect an important aspect of sin or focus too much on the systemic and structural aspects of it.

Another criticism leveled by Anyabwile is that Cone has too narrow a view of the Black community and its experiences. Perhaps because of his own history of growing up during the worst of Jim Crow and segregation, Cone saw the essence of the Black community largely in terms of struggle, suffering, and humiliation.[89] While this depiction certainly

captures major experiences of Black people, among struggle and suffering, there are also stories of strength and success. Those become fodder
for a deepening of the liberation approach to justice, as we shall see in
the next chapter. But it is notable that Cone himself argued that survival
was not the only occupation of Black people; the real question was how
to survive with *dignity* in a White supremacist society.[90]

Ironically, while Cone argued so strongly for God's liberating activity on behalf of those oppressed, his theology may have remained too
"middle-class" to reach many churches that serve poor and oppressed
Blacks. A survey of Black church leaders some twenty years after Cone's
Black Theology of Liberation found that only about a third of them had
been influenced by the Black theology movement.[91]

Finally, while Cone worked from a foundation in the Black community in general, he did not free himself from the sexism that was
prevalent in theological circles in the 1970s. Black women did not figure
prominently in his work even though they figure prominently in the
work of the Black church, to which he gave such strong allegiance.[92]
It would remain for womanist theology to bring a corrective vision at
this point.

ASSESSMENT

As was true of other liberation theologies emerging around the world
at the same time, the introduction of *oppression* as a key category for
thinking about justice is a genuine contribution. Where there is a history of wrongdoing, justice cannot be simply about rules for current
distribution of goods or even about the basic structure of society (Rawls).
Justice cannot ignore history, nor can it reside simply in individual
exchanges of goods (Nozick). Cone may have been too strident in some
of his claims, but he was right to understand the lingering and devastating consequences of slavery, segregation, and Jim Crow laws in North
America and, hence, the need for any view of justice to address oppression as a primary category.

Cone, like other liberation theologies, was correct to note that all
theology—and, by implication, all philosophy as well—reflects social

and cultural conditioning. It is notable that Cone did not draw heavily on Marxist philosophy, as did some Latin American liberation theologians. But he understood clearly that no one is free from cultural influences that determine what we see, what questions we ask, and therefore what answers are possible. Racism distorts vision.

Cone was also correct to focus on White domination and racial oppression as keys to justice. "The one constant factor in any survey of the relationship between black churches and politics is the history of white domination and racial oppression," declare C. Eric Lincoln and Lawrence H. Mamiya. Whatever the specific tactics and political strategies that have unfolded over the decades, "the target has always been the white system of domination and oppression."[93] If there is to be justice in the United States, oppression of Black people must end.

Further, Cone was correct that racism shows up not just in explicit hatred of Blacks or in systems that ensure Blacks are underrepresented in places of power. Racism also shows up in the *invisibility* of the Black community in White thinking.[94] When value systems are entirely based on White values, this is racism. When the pains of the Black community are simply ignored and not mentioned, this is racism. Cone pushed for a broad understanding of how racism functions in the United States. Such an understanding helps us to see why the emancipation declaration after the Civil War was not sufficient to undo racism and why it is still appropriate today to speak of the oppression of the Black community despite advances in employment, housing, and distribution of goods in society.[95]

Moreover, Cone was prescient in seeing that a movement of antiwhiteness would be necessary. His argument here is somewhat reminiscent of Reinhold Niebuhr's insistence that education and rationality alone would not undo centers of power. Racism cannot be undone by racism training or efforts at integration. Both of those tend to leave White values as *the* values, to which Black people must adjust. Since the murder of George Floyd in 2020, there have been a spate of books on antiracism and antiwhiteness that concur with the need to probe to a fundamental level of undoing whiteness in American culture.[96]

It is also notable that *liberation* gains meaning as it is connected to "self-determination, dignity, and a pride in the African and African

American heritage and institutions" of the Black community and experience.[97] Thus, liberation requires not just economic well-being but political self-determination. It requires not just external changes but an internal change in the understanding of self-worth. It requires acknowledgment of the value of history and the positive forces that Black people and communities have forged.

Where Roman Catholic theology finds ethical principles in our human nature, Cone's explicit dependence on the Bible as a source for understanding God and Cone's history in and allegiance to the Black church both position him within the Protestant Reformation tradition. Not all Protestants would interpret the core of the biblical story the way Cone does, but his strong voice for the oppressed will resonate with many Christians and perhaps especially with those who find the Exodus a compelling story of God's actions in history and who see the clear connections between the God of the Hebrew Scriptures and the God of the New Testament. To be sure, such a central dependence on the Bible may also alienate many in the United States who are now increasingly unchurched. The explicit turn to religion can be problematic. However, if Cone is correct that much of the Black community retains influences from its Christian past, his compelling interpretation of the core of the Bible may yet resonate with that community.

We judge Cone to be correct in one additional argument: that racism—or, perhaps more accurately, White supremacy—raises not just *moral* questions but also *theological* questions. It forces us to ask, "Who is God?" Niebuhr identified two basic forms of sin: idolatry and injustice. One might think that racism simply fits into the category of injustice, but Cone argues that racism is also idolatry—it represents a false understanding of the God of the Bible.[98] This is a very important point, and it raises a significant challenge not just for theories of justice but for theology in general.

Cone argues that theology must be passionate.[99] Here, he joins with feminists and others who believe that the dispassionate language of philosophical reason is itself one of the elements of oppression. Oppression begins with language. All liberation theology argues for an involved and passionate approach to justice. Cone acknowledged that he was angry and disgusted "with the oppression of black people in America and with the scholarly demand to be 'objective' about it."[100] As Cornel West puts it in his introduction to the fiftieth anniversary of Cone's *Black Theology and Black Power*, "We need more intellectual work like this: work that comes from the heart and the soul and mind, the type of intellectual work that the academy does not know what to do with it."[101]

Finally, while Cone's rejection of universal ethical norms is worrisome, he does us a service in highlighting the ways in which oppressed people find that they must live by a different set of norms where stealing, lying, and cheating might sometimes—even often—be justifiable responses to circumstances of injustice and oppression.[102] It remains to be seen whether this basic insight can be complemented by a more critical analysis of the conditions and circumstances that justify actions generally considered wrong.

Cone raised challenges that reverberated widely throughout the theological community in North America and elsewhere.[103] While his strident critiques of mainstream theology angered many at the time, some of his striking analyses and pungent charges remain cogent today and raise crucial challenges for any theory of justice. It is notable that some fifty years after the publication of his first book, Cone's *A Black Theology of Liberation* is still credited with bringing liberation into the lives of oppressed people. On reading *A Black Theology of Liberation*, Talique Taylor, who self-identifies as both Black and queer, writes, "It was as if Cone's words lit a fire in the depths of my soul and I came alive again."[104] Similarly, Matthew Burdette speaks of the "redeeming power of Cone's words" and declares that "Cone's work transformed my faith, my life."[105] Such testimonies from contemporary Black scholars indicate the enduring importance of Cone's liberation theology.[106]

Ironically, however, Cone's recognition that social location affects theology did not originally make him aware of his own failure to bring women's concerns to the fore. In the introduction to the 1989 edition of *Black Theology and Black Power*, Cone takes note of this. A weakness of the original edition, he writes, was its sexist language and patriarchal perspective: "There is not even one reference to a woman in the whole book."[107] But while Cone did later devote a chapter of *The Cross and the Lynching Tree* to the role of Black women,[108] he purposefully did not change the language of *Black Theology and Black Power*, partly as a reminder that "amnesia is an enemy of justice." We need to recall our mistakes of the past to know what justice requires in the present. The failure to address Black women's situation becomes fodder for our final view of justice in the next chapter.

NOTES

1 See Gustavo Gutierrez, *A Theology of Liberation* (Maryknoll, NY: Orbis, 1973) and *The Power of the Poor in History* (Maryknoll, NY: Orbis, 1983). Karen Lebacqz's *Six Theories of Justice* (Minneapolis: Augsburg, 1986) dealt with the Latin American version of liberation theology, focusing on Jose Porfirio Miranda because of his specific attention to justice in the Bible and his use of Marx as a tool for understanding social context.

2 Ernesto Cardinal, "The Gospel in Solentiname," *Concilium* 5 (May 1974): 107; he quotes a woman identified as Rebecca.

3 Enrique Dussel, *Ethics and the Theology of Liberation* (Maryknoll, NY: Orbis, 1978), 2.

4 Allan Aubrey Boesak, *Farewell to Innocence* (Maryknoll, NY: Orbis, 1977), 12: "Theology is passionately involved."

5 In the quote above, Gutierrez stresses reflection on *faith* from the perspective given in praxis. However, elsewhere (e.g., in *Power of the Poor*, 79), he stresses reflection on *practice* in the light of faith.

6 Gutierrez, *Power of the Poor*, 37.

7 Gutierrez, *Power of the Poor*, 7, 193. In *A Theology of Liberation*, 291, Gutierrez reviews the various biblical applications of the term *poor* to the beggar, the weak one, the one bent over or laboring under a weight. Dussel (*Ethics*, 36–37) offers three categories of the poor: the oppressed, the servants or prophets, and those outside the system. The Third General Conference of the Latin American Episcopate at Puebla in 1979 named a range of victims of institutionalized injustice: young children whose chances for development are blocked, laborers ill-paid and kept from organizing, old people disregarded because they are not productive, etc. (§§31–40). Any of these would qualify as poor here. The final document from Puebla can be found in John Eagleson and Philip Sharper, eds., *Puebla and Beyond* (Maryknoll, NY: Orbis, 1979).

8 Gutierrez, *Power of the Poor*, 50.

9 These two circumstances take different forms in different contexts where liberation theology is emerging, but they remain constant elements.

10 Black South African theologian Boesak (*Farewell to Innocence*, 29) gives a parallel description of his situation: "This is the situation in which black

people find themselves. Slavery, domination, injustice; being forced to live a life of contradiction and estrangement in their own country and 'in exile,' where fear and the urge to survive made deception a way of life; being denied a sense of belonging; discrimination--all these were realities which have almost completely broken down the sense of worth of black personhood."

11 Gutierrez, *Theology of Liberation*, 89.

12 Gutierrez, *Power of the Poor*, 93.

13 Gutierrez, *Power of the Poor*, 84, 192. For an excellent introduction to these issues, see Penny Lernoux, "The Long Path to Puebla," in Eagleson and Sharper, *Puebla and Beyond*.

14 Gutierrez, *Theology of Liberation*, 84.

15 Dussel, *Ethics*, 26.

16 See, e.g., reports from the Second General Conference of the Latin American Episcopate at Medellin, 1968, in Joseph Gremillion, ed., *The Gospel of Peace and Justice: Catholic Social Teaching since Pope John* (Maryknoll, NY: Orbis, 1976).

17 The exact form of such grassroots communities differs from context to context. Note also that Ferm suggests that liberation theology is "rice-roots" theology in the Asian context; Deane William Ferm, "Outlining Rice-Roots Theology," *Christian Century* 101 (January 1984): 78–80.

18 Gutierrez, *Theology of Liberation*, 133.

19 Gutierrez, *Power of the Poor*, 92.

20 An extensive discussion of the hermeneutic of suspicion is provided by Juan Luis Segundo, *Liberation of Theology* (Maryknoll, NY: Orbis, 1976), chap. l. Dussel (*Ethics*, 166) suggests that what is needed is a "suspicionometer."

21 For this reason, the original *Six Theories of Justice* used Jose Porfirio Miranda's *Marx and the Bible: A Critique of the Philosophy of Oppression* (Maryknoll, NY: Orbis, 1974) as its prime example of Latin American liberation theology.

22 Gutierrez, *Theology of Liberation*, 273.

23 Gutierrez, *Theology of Liberation*, 87.

24 Gutierrez, *Power of the Poor*, 117.

25 Gutierrez, *Theology of Liberation*, 174.

26 Boesak, *Farewell to Innocence*, 34.

27 Gutierrez, *Theology of Liberation*, 88.

28 "Beyond—or rather, through—the struggle against misery, injustice, and exploitation the goal is *the creation of a new man*" (Gutierrez, *Theology of Liberation*, 146; emphasis added).

29 Dussel, *Ethics*, 2.

30 Jose Miguez Bonino, *Toward a Christian Political Ethic* (Philadelphia: Fortress, 1983), 32.

31 Dussel, *Ethics*, 43. However, though almost all liberation theologians would join Dussel in urging a different moral judgment on the violence perpetrated

by oppressors and that perpetrated in response by the oppressed, not all would support violent revolution.

32 Gutierrez, *Power of the Poor*, 45.

33 Gutierrez, *Power of the Poor*, 197.

34 James H. Cone, *God of the Oppressed* (New York: The Seabury Press, 1975), 5. The capitalization of "Black" and "White" varies widely and each interlocutor in this book has their own approach. Our practice in this book is to follow the Chicago Manual of Style guidance for capitalizing "Black" and "White" for our own words, but to maintain the style of our interlocutors when directly quoting others.

35 James H. Cone, *Black Theology and Black Power*, 50th anniversary ed. (Maryknoll, NY: Orbis, 2019), Introduction, Kindle.

36 James H. Cone, "Black Theology and Black Liberation," in Basil Moore, *Black Theology: The South African Voice* (London: C. Hurst, 1973), 49.

37 James H. Cone, *The Spirituals and the Blues: An Interpretation* (New York: The Seabury Press, 1972), 20.

38 James H. Cone, *The Cross and the Lynching Tree* (Maryknoll, NY: Orbis, 2011), xiii.

39 James H. Cone, *A Black Theology of Liberation* (Philadelphia: J. B. Lippincott, 1970), 108.

40 Cone, *The Cross*, 41, 71.

41 Cone, *God of the Oppressed*, 218.

42 Cone, *Black Theology and Black Power*, 26.

43 Cone, *Black Theology and Black Power*, 6.

44 Cone, *A Black Theology of Liberation*, 177.

45 Cone, *Spirituals and Blues*, 27; *God of the Oppressed*, 209. In *Ownership: Early Christian Teaching* (Maryknoll, NY: Orbis, 1983), Charles Avila argued that giving to the poor was not charity but justice—returning to them what was rightfully theirs.

46 Cone, *A Black Theology of Liberation*, 33.

47 Cone, *Spirituals and Blues*, 102.

48 Cone, *A Black Theology of Liberation*, 121.

49 Cone, *Black Theology and Black Power*, 48.

50 Cone, *A Black Theology of Liberation*, 214: "Christ is black."

51 Cone is not the first to declare a Black God. In the late 1800s, Bishop Henry McNeal Turner declared that Blacks needed a God who reflected them if they were to believe that they were made in God's image. See Thabiti M. Anyabwile, *The Decline of African American Theology: From Biblical Faith to Cultural Captivity* (Downers Grove, IL: Intervarsity Press, 2007), 88.

52 Cone, *A Black Theology of Liberation*, 120.

53 Cone, *A Black Theology of Liberation*, 157.

54 Cone, *A Black Theology of Liberation*, 192.

55 Cone, *God of the Oppressed*, 10, 34.

56 Cone, *God of the Oppressed*, 97. He does, for example, note with some approval Frederick Herzog's *Liberation Theology* (New York: The Seabury Press, 1972), suggesting that White theologians do not have to "remain in their little white boxes." Cone, *God of the Oppressed*, 50.

57 Cone, *The Cross*, 92.

58 Cone, *A Black Theology of Liberation*, 54–60.

59 Cone, *A Black Theology of Liberation*, 66.

60 Cone, *A Black Theology of Liberation*, 71.

61 Cone, *A Black Theology of Liberation*, 90.

62 Cone, *A Black Theology of Liberation*, 153.

63 Cone, *Black Theology and Black Power*, 60. We retain the language of *man* here because it is Cone's language.

64 Cone, *Black Theology and Black Power*, chap. 3.

65 Cone, *Black Theology and Black Power*, 100.

66 Cone, *Black Theology and Black Power*, 125.

67 Lebacqz, *Six Theories of Justice*, 104.

68 Cone, *Spirituals and Blues*, 27.

69 Cone, *God of the Oppressed*, 195.

70 Cone, *A Black Theology of Liberation*, 91.

71 Cone, *A Black Theology of Liberation*, 193.

72 Cone, *God of the Oppressed*, 37.

73 In *God of the Oppressed*, Cone mentions criticisms made by White scholars but does not reference them directly, as though only criticisms from the Black community are worthy of specific reference. We take heart in bell hooks's view that White people *can* write about other groups as long as they do not presume to be authoritative about them. See bell hooks, *Talking Back: Thinking Feminist, Thinking Black* (Boston: South End Press, 1989), 46.

74 Katie Geneva Cannon, *Katie's Canon: Womanism and the Soul of the Black Community* (New York: Continuum, 1995), 129.

75 Sharon D. Welch, *Communities of Resistance and Solidarity* (Maryknoll, NY: Orbis, 1985), 27. Her argument is not made in direct response to Cone but is a general argument about liberation theology.

76 James Ellis III, "A Critique of Cone's Black Liberation Theology," July 9, 2011, 7, https://day1.org/articles/5d9b820ef71918cdf2002e8f/faith_seeking _understanding_a_critique_of_cones_black_liberation_theology.

77 Kelly Brown Douglas, *The Black Christ*, 25th anniversary ed. (1994; repr., Maryknoll, NY: Orbis Books, 2019), 96.

78 See Welch, *Communities*, 81. Welch argues that all definitions of justice are therefore only provisional.

79 Karen Lebacqz, *Justice in an Unjust World* (Minneapolis: Augsburg, 1987), chap. 1; Ellis, "A Critique of Cone's Black Liberation Theology," 7.

80 Preston Williams, "James Cone and the Problem of a Black Ethic," *Harvard Theological Review* 65, no. 4 (October 1972), 485–488.

81 Cone, *God of the Oppressed*, 204.

82 Ellis, "A Critique of Cone's Black Liberation Theology," 6.

83 This is a place where Cone's double use of *black* becomes important. If "blackness" means literal dark skin, then it is clear that "white" people cannot be part of the Black community. But Cone also uses "black" in a symbolic sense, meaning an orientation toward the liberation of the oppressed. In this sense, some of those with "white" skin might be part of the "black" community.

84 Anyabwile, *The Decline*, chap. 2. At issue here is partly the question of whether all revelation of God is contained in the Bible or whether God's revelation extends to cultural and social practices beyond the Bible. Speaking from the perspective of the United Church of Christ, Lebacqz would argue that "God is still speaking" and that there are sources of revelation outside the Bible.

85 Anyabwile, *The Decline*, 170. Anyabwile sees Jesus's mission as primarily spiritual. The divide between "other-worldly" Christians and "justice and social change" Christians in the Black community has a long history. See Anyabwile, *The Decline*, 83.

86 Dennis P. McCann, *Christian Realism and Liberation Theology: Practical Theologies in Creative Conflict* (Maryknoll, NY: Orbis, 1981), 205.

87 James M. Wall, "Liberation Ethics: Insisting on Equality," *Christian Century* 99 (November 10, 1982): 1123.

88 Carl E. Braaten, *The Apostolic Imperative* (Minneapolis: Augsburg, 1985), 101.

89 Anyabwile, *The Decline*, 51.

90 Cone, *The Cross*, 139.

91 C. Eric Lincoln and Lawrence H. Mamiya, *The Black Church in the African American Experience* (Durham, NC: Duke University Press, 1990), 179. Since more than 50 percent of Black churchgoers are women, the failure of Cone and other Black theologians to address the issue of sexism may also explain why this theology did not take more root in Black churches.

92 See Douglas, *The Black Christ*, 100–105.

93 Lincoln and Mamiya, *The Black Church*, 199.

94 Cone, *God of the Oppressed*, 201.

95 One of the lessons of the COVID-19 pandemic of 2020, however, was to highlight how very unequal is access to health care and treatment for major diseases. Racism shows up in health distribution statistics and in health-care practices.

96 See, e.g., Ibram X. Kendi, *How to Be an Anti-Racist* (London: One World, 2019); Faith Brooks, *The Anti-Racism Journal: Questions and Practices to Move beyond Performative Allyship* (Boston: Page Street Publishing, 2022); W. Kamau Bell and Kate Schatz, *Do the Work!: An Anti-Racist Activity Book* (New York: Workman Publishing, 2022). These are only a few of the many volumes now available.

97 Lincoln and Mamiya, *The Black Church*, 241.

98 For a clear statement of this thrust, see Matthew Burdette, "The Glorious, Complicated Legacy of James H. Cone," *Living Church*, May 14, 2018, https:// livingchurch.org/2018/05/14/the-glorious-complicated-legacy-of-james-h -cone/.

99 Cone, *A Black Theology of Liberation*, 45.

100 Cone, *Black Theology and Black Power*, 2.

101 Cornel West, "Introduction" to Cone, *Black Theology and Black Power*, Kindle. Later, West calls this book "a frenetic and frantic text" unconcerned about fitting into academic disciplines (Introduction by West, Kindle).

102 In *Justice in an Unjust World* (94–95), Lebacqz notes the biblical story in which Abram lies when he claims that Sarai is not his wife but his sister. "Deception serves the cause of justice," Lebacqz argues.

103 For example, African theologian Boesak credits Cone with being the first Black theologian to focus on liberation as the central message of the Gospel. Boesak follows Cone in stressing that liberation "is not only a 'part of' the gospel or 'consistent with' the gospel; it is the content and framework of the gospel of Jesus Christ." Boesak, *Farewell to Innocence*, 9. Similarly, Basil Moore echoes many themes found in Cone. See Basil Moore, "What Is Black Theology?" in Moore, *Black Theology: The South African Voice*.

104 Talique Taylor, "Who Is James Cone?" *Earth and Altar* (blog), May 8, 2023, 1, https://earthandaltarmag.com/posts/who-is-james-cone.

105 Burdette, "The Glorious, Complicated Legacy," 2. In *Psalms from Prison* (Cleveland: The Pilgrim Press, 2024; first published 1983), Benjamin F. Chavis Jr. also credits James Cone with being an inspiration and calls Cone's *God of the Oppressed* "one of the most impressive works of systematic theology in the context of the global evolution of liberation theology." Chavis, *Psalms*, 320.

106 Indeed, four authors—Kelly Brown Douglas, Nicole M. Flores, Joi R. Orr, and Lincoln Rice—in the Fall/Winter 2023/2024 issue of the *Journal of the Society of Christian Ethics* 43 (no. 2) refer directly to the work of James Cone, and his influence is implicit in other essays in that volume.

107 See Cone, *Black Theology and Black Power*, Preface, Kindle.

108 Cone, *The Cross*, chap. 5.

CHAPTER EIGHT

A Womanist Critique

Katie Geneva Cannon

James Cone illuminated oppression and liberation as the core of biblical justice, yet he ignored the plight of Black women in the struggle for liberation. That there was no immediate outcry from Black women might be because racism overshadowed the oppressions of sexism.[1] Given the tribulations that all Black people experience in a racist society, Black women may not have wanted to push the issue of sexism but rather to stand in solidarity with their men. Nonetheless, at the same time as Cone was raising his Black theology flag and Gutiérrez was arguing for class-based liberation theology, a strong second wave of feminism was sweeping the United States, urging full equality and rights for women and focusing on sexism as a key form of oppression. By the 1990s, a new, womanist theological tradition, led by Katie Geneva Cannon, would bring the concerns of race, class, and gender together in an intersectional view of oppression and justice. A quick review of some key tenets of feminism will set the stage for seeing the contribution of Katie Cannon.

THE FEMINIST CONTEXT

The term *feminism* was probably coined in France and came into common use in the late 1800s, but it has also been applied to earlier advocates of justice for women such as Mary Wollstonecraft and Elizabeth Cady Stanton.[2] Braidotti summarizes the core of feminism this way: "the expression of a political will to achieve justice for women."[3] While early feminists focused largely on political rights for women and their inclusion in the public sphere, the second wave of feminists in the 1960s and beyond challenged not just the exclusion of women and denial of rights but "the very methods and frameworks by which things are studied."[4] Feminists developed the concept of the knowing subject as embodied and passionate and focused on strategy or praxis rather than theory.[5] Instead of looking for trans-historical and transgeographic "truth," feminists sought effective forms of intervention into systems of power. Thus, while feminism begins with a recognition of the oppression of women and a commitment to overcome oppression and seek justice for women, it incorporates significant challenges both to some traditional ways of understanding justice and to methods for developing knowledge.[6]

In that regard, the 1982 publication of Carol Gilligan's *In a Different Voice*[7] was a watershed moment in the United States. At the time, Lawrence Kohlberg's theory of moral development was dominant. Kohlberg, following Jean Piaget, studied children and young adults, both male and female. He posited six stages of moral development, of which the highest was making ethical decisions based on universal principles.[8] He also found that girls often did not move beyond relationship concerns to arrive at the sixth stage. Thus, it appeared that girls were less advanced than boys in moral development.

Gilligan argued that Kohlberg's framework assumed only one right way to make ethical decisions but that in fact there was another way or "voice" often used by girls. Further, she contended that this different voice was not "less developed" than reasoning focused on principles and justice. Appealing to relationships rather than principles was not an inferior mode of ethical reasoning, she charged.[9] Gilligan called the second voice an *ethic of care*: "In the different voice of women lies the truth of an ethic of care."[10]

Gilligan's methods and conclusions were scrutinized and criticized,[11] but her basic argument that there are two different and equally advanced methods of moral decision-making created a firestorm within feminism in the United States.[12] Was Gilligan correct to identify a second "voice" in ethical reasoning? If so, is that "different voice" associated with *gender*, as she seemed to imply,[13] or is the relational and "caring" mode of decision-making more the result of being oppressed or powerless, as others suggested?[14]

For our purposes, the significance of Gilligan's work lies in its challenge to the dominance of theories of justice, especially those that focus on principles and individual rights. An "ethic of justice," she argued, was based on a premise of separation and equality, while an "ethic of care" was based on connection and a premise of not harming.[15] Valuing relationships, connection, and feelings as valid modes of ethical reasoning stood against the abstract and "objective" view sought by most philosophers and theorists of justice.[16] Some feminists expressed concern that the association of a different voice with women's ways of reasoning would simply reinforce old dualisms that contributed to women's oppression.[17] But others applauded the idea of new ways of thinking: Sara Ruddick proposed a mode of "maternal thinking"[18]; Belenky and colleagues posited "two contrasting epistemological orientations: a separate epistemology, based upon impersonal procedures for establishing truth, and a connected epistemology, in which truth emerges through care."[19]

A crucial substrate for this understanding was the rejection of the notion that obligation comes through choice and free will. Nancy Hirschmann rightly observed that many women, especially if they have children, experience obligations that are not necessarily chosen but imposed by circumstance.[20] Thus, if free will and autonomy are the foundation for most theories of justice, those theories will be found wanting. Justice may be more about social circumstances that are *not* chosen than about the choices we make.[21]

Crucial among those social circumstances are situations of oppression and injustice. Thus, justice and care may not be mutually exclusive voices or ethical orientations.[22] Is feminist thought dominated by care to the exclusion of justice, or are care and justice linked in important ways?[23] While some feminists were engaging with an ethics of care, others developed approaches that still highlighted justice, which remains a central concern of feminist efforts to overcome sexist oppression. This was certainly true in the theological arena. In *Our Passion for Justice*, Carter Heyward introduced the term *right relationship* as the key to what justice requires.[24] In *Justice in an Unjust World*, Karen Lebacqz took listening to the voices of the oppressed as the beginning point for developing a biblically informed approach to justice.[25] Both of these thinkers stood within a liberation context, both argued for an option for those who are poor, and both linked biblical mandates to the need to topple unjust structures.

But while both of these thinkers recognized racism, sexism, and poverty as central to the injustices and oppression, neither began from explicit personal experiences of the interplay of racist, sexist, and economic oppressions. As Beverly Harrison put it, "No white feminist dares deny the failure of white feminism . . . to name and integrate racism and class privilege."[26]

KATIE CANNON AND WOMANIST JUSTICE

Enter Katie Cannon. Where W. E. B. DuBois declared that "the problem of the 20th century is the problem of the color line," Cannon declared that "the problem of the 21st century is the problem of the color line, the gender line, and the class line."[27] She understood clearly that any approach to justice had to take seriously racism, sexism, and classism.

Cannon saw a lacuna in "the cracks between feminist ethics and Black male theology."[28] She stepped into the unenviable task of speaking in terms that the "academy" would recognize and yet, as a womanist liberation ethicist, seeing her task to be precisely that of "debunking, unmasking, and disentangling" the historically conditioned value judgments, power relations, and thought processes that operated within the academy and society to create a triple oppression for Black women.[29] "The accepted canonical methods of moral reasoning," writes Cannon, "contain deeply hidden biases."[30] Her academic mentor, Beverly Harrison, championed the need "for a moral theology shaped and informed by women's actual historical struggle."[31] This was the task that Cannon set for herself. In assembling the essays that comprise her signature work, *Katie's Canon*, she writes, "My overall goal in this project is to recast the very terms and terrain of religious scholarship."[32]

Cannon does this by developing a womanist methodology. As the editors of *Walking through the Valley* note, Cannon "was the founding figure in exploring how the concept of womanism can be used in moral thought."[33] The term *womanism* is attributed to Alice Walker.[34] It connotes not just Black feminism but a seriousness that befits a grown woman and even a kind of feisty or outrageous behavior.[35] To be a womanist, then, is to be a Black woman who may or may not accept feminism and who is willing to take risks and stand against mainstream concepts of right behavior and right thinking. This is what Cannon does.

The difficulty for Cannon's project is how to access or create a moral theology or theory of justice based on Black women's actual historical struggles and survival strategies.[36] Black women are often among the poorest of the poor—"the most vulnerable and the most exploited members of the American society"[37]—and they must cope with the "irrational facticity of life."[38] Although some slave narratives have survived, for instance, in general, Black women neither write their life stories nor achieve publication if they do. Cannon therefore turned to Black women's literary tradition, especially the work and life of Zora Neale Hurston, as a primary source for seeing the reality of Black women's lives. She opined that Black women's literature was an unparalleled source for understanding the daily struggle of Black women's lives because Black women writers used oral tradition and focused on issues within the Black community rather than on the conflict between Black and White.[39] Hurston included many sermons in her novels, and Cannon argues that these sermons "are not just fictional tools but cultural truths" that illuminate Black lives by showing what *is* in contrast to what *should be*.[40]

From Black women's literary tradition, then, Cannon excavated some unusual strengths or virtues for those living under circumstances of oppression: "invisible dignity," "never practiced delicacy," "quiet grace," and "unshouted courage." It is important to note that each of these virtues begins with a negative, indicating that these virtues are often hidden from sight or sound—they are "invisible" or "quiet," "unshouted" or "never practiced." They may even be inversions of the virtues that were touted for White women in those days (e.g., delicacy and grace). In short, they would be noticed only by those who were looking and listening very attentively and were ready to find strength or courage where it was not overtly apparent, and they were virtues that did not fit dominant norms of the day.

Cannon's investigative technique thus has two foci: on the one hand, describing and analyzing the various ways in which Black women have been oppressed by racism, sexism, and classism, and on the other hand, mining Black women's stories to see how Black women resist their oppression and shape their destinies. In short, hers is both a deconstructive and a constructive task focused on the triple oppression of Black women in the United States.

To accomplish the deconstructive task, Cannon reviews "the Black woman's moral situation" from 1619 to the present, noting how Black women were seen during the time of slavery as "brood sows" and "work oxen."[41] As domestic workers, they were often at the mercy of slave owners or White bosses, both men and women. Rape was common, and any children they bore might be taken away and sold. Peter Paris notes that Cannon's "vivid descriptions of the historical sufferings of Black women lead me to conclude that the women must have fared much worse than the men."[42]

Even after the Civil War with its presumed emancipation, Black women had to work, often in the most menial jobs, as they were denied education or received vastly inferior education. Indeed, as Cone also notes in his review of Jim Crow and segregation, Cannon argues that racism heightened during this period.[43] Perpetual indebtedness resulted in involuntary servitude. The 1896 decision in *Plessy v. Ferguson* established the devastating effects of "separate but equal," which gave no equality at all to Blacks. As Cannon puts it, "The Black woman began her life of freedom with no vote, no protection, and no equity of any sort."[44] To her day, Cannon argues, Black women face the triple oppression of poverty, gender discrimination, and racial prejudice.[45] With "justice denied, hopes thwarted, and dreams shattered,"[46] Black women had to find resources to stand against cruelty and oppression.

Yet despite triple oppression, Black women carve out meaningful lives and even lives of stellar achievement. Crucial to the constructive task is Cannon's unearthing of strategies and tactics employed by Black women that might ordinarily be seen as vices and claiming them as virtues instead. Unctuousness is a prime example.[47] In its simplest definition, to be unctuous is to be insincerely smooth in speech and manner.[48] Such insincerity would normally be considered a false representation of oneself or even an outright lie, and being unctuous would hardly be considered a virtue. Under circumstances of oppression, however, Black women must balance the complexities of life, where every movement and word might put them in jeopardy. When you have little or no power, sometimes being false is the only way to survive.[49] To appease her White benefactor, for example, Hurston might have to announce her gratitude when in fact she felt resentment. Thus, what might ordinarily seem a vice or a wrong way to present oneself can be, under certain circumstances, a creative way to navigate the trials and tribulations of life. Powerless people curry favor and avoid antagonizing others by presenting a smooth and favorable surface, even as they resist oppression. As Stacey Floyd-Thomas puts it, for womanist ethicists, "unctuousness" came to connote "the unapologetic, unashamed venture of putting knowledge to work in such a way that one was to use their unmitigated gall to name the oppressions that disrupt lives, wound souls, destroy communities, and forestall liberation."[50]

Cannon therefore rejected "absolute principles of what is right or wrong and good or bad."[51] Noting that "the cherished assumptions of dominant ethical systems predicated upon both the existence of freedom and a wide range of choices have proven to be false in the real-lived texture of Black life,"[52] she argued that lying, stealing, and cheating might be virtues in some circumstances:[53] "Our womanist work is to draw on the rugged endurance of Black folks in America who outwit, outmaneuver, and outscheme social systems and structures that maim and stifle mental, emotional, and spiritual growth."[54] Here, Cannon echoes themes that were also struck by Cone in his analysis of acceptable behavior for those who are oppressed.

Like Cone, Cannon also paid considerable attention to the Black church, as it was often the sole institution of power for Black people, and it was one of the sources of Black women's strengths—a "citadel of hope."[55] To represent this tradition, she drew on the work of both Howard Thurman and Martin Luther King Jr. It is notable that, for King, love and justice are inseparable, and both must be integrally related to power.[56] While neither of these Black male theologians reflected specifically on Black women's lives, their theologies gave rise to a strong affirmation of the dignity of all Black people.[57] Unlike Cone, however, Cannon also took note of the specific contributions of Black women to the life and well-being of the Black church. She also took note of the fact that Black men, including those in the literary guild, often were the source of oppression for Black women, including Hurston.[58] Thus, for Cannon, Black men and women cannot simply be lumped together as the oppressed since Black men are sometimes the oppressors of Black women. Justice requires particular attention to the plight of Black women and the ability to discern virtue in the strategies they employ to combat injustice and oppression: "Black women are still the victims of the aggravated inequities of the tridimensional phenomenon of race/class/gender oppression."[59]

REVIEW

If Cannon were following directly in Cone's footsteps, she might have insisted not simply that God is Black but that God is a Black *woman*. If God is a god of the oppressed, and if Black women face triple oppression and are among the poorest of the poor, then perhaps the God who sides with those who are poor is best imaged as a Black woman. This is the approach taken by Jacquelyn Grant.[60] But this is not Cannon's approach. Rather, her approach is to take Black women's liberation as the requirement of justice and ask which qualities and characteristics we can find in history that show Black women's strengths and strategies to achieve liberation—or at least to mitigate oppression. Hers is not a new

Black *theology* but a womanist *ethic*. She does not present a new image of God but rather a picture of the injustices faced by Black women and then a method for mining the strengths of Black women in the face of those injustices. Her approach requires that theories of justice include consideration of some unusual virtues.

Perhaps Cannon's approach is best summarized in her own words: "The particular usefulness of womanist ethics is (1) to know and do justice to the moral resources and tradition of Black women's lives; (2) to help Black women remember, redeem, and reproduce the moral wisdom that they utilize; and (3) to engage Black women and other feminists of color who have given up on the community of faith so we might gain new insights concerning the reasonableness of theological ethics in deepening our character, consciousness, and capacity in our collective struggle for survival."[61]

In short, Cannon's approach intended to mine both theology and history for wisdom and strategies to support Black women's survival and bring about their liberation. She is not concerned with the whole discussion of the "black Christ" but rather with what Kelly Brown Douglas calls the "spirituality of resistance."[62] Cannon's approach to justice attempts to give the rich texture that Sandel suggests is crucial to understanding justice from a communitarian view. What is the situation in which Black women find themselves? What are the qualities that allow them to survive or thrive in the face of triple oppression? What facilitates the development of those qualities and moves them toward liberation?

In this approach, the Black church remains central as the Black community's sole institution of power and as an important formative influence: "In essence, the Bible is the highest source of authority for most Black women. . . . Jesus provides the necessary soul for liberation."[63] And yet the Black church itself has a mixed history where Black women are concerned. Black women are often the stalwarts of the church and yet not always honored as leaders or even permitted into positions of leadership.[64] Sexism can be present even in institutions among oppressed people. Thus, no liberation theology will be complete unless it takes account of the intersections of different oppressions, such as racism, classism, and sexism.

Feminism is not a complete corrective to oppression, either, as White women were and are among those who oppress Black women. Cannon does not repudiate some of the central insights of White feminism and indeed suggests that there can be a collaborative "back and forth" between womanist scholarship and White feminist liberationists.[65] But she also urges that we never forget that "key to the racial discrimination that the Black Woman experienced was the vindictiveness of white women."[66] Because Black women face triple jeopardy and cannot depend on either White feminism or Black theology as sources that comprehend and combat this triple oppression, they must develop their own approaches to justice. One of Katie Cannon's enduring legacies in this regard is the establishment of the Center for Womanist Leadership (now the Katie Geneva Cannon Center for Womanist Leadership), which helps Black women scholars search for new ways of envisioning what justice requires and which strategies will help to accomplish it.

In short, what Katie Cannon adds to liberation theology is a womanist perspective that requires that any approach to justice must attend to the multiple forms of oppression faced by Black women and must also locate and amplify the survival strategies and virtues that Black women have exhibited as they struggle against those multiple oppressions and toward full liberation.

CRITIQUE

Cannon has been lauded both within the womanist community and outside it for establishing a new *method* in studies of justice—the use of Black women's literary tradition.[67] This is certainly the use of a new *resource*. But this use raises some questions. First, Cone also drew on folk stories, music such as the blues and spirituals. While Cannon's use of Black women's literary tradition introduces a new *source*, it is not clear whether it presents an entirely new *method*. Second, is her use of this source—for instance, her reading of Hurston—correct? To the best of our knowledge, no serious challenges have yet been raised at this point; nonetheless, literary criticism is always open to alternative interpretations. Third, is she correct that Black women's literary tradition is true to Black women's lives? There are always possible distortions in the transition from oral to written story, as Cannon herself notes.[68] The use of Black women's literary tradition is a new and important resource, but its possibilities and limits have yet to be fully delineated.

Cone also argued that some actions that would normally be considered wrong might be right under conditions of oppression and that some characteristics that would normally be considered vices might then be virtues. Thus, Cannon's "paradigmatic ethical inversion," as Nikia Smith Robert calls it,[69] is not the first inversion in liberation theology. What makes it important is the naming of particular virtues that come out of this inversion. Cannon names at least the following, as noted above: "invisible dignity," "quiet grace," "never practiced delicacy," and "unshouted courage." The first term in each of these names refers to the fact that these virtues are often hidden and not readily noticed. Their definitions seem rather vague, however. "Quiet grace" is fashioning values in your own terms and refusing to be brutalized.[70] "Unshouted courage" is fortitude or having "staying power."[71] Clearer delineations would be helpful so that observers could assess when each virtue is being exhibited and whether there are other virtues that also could be mined from oral or textual tradition. Any turn to virtue theory around women's lives also runs the risk of assuming that virtue is gendered, following Jean-Jacques Rousseau's influential division of virtues into those appropriate for men and those appropriate for women.[72] Historically, seeing women's virtues as different from men's virtues has *not* been liberating for women.

Part of the difficulty here is that Cannon's work is not systematic. Often considered her signature work, *Katie's Canon* is a collection of essays that are rather loosely tied together.[73] Even *Black Womanist Ethics*, her published dissertation, has a somewhat disjointed feel. Its focus is Hurston. Hurston sank into "unreboundable brokenness" following an unsubstantiated sex slander, and Cannon asks whether resources from Black theology—notably Howard Thurman and Martin Luther King Jr.—might have helped sustain Hurston's uncompromising struggle to fulfill her capacities.[74] Hence, the introduction of theology at this point has purpose. Nonetheless, the theological reflections and the literary examinations seem less well integrated than they might be. Nonetheless, we believe that Cannon chose Hurston as a major interlocutor precisely because Hurston did not wallow in the suffering of Black women but sought to locate their ability to thrive. We therefore see Cannon's choice of Hurston as a reflection of Cannon's own faith-filled understanding of what constitutes the *imago Dei*—a feistiness in the face of oppression. Such feistiness is part of what womanism brings to the exploration of justice.

Overall, we find in Cannon's work a rich panoply of thoughts and resources for deeper consideration of what justice requires but not the systematic approach that would lend itself to a more developed analysis of the requirements of justice.

Cannon's refusal of rules and principles also raises the question of whether there are standards for criticizing tactics, strategies, and characteristics that are used within the oppressed community of Black women. If a subversive style of leadership is sometimes necessary, or if lying, cheating, and stealing are sometimes right rather than wrong, we are pushed to ask *when* these are necessary or *what* makes them right rather than wrong. Is any strategy utilized within the oppressed community *ipso facto* right? This criticism was noted in examining James Cone's theology: just because something comes from an oppressed community, that does not necessarily make it right or true.[75] Cannon's interest may not have been the particularities of defining when something that is normally a vice becomes instead a virtue, but the need for further guidelines remains.[76]

Peter Paris, in an otherwise very laudatory review of Cannon's work, raises an additional critique at this point. Does Cannon's womanist ethics focus so much on *survival* skills among Black women that it does not sufficiently address "the art of living well"? Or, perhaps better, in his words, "what is the relationship between an ethic of survival and an ethic of liberation?"[77] Justice is clearly not satisfied by simple survival. "Making do" is not enough; people must also "do better."[78] If the goal is liberation, then a focus on character and virtue must also locate those strategies, strengths, and virtues that move people beyond survival into the abundant life that Christianity proclaims for God's people. Are Cannon's virtues as stated sufficient?

Ironically, Cannon's own life is an excellent model of what it means to break boundaries, refuse limits, and carve new paths of liberation, yet she made little of her own story in her writing. Her story includes grandparents who were sharecroppers, the birth of one "white" child to her grandmother, some racial prejudice within her family, White people stealing land from her grandfather, and the expectation that Katie herself would automatically grow up knowing how to be a good "house servant."[79] When Katie Cannon was a child, Blacks were not allowed to go to the library, eat at restaurants, drink from public fountains, sit downstairs in movie theaters, or swim in local pools.[80] During her life, Cannon triumphed over many instances of racism and discrimination both within the academy and outside it in her journey toward becoming a leading womanist scholar.[81] Cannon's own life story thus reflects the triple oppression of which she writes: racism, sexism, and economic poverty. In feminist fashion, Cannon might have chosen to utilize her own story as a beginning point for her academic explorations or as a major example of some of the strengths exhibited among Black women. Yet she makes little of her powerful story. Perhaps at this point she bowed to the academic expectation that personal story does not provide sufficient "evidence" of claims and arguments.[82] It remains for her followers to develop such links more fully, integrating reason and personal experience in new and compelling ways.

Finally, because of her interest in the hidden strengths of Black women, Cannon's work seems to turn us from theories of justice to virtue theory. Yet there are traditions of understanding justice *as a virtue* that could be mined here and connected to her work. This is a place where both Protestant work on virtue theory and Roman Catholic theology and ethical analysis might challenge or strengthen Cannon's contribution.[83] If lying is sometimes right though often wrong, perhaps it is justice as a virtue that permits one to know the difference and choose rightly. Cannon beautifully parsed some of the experiences that form womanist strengths and character, but there is still work to be done. And there is always the danger that virtue theory turns us toward a private realm and away from the social justice that liberation demands. How to hold the two in creative tension is a task for additional ethical reflection.

ASSESSMENT

It may seem strange to include Katie Cannon in a book on theories of justice. Clearly, Cannon never set out to offer a theory of justice, nor does she. But her attention to the nexus of sex, race, and class oppression implies that any adequate theory of justice must attend to that nexus. Her work suggests that only an intersectional approach to justice will do.[84]

Further, her naming as virtues some actions that promote justice but would normally be considered vices does indeed turn much traditional ethical theory upside down or at least present challenges that require response. She claimed in *Katie's Canon* that "each essay in this book is a challenge to systems of domination."[85] The somewhat scattered nature of her reflections may therefore itself be a strength in her work, for systems of domination exist in all arenas of human life, and different approaches may be needed to address them in different arenas. Cannon claims that the cumulative effect of the work of womanist scholarship is a "fundamental reconceptualization of all ethics."[86] Minimally, we would argue that she has added to the liberation approach a concern for the virtues and spirituality that sustain the struggle for liberation and a focus on the everyday lives of Black women that is unique in the academy. She offers one example of the "thick" approach to understanding a community and its requirements for justice to be done. Finding strengths in the lives of everyday Black women recenters the approach to justice from academic halls to the streets of our cities and takes us to new places for insight into the requirements of justice.

Indeed, Cannon's approach may fit well into the suggestion made by Nancy Fraser and Linda J. Nicholson that feminists should create an approach to justice that takes seriously the postmodern critique of meta-theories without giving up on the idea that social criticism is possible.[87] Postmodernism left social critics with the problem of having no meta-narrative that provides *one* explanation for the cause of social injustices such as racism or sexism. The danger for any feminist work is the temptation to search for one key factor that explains sexism cross-culturally and that illuminates women's oppression in all social life (e.g., the notion that women's morality is based in caring rather than in principles of justice). Such approaches tend toward an essentialist reading of human nature. Fraser and Nicholson propose that there can be a postmodern feminism that is explicitly historical, attuned both to the cultural specificity of different societies and periods and to the plight of different groups within those societies and periods. That is precisely what Cannon does in her womanist approach to liberation and justice.

Cannon's work, as is true of other feminist and womanist work, makes clear that justice requires attention to community, relationship, and connection. Justice is not satisfied by a focus on honoring human rights, however difficult and crucial that task alone might be. As Peter Paris puts it in his commendation of Cannon, "Individuals are never alone but integrally related to the family and the larger community, apart from which they could not exist."[88] People are embedded in communities and shaped by family and community. Any theory of justice that takes people as isolated individuals misses something very important, especially in the struggle for liberation.

In addition to the role of family and community, Cannon's womanist ethics also takes very seriously the impact of *history* on contemporary lives, structures, and ideologies. Slavery may have been abolished, but its legacy lives on. Jim Crow laws may no longer dominate the landscape, but their legacy also endures. Only a serious appropriation of the lessons of history and the remarkable survival of those who are oppressed can give us an adequate approach to justice. Nozick criticized Rawls for focusing on end-state principles rather than on the process by which distributions came about, yet Nozick never looked carefully at some of the most egregious and important elements of that process in America: slavery and segregation and their enduring impact on current distributions. Cannon's focus on history stands out as a crucial contribution to any theory of justice.

Further, while language of the "option for the poor" became common in "Third World" approaches to liberation, the identity of the "poor" in

America needs to be named. Cannon's focus on Black women locates one clear place where the "option for the poor" might focus.

In short, Cannon gives us a view of what it means to approach a thick conceptualization of justice that takes seriously the history, values, "irrational facticity," and obstacles that particular communities face as they struggle for freedom, rights, liberation, and all the other goals that might be included in a rich description of justice.

As is true of James Cone, Katie Cannon's life and work continues to have a significant impact on other scholars. Stacey Floyd-Thomas puts it succinctly: "Her explicit naming of her approach as 'womanist ethics' quickened my soul, opened my mind, and set my feet on a course toward becoming the womanist ethicist I am today."[89] The Katie Geneva Cannon Center for Womanist Scholarship remains an ongoing legacy of the attempt to break open the field of ethics into new modes of learning and new epistemologies. Indeed, as Mary Hunt notes, Cannon's legacy is "multivalent—scholarship, style, spirituality, and solidarity."[90] Cannon may not have given us a "theory" of justice, but she has left us a vision of how we might approach intersectional justice in an unjust world.

NOTES

1 As Lincoln and Mamiya put it, "Racism in American Society is so pervasive and controlling in the lives of African Americans that the problem of sexual discrimination often gets considerably less attention." C. Eric Lincoln and Lawrence H. Mamiya, *The Black Church in the African American Experience* (Durham, NC: Duke University, 1990), 307.

2 Carole Pateman, "Introduction: The Theoretical Subversiveness of Feminism," in *Feminist Challenges: Social and Political Theory*, ed. Carole Pateman and Elizabeth Gross, (Boston: Northeastern University Press, 1986), 1–10, at 5.

3 Rosi Braidotti, "Ethics Revisited: Women and/in Philosophy," in Pateman and Gross, *Feminist Challenges: Social and Political Theory*, 44–60 at 60.

4 Elizabeth Gross, "Conclusion: What Is Feminist Theory?" in Pateman and Gross, *Feminist Challenges: Social and Political Theory*, 190–204, at 192.

5 Gross, "Conclusion: What Is Feminist Theory?" 196.

6 For an excellent introduction to types of feminism, see Gale A. Yee, "Introduction: Definitions, Explorations, and Intersections" in *The Hebrew Bible: Feminist and Intersectional Perspectives*, ed. Gale A. Yee (Minneapolis: Fortress, 2018).

7 Carol Gilligan, *In a Different Voice: Psychological Theory and Women's Development* (Cambridge, MA: Harvard University Press, 1982).

8 Lawrence Kohlberg, *The Philosophy of Moral Development: Moral Stages and the Idea of Justice (Essays in Moral Development v. 1)* (New York: Harper & Row, 1981). Kohlberg later added a seventh stage, but it was his original work that sparked Carol Gilligan's critique.

9 Jean Grimshaw, "The Idea of a Female Ethics," *Philosophy East and West* 4, no.2 (April 1992): 221–238 at 225.

10 Gilligan, *Different Voice*, 173.

11 Mary Jeanne Larrabee, ed., *An Ethic of Care* (New York: Routledge, 1993); Cynthia S. W. Crysdale, "Gilligan and the Ethics of Care: An Update" *Religious Studies Review* 20, no. 1 (January 1994): 21–28; *Hypatia* 15, no. 1 (Spring 1992); Dianne Romain, "Care and Confusion," in *Explorations in Feminist Ethics: Theory and Practice*, ed. Eve Browning Cole and Susan Coultrap McQuin (Bloomington: Indiana University Press, 1992), 27–37.

12 The impact of Gilligan's thesis reached into practical ethics such as arguments about nursing ethics. See Hilde L. Nelson, "Against Caring," *Journal of Clinical Ethics* 3 no. 1 (Spring 1992): 8–15, with responses by Nel Noddings and Toni M. Vezeau.

13 In the introduction to *In a Different Voice*, Gilligan is careful to say that the "different voice" is characterized not by gender but by theme (Gilligan, *Different Voice*, 2). However, in the concluding chapter, she does appear to identify the "different voice" of care very explicitly with women (Gilligan, *Different Voice*, 171–174).

14 Sandra Harding, "The Curious Coincidence of Feminine and African Moralities," in Eva Feder Kittay and Diana T. Meyers, *Women and Moral Theory* (Totowa, NJ: Rowman & Littlefield, 1987), 296–315 at 311.

15 Gilligan, *Different Voice*, 174.

16 Recall that one of Sandel's criticisms of Rawls was precisely that Rawls had a disembodied self who was disconnected from community. Feminists championed connections and embodiment.

17 For example, Katzenstein and Laitin argue that moralities of caring have "ambiguous implications." See Mary Fainsod Katzenstein and David D. Laitin, "Politics, Feminism, and the Ethics of Caring," in Kittay and Meyers, *Women and Moral Theory*, 261–281 at 263. Similarly, Jean Grimshaw argues that the idea that women "reason differently" runs the risk of "recapitulating old and oppressive dichotomies." Jean Grimshaw, "The Idea of a Female Ethic," *Philosophy East and West* 42, no. 2 (April 1992): 221–238 at 231.

18 See Sara Ruddick, "Maternal Thinking," in *Women and Values: Readings in Recent Feminist Philosophy*, ed. Marilyn Pearsall (Belmont, CA: Wadsworth, 1986), 340–351; Ruddick, "Remarks on the Sexual Politics of Reason," in Kittay and Meyers, *Women and Moral Theory*, 237–260.

19 Mary Field Belenky et al., *Women's Ways of Knowing: The Development of Self, Voice, and Mind* (New York: Basic Books, 1986), 102.

20 Nancy J. Hirschmann, "Freedom, Recognition, and Obligation: A Feminist Approach to Political Theory," *American Political Science Review* 83, no. 4 (December 1989): 1227–1244.

21 Indeed, one of the strengths of Sandel's approach to justice is his recognition that not all obligations are freely chosen.

22 E.g., Emilie M. Townes uses the language of "ethic of care" in her analysis of the injustices present in the American health-care system and its impact on Black lives. See *Breaking the Fine Rain of Death: African American Health Issues and a Womanist Ethic of Care* (New York: Continuum, 1998).

23 Nelson points out that Gilligan herself never rejected concerns for justice, though some subsequent feminists spoke as though care alone was sufficient. Because of its focus on intimates, Nelson argues, the ethics of care can be dangerously narrow in scope and too easily permits racism, xenophobia, and disregard for future generations. Nelson, "Against Caring," 10.

24 Carter Heyward, *Our Passion for Justice: Images of Power, Sexuality, and Liberation* (New York: Pilgrim Press, 1984).

25 Karen Lebacqz, *Justice in an Unjust World* (Minneapolis: Augsburg, 1987).

26 Beverly Wildung Harrison, *Making the Connections: Essays in Feminist Social Ethics*, ed. Carol S. Robb (Boston: Beacon Press, 1985), 238.

27 Katie Geneva Cannon, *Katie's Canon: Womanism and the Soul of the Black Community* (New York: Continuum, 1995), 25.

28 Cannon, *Katie's Canon*, 126.

29 Cannon, *Katie's Canon*, 138.

30 Cannon, *Katie's Canon*, 123.

31 Harrison, *Making the Connections*, 6.

32 Cannon, *Katie's Canon*, 23.

33 Emilie M. Townes et al., eds., *Walking through the Valley: Womanist Explorations in the Spirit of Katie Geneva Cannon* (Louisville, KY: Westminster John Knox, 2022), xv. [hereafter: *Valley*]

34 Walker's definition included four elements: (1) being "grown up" rather than childish, with behavior that could even be seen as *willful*; (2) loving women, sexually and/or nonsexually; (3) loving music, dance, the Spirit, and oneself; and (4) "womanist is to feminist as purple to lavender." See Cannon, *Katie's Canon*, 22.

35 Townes et al., *Valley*, 22.

36 As in the previous chapter, we have followed the Chicago Manual of Style guidance for capitalizing "Black" and "White" for our own words, but when quoting others we have maintained the style of our interlocutors.

37 Cannon, *Katie's Canon*, 60.

38 Katie G. Cannon, *Black Womanist Ethics* (Atlanta: Scholars Press, 1988), 99.

39 "The work of Black women writers can be trusted as seriously mirroring Black reality" (Cannon, *Katie's Canon*, 61); "In the quest for appreciating Black women's experience, nothing surpasses the Black women's literary

tradition" (Cannon, *Katie's Cannon*, 60); "There is no better source for comprehending the 'real-lived' texture of Black experience and the meaning of the oral life in the Black context" (Cannon, *Black Womanist Ethics*, 90).

40 Cannon, *Katie's Cannon*, 108–109.

41 Cannon, *Black Womanist Ethics*, 31.

42 Peter J. Paris, "Katie Cannon's Non-Canonical Canon," *Interpretation: A Journal of Bible and Theology* 74, no. 1 (2020): 3.

43 Cannon, *Black Womanist Ethics*, 43.

44 Cannon, *Katie's Canon*, 51.

45 Cannon, *Black Womanist Ethics*, 66.

46 Cannon, *Katie's Canon*, 48.

47 Cannon, *Katie's Canon*, 92: "The primary ethical principle or action guide is 'unctuousness.'"

48 *Merriam-Webster Dictionary* (Springfield, MA: Merriam-Webster, 2004), 780. See Cannon, *Black Womanist Ethics*, 105.

49 In *Justice in an Unjust World* (94–95), Karen Lebacqz draws on the story of Abram and Sarai in Egypt to argue that lying can serve the cause of justice.

50 Stacey M. Floyd-Thomas, "Enfleshing Womanism, Mentoring, and the Soul of the Black Community," *Journal of Feminist Studies in Religion* 35, no. 1 (Spring 2019): 101–104 at 102.

51 Cannon, *Black Womanist Ethics*, 75.

52 Cannon, *Black Womanist Ethics*, 75.

53 Nikia Smith Robert notes that her mother bent rules and broke laws (e.g., cheating on income tax reports) to have money to feed her children. This subversive approach is akin to what Cannon calls "living an ethics under oppression." Nikia Smith Robert, "'Not Meant to Survive': Black Mothers Leading beyond the Criminal Line," in Townes et al., *Walking Through the Valley* 107.

54 Cannon, *Katie's Canon*, 135.

55 Cannon, *Black Womanist Ethics*, 19, 53.

56 Cannon, *Black Womanist Ethics*, 22.

57 Cannon, *Black Womanist Ethics*, 174.

58 Cannon, *Black Womanist Ethics*, 109.

59 Cannon, *Katie's Canon*, 56.

60 Jacquelyn Grant, "Womanist Theology: Black Women's Experience as a Source for Doing Theology, with Special Reference to Christology," *Journal of the Interdenominational Theological Center* 13, no. 2 (Spring 1986): 195–212 at 210.

61 Private communication, quoted in Floyd-Thomas, "Enfleshing Womanism," 101–104 at 102.

62 Kelly Brown Douglas, *The Black Christ*, 25th anniversary ed. (Maryknoll, NY: Orbis Books, 2019), 123.

63 Cannon, *Katie's Cannon*, 56.

64 See Lincoln and Mamiya, *The Black Church*, chap. 10.

65 Cannon, *Katie's Canon*, 132.
66 Cannon, *Black Womanist Ethics*, 38. Indeed, Cannon suggests that Black women even contribute to each other's oppression when they rank each other in accord with criteria such as hair texture and skin color. See *Katie's Canon*, 71.
67 E.g., Renita J. Weems declares that Cannon pioneered a totally new field of inquiry in Christian ethics. Renita J. Weems, "The Biblical Field's Loss Was Womanist Ethics' Gain: Katie Cannon and the Dilemma of the Womanist Intellectual," in *Valley*, 3. Similarly, David Gushee opined that Katie Cannon created "an entirely new and lasting methodology." David P. Gushee, "Katie Cannon's Enduring Contribution to Christian Ethics," *Interpretation: A Journal of Bible and Theology* 74, no. 1 (2020): 27.
68 Cannon, *Katie's Canon*, 134.
69 Smith Robert, "'Not Meant to Survive,'" 118.
70 Cannon, *Black Womanist Ethics*, 126–127.
71 Cannon, *Black Womanist Ethics*, 144.
72 Jean-Jacques Rousseau, *Emile: Or, Treatise on Education* (1762; repr., Totowa, NJ: Biblio Distribution Centre, 1972). See Grimshaw, "The Idea of a Female Ethic," 221–238. It was the litany of women's virtues, such as obedience, modesty, and chastity, that Mary Wollstonecraft attacked in her *Vindication of the Rights of Woman* in 1792. Cannon's womanist ethics echoes Wollstonecraft but with a twist.
73 Indeed, the order of essays has been changed in recent editions in an effort to bring more sense of cohesion and flow.
74 Cannon, *Black Womanist Ethics*, chap. 6..
75 See Patricia Hill Collins, *Black Feminist Thought* (New York: Routledge, 1991), chap. 10.
76 For example, in *Justice in an Unjust World* (94–95), Karen Lebacqz also suggests that lying is not always wrong, and she references James Cone. But she uses W. D. Ross's concept of "prima facie" duties to suggest a way to determine when lying might be considered acceptable. One need not have *absolute* rules or principles in order to have *some* rules.
77 Paris, "Katie Cannon's Non-Canonical Canon," 8.
78 Douglas, *The Black Christ*, 137.
79 Cannon, *Katie's Canon*, appendix.
80 Sara Lawrence-Lightfoot, "Forward" to *Katie's Canon*, 12. See also Paris, "Katie Cannon's Non-Canonical Canon."
81 See Weems, "The Biblical Field's Loss."
82 In *Talking Back: Thinking Feminist, Thinking Black* (Boston: South End Press, 1989), bell hooks makes a powerful argument regarding the danger of any personal revelation from Black women: "Moving from silence into speech is for the oppressed . . . a gesture of defiance" (9).
83 See, for example, Josef Pieper, *The Four Cardinal Virtues* (Notre Dame, IN: University of Notre Dame Press, 1975); Joseph J. Kotva, *The Christian*

Case for Virtue Ethics (Washington, DC: Georgetown University Press, 1996).

84 The term *intersectionality* was coined by Kimberle Crenshaw in 1989 to show how a group or individual identity can be a unique combination of discrimination and privilege based on factors such as sex, race, class, sexual orientation, physical appearance, disability, age, and so on. Accessed May 2, 2024, https://en.wikipedia.org/wiki/intersectionality.

85 Cannon, *Katie's Canon*, 25.

86 Cannon, *Katie's Canon*, 128.

87 Nancy Fraser and Linda J. Nicholson, "Social Criticism without Philosophy: An Encounter between Feminism and Postmodernism," in *Feminism/Postmodernism*, ed. Linda J. Nicholson (New York: Routledge, 1990), 19–38.

88 Paris, "Katie Cannon's Non-Canonical Canon," 7.

89 Floyd-Thomas, "Enfleshing Womanism," 101–104 at 101.

90 Mary E. Hunt, "Katie Geneva Cannon Incarnate," *Journal of Feminist Studies in Religion* 35, no. 1 (Spring 2019): 109–111 at 109.

Conclusion

So where have we come with our explorations of the elephant? What are the gifts and legacies of each approach? What are the possibilities for a theory of justice? Let us begin with a quick review.

EIGHT FRAGMENTS ON JUSTICE

From Mill and the utilitarians, we get a vision of a good that transcends and yet incorporates individual rights. Claims are accepted as the core of justice, but claims are always derived from and dependent on maximizing utility. To be sure, justice, for Mill, includes a fundamental sense of equality since each person's good is to count as much as each other's. Yet there is no standard of equality as the goal or pattern of distribution. Further, there is no protection for those who are vulnerable as the greatest good overall might permit huge gaps between those who are rich and poor. Such lacunae present the challenge that all subsequent theories of justice must address.

Rawls responds to this challenge. The vision of a greater good overall is not alone sufficient; it matters who receives the benefits and who bears the burdens. Rawls begins with two basic assumptions: first, that there is no shared agreement about what constitutes the good life, and therefore, justice cannot be derived from conceptions of the good; and second, that our starting places in society seriously impact our opportunities and outcomes. He therefore attempts a "pure procedural" justice in which the demands of justice are derived by a thought experiment based on a minimum of agreements about what constitutes a fair setting (e.g., that those with power should not be able to use their power to disadvantage others). The result is two basic rules: one that requires equal opportunity in certain arenas and the other that permits some inequality in distribution of goods for the sake of a greater gain so long as everyone is better off than they would otherwise be. The concern is how the basic structures of society distribute benefits and opportunities, and for Rawls, the litmus test is what happens to the person in the worst position. In Rawls's view, the theory thus orients society toward an equality of distribution, though it does not require equality as its sole distributive principle.

Nozick wants to endorse the same Kantian presuppositions as Rawls, respecting the rights and reasons of individuals. But he utterly rejects any substantive equality as the requirement of justice. Justice in holdings and justice in transfer are the only standards, so justice becomes the product of free choice and exchange. Similarly to Mill, Nozick sees justice as rooted in people's legitimate claims. An important basis of claims for Nozick is the contribution of labor, for our labor is the one thing to which no one else can lay a claim. But individuals need to be free to determine how and when their labor is deployed. Thus, it is freedom, not fairness or utility, that constitutes the core of justice. To set any requirements that maximize the total output or to require distributions to help the least advantaged is to violate human freedom.

Sandel takes the maintenance and promotion of the community as the end of justice. To know what justice requires, we must first have a vision of a good society. Sandel follows Aristotle in asking about the *purposes* of an institution or system. For Sandel, the purpose of society is the common good, and justice is whatever serves or fits with this end. But the common good should not be mistaken for the utilitarian greatest good for the greatest number. When the community is the focus, then bonds between individuals are as important as, and cannot be isolated from, the individuals themselves. Utility, fairness, and freedom are all valued in their own right, but these are also tempered by social values of solidarity, trust, and mutual respect. In the communitarian view, each social good ought to be distributed by a logic intrinsic to the good itself—some by need, others by free choice, and still others by merit.

Such logics are determined by the way in which the community *values* that good.

Like Sandel, Francis also grounds his understanding of justice in a vision of the common good. And like Rawls, he is concerned with protecting those in the minimum position, especially the economic poor. For the Catholic social teaching tradition, however, the beginning point for justice is the fundamental dignity of the human person. Francis's contribution to this living tradition affirms human dignity, especially against the "technocratic paradigm" that dominates many cultures today. The technocratic paradigm prioritizes individualism, market economics, and technology as the solutions to the world's ills. In response, Francis calls us back to recognizing the dignity in each person (even those who are not "useful" and those not in our group) and to strengthening the bonds not just of solidarity but of fraternity—a genuine identification with the other who suffers. Francis also includes in the arena of justice not simply the human community but the "integral ecology" of the entire global ecosystem.

Into the rather irenic picture painted by Sandel and Francis, Niebuhr introduces the discordant note of sin. While "love" is the Christian command, we live in circumstances of sin and discord. Individual rights and group interests are not so easily compatible with the greater good or the common good as Mill, on the one hand, and Francis and Sandel, on the other, might have it. Worse, as reasoning and theory themselves become suspect, philosophical theories cannot yield an adequate understanding of justice. Justice in the "real" world is a constant process of balancing powers and compromising with the realities of sin and conflict. Niebuhr leaves us with the need for justice to be able to address real problems in the world and a sense of the necessity for historical compromise. We become aware of the inadequacies of every concrete achievement of justice and the paradox that every justice achieved contains an injustice yet to be addressed.

Cone and other liberation theologians accept and advance Niebuhr's focus on sin but with a twist. Justice begins neither with philosophical theory nor with Niebuhr's Christian love, but with the concrete realities of injustice experienced by the oppressed and illumined by the God of the Bible. Niebuhr's distrust of reason is carried to its full implications for the epistemological privilege of those oppressed: only those who suffer injustice and are involved in the struggle for justice can know what justice is. For Cone in particular, this means that in the United States, only the Black community can know what justice requires. Justice has become not merely *structural*, as it would be for Rawls, but *systemic*, and the finger is pointed clearly at White supremacy.

From feminist and womanist theologians, we get a further critique and correction: none of the previous theorists has taken seriously the suffering and oppression of women and of Black women in particular. In response, Cannon carefully delineates how, despite their oppression, Black women have carved out meaningful and even exemplary lives that move toward justice for themselves and their communities. Their strategies, their tactics, and their ways of thinking and being in the world have a lot to teach us about what justice requires. Minimally, justice requires an intersectional view that takes seriously oppressions based on race, sex, and class.

OF ELEPHANTS AND JUSTICE

Here, in brief, are eight frames of justice—eight perspectives, each of which gives us a different way to see the elephant. What, then, is the nature of the beast? If the elephant metaphor has any salience, then the first thing we can say is that no single theory presented in these pages has the whole of justice described. Just as our blindfolded explorers each came to discover a part of the elephant, so, too, we might suggest, have our theologians and philosophers each offered a piece of the larger whole. This, of course, runs us afoul of the intentions of our scholars. Mill, Rawls, Nozick, and Sandel each sought to show that their take on justice was not simply an alternative to but actually superior to those that came before. Francis and Niebuhr each claim how certain theological beliefs—human dignity and sin, respectively—inform our understanding of God's will for a just world in a way the philosophers could not fully comprehend. And Cone and Cannon privilege the position of those oppressed—Blacks and Black women, respectively—as the only true place from which justice can be fully comprehended. None would accept the way the elephant metaphor limits their work to only a piece of the whole, and yet that is precisely what we suggest. None of these eight theories has the whole of justice, nor do we.

Still, this recognition of intellectual humility is, itself, reflective of perspectives offered in this book. If justice is God's will for the community, then we imperfect and sinful humans are incapable of knowing the whole of it. If justice is reflective of the common good, then we as situated individuals are similarly limited. And if justice can only be truly known from the margins, then who among us is never in a position of privilege and therefore ignorance? At the same time, if we set the purpose of this book to be to *know justice better* rather than to solve what justice is or find absolute principles for justice, then each of the perspectives offered in these chapters helps us toward this goal.

Some Differences and Commonalities

Examining some commonalities and differences may help us move toward a better understanding of what justice encompasses. Our knowledge of the elephant will be only as good as our ability to put the different perspectives together in some meaningful way so that we do not mix up the trunk and the tail, for instance. At first glance, this might seem difficult. Several of our theories are teleological (Mill's utilitarianism and Sandel's communitarianism), while others are starkly deontological (Rawls's liberalism and Nozick's libertarianism). Several prioritize rational deliberation (Rawls, Mill, and Nozick), while others appeal to experience and community context (Sandel, Cone, and Cannon in particular). Rawls's focus is directed to the basic structure of liberal society, while both Niebuhr and Francis directed their gaze toward a fundamental view of human nature. Cone, Cannon, and Sandel give the most attention to the values and commitments that derive from the community, while Rawls appears to derive justice from the perspective of one properly situated individual, and Nozick limits justice to exchanges between individuals. Both Francis and Cone stress human dignity, but for Francis, that is a universal value, while for Cone, it is a very focused value directed toward the dignity of oppressed Black people. Sandel and Francis hold out hope for social harmony, while Niebuhr sees human community as essentially conflictual. Cone and Cannon refine that conflict and give it sharp focus, while Rawls and Mill, for all their differences, seem utterly to ignore human conflict and its implications for justice.

Yet in spite of such obvious differences, some commonality emerges around specific issues, at least for some of our interlocutors. One of these issues is the justice of market systems.

Three of the philosophical approaches considered here include at least tacit support for and affirmation of a market-based, capitalist economic system such as that which pervades the United States. Advocating the "greatest net good," utilitarianism became the base for much economic theory that supports capitalism. Cost-benefit analysis dominates many arenas of modern life. Problems experienced by workers in such a system are not easily recognized by a theory in which gains to some can outweigh losses to others. As long as the overall economic system is thought to work for the greater good in the long run, losses to the poor in the short run are deemed a "necessary trade-off" that does not make a system unjust.

Rawls, too, appears to defend democratic capitalism. Although he argues that his principles of justice are compatible with both capitalist and socialist economic systems, basic acceptance of capitalism is assured: as long as the least advantaged are thought to "benefit" from the market system, no injustice has been done. In what has been dubbed a trickle-down theory, benefits to those at the top in a capitalist economy are always thought to trickle down to some benefits for those at the bottom. By Rawls's theory, this makes capitalism basically a just economic system.

Nozick gives the most explicit support for a capitalist market exchange system based on the right to private property. Indeed, he indicates that he believes contemporary capitalist societies do not violate the principles of justice in exchange. Whatever distribution of goods occurs within an economy will be considered just, as long as it is the consequence of proper market exchanges. Aside from the "Lockean proviso" that might limit the original acquisition of a scarce good, there is no sense of any limits necessary to protect those who are poor.

Thus, although the utilitarians, Rawls, and Nozick hold very different basic theories of justice, in practice they all support forms of capitalist "free market" exchange and private property. Of our philosophers, only Sandel appears to move toward explicit criticism of market systems, arguing that certain goods (e.g., donor organs, elite educational opportunities) should never be left to market forces. Instead, the logic of distribution should be determined by how we value the good itself (e.g., organs should be distributed by need and opportunities by merit).

The picture changes quickly when we turn to our theological theories. All of them are suspicious of capitalism and its impact on those who are poor. Though Catholic social teaching generally supports the right of private ownership, that right has always been subject to constraints on the use of property for the sake of the common good.[1] Francis offers some crucial criticisms of capitalism, particularly in his concern for protection of the environment and its impact on poor people. For Niebuhr, a "free exchange" system based on private property would not represent economic justice. It gives too much power to those in control of capital, and, for Niebuhr, justice always requires a balancing of such power.

Latin American liberation theologians extend the Catholic perspective but use Marxist analysis to excoriate capitalism. They generally see the capitalist system that permits "differentiating" ownership and the development of classes as intrinsically evil. Justice is antithetical to any system that permits poor people to suffer so much.

Because of the specific history of White supremacy in the United States, Cone does not focus his critique on capitalism but on racism. However, both Cone and Cannon take seriously the economic impact of racism, and Cannon's explicit concern for classism brings a sharp critique to the impact of market capitalism in the United States. Once again, although the Christian perspectives examined here offer quite different approaches to and perspectives on justice, in practice, they appear to agree at least on the question of unfettered market capitalism.

The Value of Dialogue

Yet even here, we venture to suggest that those who describe the elephant so differently nonetheless may profit from dialogue with each other. In bringing our eight perspectives together, we shall follow the model of several of our interlocutors—Niebuhr, Francis, Sandel—who made it a point to let stand the paradoxes and tensions in their views of justice. There is not just contradiction but wisdom in those points of tension.

Let us illustrate with a case. Eleanor Windsor, a White middle-class quilter from Northern California, buys cotton fabric, cuts it up, puts the pieces together in what she hopes are pleasing patterns, and sews them back together on her machine, making a three-layer object called a *quilt*. Typically, she sells a lap-sized quilt for around one hundred dollars.

Ida Pettway, a Black woman from Gee's Bend, Alabama, also makes quilts.[2] But she does not buy fabric as she lives in dire poverty and has no money to purchase fabric. Her quilts are made from the relatively unspoiled edges of sheets or jeans that have been otherwise worn threadbare. With no electricity in her house, her quilts are made by hand, not on a sewing machine. Her quilts are fully as beautiful and artistic as Eleanor's—indeed, even more so—and they are larger in size, but they are sold by the roadside for five dollars each.

Nozick would say that as long as she has acquired the fabric fairly and put her own labor into creating the quilt, Eleanor is entitled to the monies from the sale. She could, of course, give away either the quilt or the monies, but in Nozick's view, the "poor" are not entitled to any of the proceeds from her work. Indeed, being taxed on the income from her quilting represents a kind of "stealing" of her labor. For Nozick, as long as each acquires materials in some "fair" way (i.e., it is not stolen), adds labor, and sells the resulting product for what the "market" permits, justice is done. There is a certain logic to this argument.

But, intuitively, something seems wrong with this picture. The discrepancy between the prices of quilts should raise an eyebrow or two, even accounting for geographic location. Ida's inability to purchase cotton fabric seems a stinging irony, given that her ancestors were slaves in the cotton fields. Despite Ida's quilting skills, she cannot sell her quilts for the same price that Eleanor can command. Several of our interlocutors would offer reasoning for our intuitive unease here. Rawls would suggest that, behind a veil of ignorance, no one would design a society in which such discrepancy exists for fear that they might occupy Ida's position once the veil is lifted. Niebuhr would argue the discrepancy reflects a sinful world, while Francis would argue that our focus is drawn too much to the quality and price of quilts and not enough to the dignity of the quilter. All three might call for corrective measures in the name of justice but perhaps without ever naming the structural racism or tragic history that seems to underlie the discrepancy in pricing.

Sandel, Cone, and Cannon might all point to the significance of the creation of the Gee's Bend Quilters Collective as a community effort to further the lives of these quilters. Cannon and Cone would further note that it is not a mistake that the quilters of Gee's Bend who were so impoverished are Black women and the descendants of slaves. While Cannon's focus might be on their tenacity and creativity as they struggle to survive and even thrive, we think she would also suggest that a look at their social and historical situation indicates why an inequality in quilt prices reveals an injustice hidden in the market system. Cone would focus less on the gender of the quilters but would certainly note the ways in which the oppression of former slave families is sustained across generations. Justice, for Cone, requires more than corrective measures; it requires liberation from longstanding mechanisms of oppression.

The story told above is as it would have been some years ago. The subsequent "discovery" of the Gee's Bend quilts by William Arnett, who recognized them as modern art and brought them to public attention with a resulting revaluation of the quilts, is an occurrence largely to be celebrated.[3] This raises questions about how goods are valued in a just society. Mill would recognize that Ida's quilts bear more utility (in both size and beauty) but would have been hard-pressed to identify why they were then originally priced lower than Eleanor's quilts. Nor is the particular value added by their "discovery" captured in the utility calculus. The quilts did not get warmer or more beautiful; the market just became more aware. Communitarians, for their part, would agree with utilitarianism that quilts are a social good that is rightly distributed by market forces but would recognize in the original pricing discrepancy that the market was not free; rather, it was "dominated" by White privilege. When Arnett drew attention to the Gee's Bend quilts, it offered a counter-narrative that helped to unlock the value of the quilts from this racist legacy.

To bring our conversation back around, however, it is worth recognizing that Nozick's theory can give some teeth to liberation and womanist concerns. Both liberation theology in general and womanist ethics in particular attend to historical injustices. But what is the nature of these injustices? Liberation theology agrees with Rawls that those who are poor would not have agreed to the system that puts them in their current poverty. But Nozick moves from the hypothetical veil of ignorance to the real history of transactions: either the original acquisition was not fair (e.g., lands, goods, or even people were stolen, expropriated, or enslaved), or the exchange was not fair (coercion was involved, grounds for setting a fair price were not mutually agreed, people were kept in ignorance of the actual value of goods). Liberation theologian José Porfirio Miranda acknowledged the importance of this history when he claimed that "commutative justice itself carries within it the whole problem of distribution."[4] Charges of economic injustice leveled by liberation theologians depend to some extent on a theory about right exchange and fairness in choice. In this sense, the liberation perspective needs Nozick (as do Rawls, Niebuhr, and Francis).

But Nozick also needs the liberation or womanist perspective. Nozick claims to establish a historical approach to justice. But his conclusion that capitalist exchange meets the demands of justice rests on speculation, not evidence. Are the Gee's Bend quilts fairly valued before or after their "discovery"? Liberation theology and womanist ethics provide the historical experiences necessary to test the truth of Nozick's basic claims about the entitlements attached to ownership, effort, and the production of goods. If Nozick provides the liberationists a way to demonstrate why the situation in Gee's Bend was "unfair" and not just "unfortunate," he needs liberation theology to put flesh on the bones of his purported historical approach to justice.

But then if it turns out that liberation and womanist theologies are correct, and that the world situation is characterized largely by injustice, something else will be needed. Sandel, Niebuhr, Cone, and Cannon all force us to see the importance of *history* to any claims for justice. Nozick nods toward the necessity for a theory of rectification of injustice, but he fails to develop that theory. Yet it is precisely this that may be the most important clue toward establishing distributive justice in our age. Perhaps one of the problems with dominant theories of justice is that so many of them come from White males who are economically and socially privileged. As Susan Bordo charges, the Western intellectual tradition that we so often take as normative or mainstream is in fact, properly speaking, a minority tradition that does not represent the majority population.[5] Most people live not in privilege but in poverty, constraints, and even oppression.

Expanding the Measures of Justice

When the first edition of this book was written in 1986, it focused almost entirely on questions of economic justice, with occasional appeals to political rights and freedoms. In hindsight, that perhaps should not have sufficed then, but it certainly does not suffice now. In the intervening decades, awareness has grown regarding the ways in which injustice pervades our societies and our structures through mechanisms that have nothing to do with economic distributions or even political rights. Indeed, there has been an explosion of books about justice among feminists[6] and an ongoing and important debate about what happens when we try to think globally rather than locally.[7] The major changes we have made in this new edition—the inclusion of communitarianism, the shift from the earlier "Economic Justice for All" to Pope Francis, the inclusion of Cone and Cannon—all reflect changes in the way we view and understand not just the answers but also the very questions that our pursuit of justice requires.

If injustice is the beginning point, then we may need different theories of justice. In rejecting classical distinctions of distributive, retributive, and commutative justice, Feinberg suggests that "an equally useful" way of classifying the data of justice and one that promises "more rewarding theoretical insights" is a classification according to types of injustice.[8] Perhaps another perspective for exploring the elephant is needed. A theory of justice is needed that is truly historical and that takes seriously the problem of rectification of injustice.[9]

To meet that challenge, we suggest that future theorists will need to adapt the concept of intersectionality and look at important forms of injustice that go even beyond Cannon's triad of sex, race, and class. Womanist ethics hints at that journey because the term *womanist* as defined by Alice Walker also included the idea that a womanist is a woman who loves other women, possibly though not necessarily in a sexual way. Heterosexism is noted by Kelly Brown Douglas as another important form of oppression.[10] When our structures are constructed with certain normative abilities in mind, we also need to be concerned with ableism, discrimination against people whose physical or mental capacities operate in nonnormative ways.[11] As Mary Hunt notes, "Experiences of race, nationality, gender, class, sexual orientation, and access to resources create conditions of inequality that persist over generations."[12] If liberation theology is correct in its basic claim that the God of the Bible is a God of liberation, then theorists of justice must look for all those places where liberation is needed. The "poorest of the poor" might be a blind Hispanic immigrant trans woman. Yet the point is not to try to locate the "most" oppressed but to see how different kinds of oppression are interlinked in people's lives and to hear their stories as they struggle for liberation and discern from those stories what justice might require. As Sandel might urge, we need thick narratives in order to see more fully what constitutes justice in community.

At the time of writing this book, states were passing legislation to limit the teaching of critical race theory in public colleges and universities. If our trajectory is correct, however, universities should instead *embrace* critical race theory that decenters whiteness and examines the intersectionality of race, class, sex, and other characteristics that have been the occasions for oppression. Only then can justice roll down like an ever-flowing stream (Amos 5:24).

NOTES

1 Francis, *Laudato Si* (Rome: Vatican Library, 2015), §93, https://www
.vatican.va/content/francesco/en/encyclicals/documents/papa-francesco
_20150524_enciclica-laudato-si.html.

2 Both names in this example are fictional, but the name Pettway is not. Many
Gee's Bend quilters bear that name, even though they are not genetically
related. Mark H. Pettway was the plantation owner of their ancestors, who
were forced to adopt his surname. Karen Lebacqz had the privilege of visit-
ing Gee's Bend some years ago.

3 The Gee's Bend quilts have been shown in museums and art galler-
ies around the world, and some now sell for thousands of dollars. Their
"discovery" is not without controversy, however, as several Gee's Bend
quilters accused Arnett of cheating them out of thousands of dollars of the value of their quilts. See "Gee's Bend," accessed August 24,
2024, https://www.soulsgrowndeep.org/gees-bend-quiltmakers and
"Quilts of Gee's Bend," accessed May 16, 2024, https://en.wikipedia
.org/wiki/Quilts_of_Gee%27s_Bend.

4 Jose Porfirio Miranda, *Marx and the Bible: A Critique of the Philosophy of
Oppression* (Maryknoll, NY: Orbis, 1974), 26.

5 Susan Bordo, "Feminist Skepticism and the 'Maleness' of Philosophy," in
Women and Reason, ed. Elizabeth D. Harvey and Kathleen Okruhlik (Ann
Arbor: University of Michigan, 1992), 143–162 at 153.

6 See, for instance, Elizabeth H. Wolgast, *The Grammar of Justice* (Ithaca,
NY: Cornell University Press, 1987); Nancy Fraser, *Justice Interruptus:
Critical Reflections on the "Postsocialist" Condition* (New York: Routledge,
1997); Susan Moller Okin, *Justice, Gender and the Family* (New York: Basic
Books, 1989); Martha Nussbaum, *Frontiers of Justice: Disability, National-
ity, Species Membership* (Cambridge, MA: Harvard University, 2006); Iris
Marion Young, *Justice and the Politics of Difference* (Princeton, NJ: Princ-
eton University Press, 1990).

7 For instance, David Miller and Sohail H. Hashimi, eds., *Boundaries and
Justice: Diverse Ethical Perspectives* (Princeton, NJ: Princeton University
Press, 2001); Thomas W. Pogge, *Global Justice* (Malden, MA: Blackwell,
2001); Will Kymlicka, *Multicultural Citizenship* (New York: Oxford, 1996);
Darrel Moellendorf, *Cosmopolitan Justice* (Boulder, CO: Westview Press,
2002); Joshua Cohen et al., *Is Multiculturalism Bad for Women?* (Princeton,
NJ: Princeton University Press, 1999).

8 Joel Feinberg, "Noncomparative Justice," in *Justice: Selected Readings*, ed. J.
Feinberg and H. Gross (Belmont, CA: Wadsworth, 1977), 55. A. D. Woozley
("Injustice," *Studies in Ethics: American Philosophical Quarterly Monograph
Series* no. 7, ed. Nicholas Rescher [Oxford: Basil Blackwell, 1973]), 109–122
also suggests that injustice is "more interesting" than justice and has been
little analyzed.

9   This is the task that Lebacqz set for herself decades ago in writing *Justice in an Unjust World*, and it remains a challenge for future theorists of justice.

10 Kelly Brown Douglas, *The Black Christ*, 25th anniversary ed. (Maryknoll, NY: Orbis Books, 2019), 115.

11 Here it is helpful to recognize the difference between impairments—the physical or cognitive condition—and disability—the ways in which society is not built for those nonnormative conditions. Cf. Matthew Gaudet, "On 'And Vulnerable': Catholic Social Thought and the Social Challenges of Cognitive Disability," *Journal of Moral Theology* 6, special issue no. 2 (2017): 36–37.

12 Mary E. Hunt, "Katie Geneva Cannon Incarnate," *Journal of Feminist Studies in Religion* 35, no. 1 (Spring 2019): 110.

Bibliography

Ackerman, Bruce J. *Social Justice in the Liberal State*. New Haven, CT: Yale University Press, 1980.

Anyabwile, Thabiti M. *The Decline of African American Theology: From Biblical Faith to Cultural Captivity*. Downers Grove, IL: Intervarsity Press, 2007.

Avila, Charles. *Ownership: Early Christian Teaching*. Maryknoll, NY: Orbis, 1983.

Barnidge, Robert P. "Against the Catholic Grain: Pope Francis Trumpets Socialism over Capitalism." *Forbes*, March 11, 2016. https://www.forbes .com/sites/realspin/2016/03/11/against-the-catholic-grain-pope-francis -trumpets-socialism-over-capitalism/.

Barry, Brian. *The Liberal Theory of Justice: A Critical Examination of the Principal Doctrines in* A Theory of Justice *by John Rawls*. Oxford: Oxford University Press, 1973.

Bartlett, Robert V., and Walter F. Baber. "Ethics and Environmental Policy in Democratic Governance." *Public Integrity* 7, no. 3 (Summer 2005): 219–240.

Bayles, Michael D., ed. *Contemporary Utilitarianism*. New York: Doubleday, 1968.

Belenky, Mary Field, Blythe McVicker Clinchy, Nancy Rule Goldberger, and Jill Mattuck Tarule. *Women's Ways of Knowing: The Development of Self, Voice, and Mind*. New York: Basic Books, 1986.

Bell, W. Kamau, and Kate Schatz. *Do the Work!: An Anti-Racist Activity Book*. New York: Workman Publishing, 2022.

Bentham, Jeremy. *An Introduction to the Principles of Morals and Legislation*. Edited by J. H. Burns and H. L. A. Hart. London: Methuen, 1982.

Boesak, Allan Aubrey. *Farewell to Innocence*. Maryknoll, NY: Orbis, 1977.

Bonino, Jose Miguez. *Toward a Christian Political Ethic*. Philadelphia: Fortress, 1983.

Bordo, Susan. "Feminist Skepticism and the 'Maleness' of Philosophy." In *Women and Reason*, ed. Elizabeth D. Harvey and Kathleen Okruhlik, 143–161. Ann Arbor: University of Michigan, 1992.

Braaten, Carl E. *The Apostolic Imperative*. Minneapolis: Augsburg, 1985.

Brandt, Richard B. *Ethical Theory*. Englewood Cliff, NJ: Prentice-Hall, 1959.

Brooks, Faith. *The Anti-Racism Journal: Questions and Practices to Move beyond Performative Allyship.* Boston: Page Street Publishing, 2022.

Brunner, Emil. *Justice and the Social Order.* London: Lutterworth, 1945.

Burdette, Matthew. "The Glorious, Complicated Legacy of James H. Cone." *The Living Church*, May 14, 2018. https://livingchurch.org/2018/05/14/the-glorious-complicated-legacy-of-james-h-cone/.

Cahill, Lisa Sowle. "Social Friendship Includes Women, but Social Change Must Engage Women." *Berkeley Forum* (blog), October 26, 2020. https://berkleycenter.georgetown.edu/responses/social-friendship-includes-women-but-social-change-must-engage-women.

Cannon, Katie Geneva. *Black Womanist Ethics.* Atlanta: Scholars Press, 1988.

———. *Katie's Canon: Womanism and the Soul of the Black Community.* New York: Continuum, 1995.

Cardinal, Ernesto. "The Gospel in Solentiname." *Concilium* 5 (May 1974): 107–112.

Chavis, Benjamin F., Jr. *Psalms from Prison.* Cleveland: The Pilgrim Press, 2024.

Clark, Megan. "'Fratelli Tutti' Shares Practical Wisdom, but Lacks Insights of Women." *National Catholic Reporter*, October 5, 2020. https://www.ncronline.org/opinion/guest-voices/fratelli-tutti-shares-practical-wisdom-lacks-insights-women.

Cole, Eve Browning, and Susan Coultrap McQuin, eds. *Explorations in Feminist Ethics: Theory and Practice.* Bloomington: Indiana University Press, 1992.

Collins, Patricia Hill. *Black Feminist Thought.* New York: Routledge, 1991.

Collins, Randall. *Four Sociological Traditions.* New York: Oxford University Press, 1994.

Cone, James H. *Black Theology and Black Power.* 50th anniversary ed. Maryknoll, NY: Orbis, 2019.

———. *A Black Theology of Liberation.* Philadelphia: J. B. Lippincott, 1970.

———. *The Cross and the Lynching Tree.* Maryknoll, NY: Orbis, 2011.

———. *God of the Oppressed.* New York: The Seabury Press, 1975.

———. *The Spirituals and the Blues: An Interpretation.* New York: The Seabury Press, 1972.

Crysdale, Cynthia S. W. "Gilligan and the Ethics of Care: An Update." *Religious Studies Review* 20, no. 1 (January 1994): 21–28

Curran, Charles E. *American Catholic Social Ethics: Twentieth Century Approaches.* Notre Dame, IN: University of Notre Dame Press, 1982.

———. *The Catholic Moral Tradition Today.* Washington, DC: Georgetown University Press, 1999.

Dalton, Max. "The Effectiveness Mindset." July 1, 2022. https://forum.effectivealtruism.org/posts/5nkeh7LWFYQ9YGdLS/the-effectiveness-mindset.

Daniels, Norman, ed. *Reading Rawls.* New York: Basic Books, n.d.

Danner, Kerry. "Saying No to an Economy That Kills: How Apathy towards Contingent Faculty Undermines Mission and Exploits Vocation at Catholic

Universities and Colleges." *Journal of Moral Theology* 8, special issue 1 (2019): 26–50.

Dorr, Donal. *Option for the Poor: A Hundred Years of Vatican Social Teaching*. Maryknoll, NY: Orbis, 1983.

Douglas, Kelly Brown. *The Black Christ*. 25th anniversary ed. Maryknoll, NY: Orbis Books, 2019.

Dussel, Enrique. *Ethics and the Theology of Liberation*. Maryknoll, NY: Orbis, 1978.

Eagleson, John, and Philip Sharper, eds. *Puebla and Beyond*. Maryknoll, NY: Orbis, 1979.

Edwards, Herbert O. "Niebuhr, 'Realism' and Civil Rights in America." *Christianity and Crisis* 46, no. 1 (February 1986): 13–14.

Ellis, James, III. "A Critique of Cone's Black Liberation Theology." *Day 1* (blog), July 9, 2011. https://day1.org/articles/5d9b820ef71918cdf2002e8f/faith_seeking _understanding_a_critique_of_cones_black_liberation_theology.

Erickson, Debra. "Adjunct Unionization on Catholic Campuses: Solidarity, Theology, and Mission." *Journal of Moral Theology* 8, special issue 1 (2019): 51–74.

Feinberg, Joel, and Hyman Gross. *Justice: Selected Readings*. Belmont, CA: Wadsworth, 1977.

Ferm, Deane William. "Outlining Rice-Roots Theology." *Christian Century* 101 (January 1984): 78–80.

Fishkin, James S. *Justice, Equal Opportunity, and the Family*. New Haven, CT: Yale University, 1983.

Floyd-Thomas, Stacey M. "Enfleshing Womanism, Mentoring, and the Soul of the Black Community." *Journal of Feminist Studies in Religion* 35, no. 1 (Spring 2019): 101–104.

Francis. "Address of His Holiness Pope Francis to the Members of the Pontifical Academy for Life." February 20, 2023. https://www.vatican.va /content/francesco/en/speeches/2023/february/documents/20230220 -pav.html.

———. *Evangelii Gaudium*. Rome: Vatican Library, 2013. https://www.vatican .va/content/francesco/en/apost_exhortations/documents/papa-francesco _esortazione-ap_20131124_evangelii-gaudium.html.

———. *Fratelli Tutti*. Rome: Vatican Library, 2020. https://www .vatican.va/content/francesco/en/encyclicals/documents/papa-francesco _20201003_enciclica-fratelli-tutti.html.

———. *Laudato Si'*. Rome: Vatican Library, 2015. https://www.vatican.va /content/francesco/en/encyclicals/documents/papa-francesco_20150524 _enciclica-laudato-si.html.

———. *Message for the Celebration of the Fifteenth World Day of Peace—Nonviolence: A Style of Politics for Peace*. Rome: Vatican Library, 2017. https://www.vatican .va/content/francesco/en/messages/peace/documents/papa-francesco _20161208_messaggio-l-giornata-mondiale-pace-2017.html.

Fraser, Nancy. *Justice Interruptus: Critical Reflections on the "Post-Socialist" Condition*. New York: Routledge, 1997.

Galston, William A. *Justice and the Human Good*. Chicago: University of Chicago Press, 1980.

Gilligan, Carol. *In a Different Voice: Psychological Theory and Women's Development*. Cambridge, MA: Harvard University Press, 1982.

Grant, George Parkin. *English Speaking Justice*. Notre Dame, IN: Notre Dame University Press, 1985.

Grant, Jacquelyn. "Womanist Theology: Black Women's Experience as a Source for Doing Theology, with Special Reference to Christology." *Journal of the Interdenominational Theological Center* 13, no. 2 (Spring 1986): 195–212.

Gremillion, Joseph, ed. *The Gospel of Peace and Justice: Catholic Social Teaching since Pope John*. Maryknoll, NY: Orbis, 1976.

Grimshaw, Jean. "The Idea of a Female Ethic." *Philosophy East and West* 42, no. 2 (April 1992): 221–238.

Gula, Richard M. *Reason Informed by Faith: Foundations of Catholic Morality*. Mahwah, NJ: Paulist Press, 1989.

Gunnemann, Jon P. "Capitalism and Commutative Justice." *Annual of the Society of Christian Ethics* 5 (1985): 101–122.

Gushee, David P. "Katie Cannon's Enduring Contribution to Christian Ethics." *Interpretation: A Journal of Bible and Theology* 74, no. 1 (2020): 23–30.

Gustafson, James. *Christian Ethics and the Community*. New York: Pilgrim, 1971.

Gutierrez, Gustavo. *The Power of the Poor in History*. Maryknoll, NY: Orbis, 1983.

———. *A Theology of Liberation*. Maryknoll, NY: Orbis, 1973.

Harland, Gordon. *The Thought of Reinhold Niebuhr*. New York: Oxford University Press, 1960.

Harrison, Beverly Wildung. *Making the Connections: Essays in Feminist Social Ethics*. Edited by Carol S. Robb. Boston: Beacon Press, 1985.

Herzog, Frederick. *Justice Church*. Maryknoll, NY: Orbis, 1981.

———. *Liberation Theology*. New York: The Seabury Press, 1972.

Heyward, Carter. *Our Passion for Justice: Images of Power, Sexuality, and Liberation*. New York: Pilgrim Press, 1984.

———. *The Redemption of God*. Washington, DC: University Press of America, 1982.

High-level Expert Group on AI. "Ethics Guidelines for Trustworthy AI." Shaping Europe's Digital Future, European Commission, April 8, 2019. https://digital-strategy.ec.europa.eu/en/library/ethics-guidelines-trustworthy-ai.

Hirschmann, Nancy J. "Freedom, Recognition, and Obligation: A Feminist Approach to Political Theory." *American Political Science Review* 83, no. 4 (December 1989): 1227–1244.

Holder, R. Ward, and Peter B. Josephson. "Obama's Niebuhr Problem." *Church History* 82, no. 3 (September 2013): 678–687.

Hollenbach, David. *Claims in Conflict: Retrieving and Renewing the Catholic Human Rights Tradition*. New York: Paulist Press, 1979.

hooks, bell. *Talking Back: Thinking Feminist, Thinking Black*. Boston: South End Press, 1989.

Hunt, Mary E. "Katie Geneva Cannon Incarnate." *Journal of Feminist Studies in Religion* 35, no. 1 (Spring 2019): 109–111.

Hypatia: A Journal of Feminist Philosophy 15, no. 1 (Spring 1992).

John XXIII. *Mater et Magistra*. Rome: Vatican Library, 1961. http://w2.vatican .va/content/john-xxiii/en/encyclicals/documents/hf_j-xxiii_enc_15051961 _mater.html.

———. *Pacem in Terris*. Rome: Vatican Library, 1963. https://www.vatican.va /content/john-xxiii/en/encyclicals/documents/hf_j-xxiii_enc_11041963 _pacem.html.

John Paul II. *Centesimus Annus*. Rome: Vatican Library, 1991. http://w2.vatican .va/content/john-paul-ii/en/encyclicals/documents/hf_jp-ii_enc_01051991 _centesimus-annus.html.

———. *Sollicitudo Rei Socialis*. Rome: Vatican Library, 1987. http://w2.vatican .va/content/john-paul-ii/en/encyclicals/documents/hf_jp-ii_enc_30121987 _sollicitudo-rei-socialis.html.

Keenan, James F. "Dignitas Infinita Falters When It Doesn't Practice What It Preaches." *Outreach*, April 19, 2024. https://outreach.faith/2024/04/james -f-keenan-s-j-dignitas-infinita-falters-when-it-doesnt-practice-what-it -preaches/.

Kegley, Charles W., and Robert W. Bretall, eds. *Reinhold Niebuhr: His Religious, Social, and Political Thought*. New York: Macmillan, 1956.

Kendi, Ibram X. *How to Be an Anti-Racist*. London: One World, 2019.

Kenehan, Sarah. "Rawls, Rectification, and Global Climate Change." *Journal of Social Philosophy* 45, no. 2 (Summer 2014): 252–269. https://doi.org/10.1111/josp.12062.

Kittay, Eva Feder, and Diana T. Meyers. *Women and Moral Theory*. Totowa, NJ: Rowman & Littlefield, 1987.

Kohlberg, Lawrence. *The Philosophy of Moral Development: Moral Stages and the Idea of Justice*. New York: Harper & Row, 1981.

Kotva, Joseph J. *The Christian Case for Virtue Ethics*. Washington, DC: Georgetown University, 1996.

Kymlicka, Will. *Multicultural Citizenship*. New York: Oxford, 1996.

Langan, John P. "Rawls, Nozick, and the Search for Social Justice." *Theological Studies* 38 (1977): 357.

Larrabee, Mary Jeanne, ed. *An Ethic of Care*. New York: Routledge, 1993.

Lebacqz, Karen. *Justice in an Unjust World*. Minneapolis: Augsburg, 1987.

———. *Six Theories of Justice: Perspectives from Philosophical and Theological Ethics*. Minneapolis: Augsburg, 1986.

Leo XIII. *Rerum Novarum*. Rome: Vatican Library, 1891. https://w2.vatican .va/content/leo-xiii/en/encyclicals/documents/hf_l-xiii_enc_15051891 _rerum-novarum.html.

Lincoln, C. Eric, and Lawrence H. Mamiya. *The Black Church in the African American Experience*. Durham, NC: Duke University Press, 1990.

Longwood, Merle. "Niebuhr and a Theory of Justice." *Dialog* 14 (1985): 253–262.

Lyons, David. *Forms and Limits of Utilitarianism*. Oxford: Clarendon, 1965.

MacIntyre, Alasdair C. *After Virtue*. Notre Dame, IN: University of Notre Dame Press, 1981.

Massaro, Thomas. *Living Justice: Catholic Social Teaching in Action*, 4th classroom ed. Lanham, MD: Rowman & Littlefield, 2024.

———. *Mercy in Action: The Social Teachings of Pope Francis*. Lanham, MD: Rowman & Littlefield, 2018.

McCann, Dennis P. *Christian Realism and Liberation Theology: Practical Theologies in Creative Conflict*. Maryknoll, NY: Orbis, 1981.

Mill, John Stuart. *On Liberty*. London: John Parker and Son, 1859.

———. *Utilitarianism*. New York: Bobbs-Merrill, 1957.

Miller, David, and Sohail H. Hashimi, eds. *Boundaries and Justice: Diverse Ethical Perspectives*. Princeton, NJ: Princeton University Press, 2001.

Miranda, Jose Porfirio. *Marx and the Bible: A Critique of the Philosophy of Oppression*. Maryknoll, NY: Orbis, 1974.

Moellendorf, Darrel. *Cosmopolitan Justice*. Boulder, CO: Westview, 2002.

Moore, Basil. *Black Theology: The South African Voice*. London: C. Hurst, 1973.

Mott, Stephen. Charles. *Biblical Ethics and Social Change*. New York: Oxford University Press, 1982.

Mudflower Collective (Katie G. Cannon, Beverly W. Harrison, Carter Heyward, Ada Maria Isasi-Diaz, Bess B. Johnson, Mary D. Pellauer, and Nancy D. Richardson). *God's Fierce Whimsy*. New York: Pilgrim, 1985.

Nelson, Hilde L. "Against Caring." *Journal of Clinical Ethics* 3, no. 1 (Spring 1992): 8–18.

Nicholson, Linda J., ed. *Feminism/Postmodernism*. New York: Routledge, 1990.

Niebuhr, Reinhold. *The Children of Light and the Children of Darkness*. London: Nisbet, 1945.

———. *Christian Realism and Political Problems*. New York: Scribner, 1953.

———. *Christianity and Power Politics*. New York: Scribner, 1946.

———. *An Interpretation of Christian Ethics*. New York: The Seabury Press, 1979. First published 1935.

———. *Moral Man and Immoral Society*. New York: Scribner, 1932, 1960. First published 1932.

———. *The Nature and Destiny of Man*. 2 vols. New York: Scribner, 1964. First published 1943.

Nozick, Robert. *Anarchy, State, and Utopia*. New York: Basic Books, 1974.

Nussbaum, Martha. *Frontiers of Justice: Disability, Nationality, Species Membership*. Cambridge, MA: Harvard University Press, 2006.

Okin, Susan Moller. *Is Multiculturalism Bad for Women?* Edited by Joshua Cohen, Matthew Howard, and Martha C. Nussbaum. Princeton, NJ: Princeton University, 1999.

———. *Justice, Gender, and the Family*. New York: Basic Books, 1989.

O'Leary, Naomi. "Pope Attacks 'Tyranny' of Markets in Manifesto for Papacy." Reuters, November 26, 2013. https://www.reuters.com /article/us-pope-document-idUSBRE9AP0EQ20131126/.

Outka, Gene. *Agape: An Ethical Analysis*. New Haven, CT: Yale University Press, 1972.

Paris, Peter J. "Katie Cannon's Non-Canonical Canon." *Interpretation: A Journal of Bible and Theology* 74, no. 1 (2020). https://journals.sagepub.com/ doi/10.1177/0020964319876577.

Pateman, Carole, and Elizabeth Gross, eds. *Feminist Challenges: Social and Political Theory*. Boston: Northeastern University Press, 1986.

Paul VI. *Octogesima Adveniens*. Rome: Vatican Library, 1971. https://www.vatican.va/content/paul-vi/en/apost_letters/documents/hf_p -vi_apl_19710514_octogesima-adveniens.html.

———. *Populorum Progressio*. Rome: Vatican Library, 1967. https://www.vatican .va/content/paul-vi/en/encyclicals/documents/hf_p-vi_enc_26031967 _populorum.html.

Pearsall, Marilyn, ed. *Women and Values: Readings in Recent Feminist Philosophy*. Belmont, CA: Wadsworth, 1986.

Pieper, Josef. *The Four Cardinal Virtues*. Notre Dame, IN: Notre Dame Press, 1975.

Pius XI, *Quadragesimo Anno*. Rome: Vatican Library, 1931. https://w2.vatican .va/content/pius-xi/en/encyclicals/documents/hf_p-xi_enc_19310515 _quadragesimo-anno.html.

Pogge, Thomas W. *Global Justice*. Malden, MA: Blackwell, 2001.

Rakoczy, Susan. "Is Pope Francis an Ecofeminist?" *openDemocracy* (blog), October 20, 2015. https://www.opendemocracy.net/en/transformation /is-pope-francis-ecofeminist/.

Rawls, John. *The Law of Peoples*. Cambridge, MA: Harvard University Press, 1999.

———. *Political Liberalism*. New York: Columbia University Press, 1993.

———. *A Theory of Justice*. Cambridge, MA: Harvard University Press, 1971.

Reiman, Jeffrey H. "The Labor Theory of the Difference Principle." *Philosophy and Public Affairs* 12, no. 2 (Spring 1983): 133–159.

Reimer-Barry, Emily. "On Naming God: Gendered God-Talk in Laudato Si'." *Catholic Moral Theology* (blog), June 30, 2015. https:// catholicmoraltheology.com/on-naming-god-gendered-god-talk-in-laudato -si/.

Rescher, Nicholas. *Distributive Justice: A Constructive Critique of the Utilitarian Theory of Distribution*. Indianapolis: Bobbs-Merrill, 1966.

Robertson, D. B., ed. *Love and Justice: Selections from the Shorter Writings of Reinhold Niebuhr*. Gloucester, MA: Peter Smith, 1976.

Ross, W. D. *The Right and the Good*. Oxford: Clarendon, 1930.

Rousseau, Jean-Jacques *Emile: Or, Treatise on Education*. Totowa, NJ: Biblio Distribution Centre, 1972. First published 1762.

Ryan, Alan, ed. *The Idea of Freedom: Essays in Honour of Isaiah Berlin*. Oxford: Oxford University Press, 1979.

Ryan, John A. *A Living Wage: Its Ethical and Economic Aspects*. London: MacMillan, 1912.

Sachs, Jeffery D. "Market Reformer: An Economist Considers Pope Francis' Critique of Capitalism." *America*, March 14, 2014. https://www.americamagazine.org/issue/market-reformer.

Sandel, Michael J. *Democracy's Discontent*. Cambridge: Cambridge University Press, 2007.

———. *Justice: What's the Right Thing to Do?* New York: Farrar, Straus and Giroux, 2009.

———. *Liberalism and the Limits of Justice*. Cambridge: Cambridge University Press, 1982. Second edition published in 2005.

———. *The Tyranny of Merit: What's Become of the Common Good?* New York: Farrar, Straus and Giroux, 2020.

———. *What Money Can't Buy: The Moral Limits of Markets*. Reprint ed. New York: Farrar, Straus and Giroux, 2013.

Scott, Nathan A., ed. *The Legacy of Reinhold Niebuhr*. Chicago: University of Chicago Press, 1975.

Segundo, Juan Luis. *Liberation of Theology*. Maryknoll, NY: Orbis, 1976.

Sherwin, Susan. *No Longer Patient: Feminist Ethics and Health Care*. Philadelphia: Temple University, 1992.

Sidgwick, Henry. *The Methods of Ethics*. London: Macmillan, 1962.

Sirico, Robert. "Pope Francis Makes an Enemy of the Poor's Best Friend—The Free Market." *Fox News*, October 24, 2021. https://www.foxnews.com/opinion/sirico-pope-francis-free-market-economics.

Stanford Encyclopedia of Philosophy. https://plato.stanford.edu/.

Stone, Ronald H. *Reinhold Niebuhr: Prophet to Politicians*. Nashville: Abingdon Press, 1972.

Taylor, Talique. "Who Is James Cone?" *Earth and Altar* (blog), May 8, 2023. https://earthandaltarmag.com/posts/who-is-james-cone.

Terrell, Ellen. "Research Guides: This Month in Business History: Formation of the American Federation of Labor." Research guide. Accessed June 6, 2024. https://guides.loc.gov/this-month-in-business-history/december/american-federation-of-labor.

Thomas, M. M. "A Third World View of Christian Realism." *Christianity and Crisis* 46, no.1 (1986): 8–10.

Townes, Emilie M. *Breaking the Fine Rain of Death: African American Health Issues and a Womanist Ethic of Care*. New York: Continuum, 1998.

Townes, Emilie M., Stacey Floyd-Thomas, Alison P. Gise Johnson, and Angela D. Sims, eds. *Walking through the Valley: Womanist Explorations in the Spirit of Katie Geneva Cannon*. Louisville, KY: Westminster John Knox, 2022.

UNESCO. "Recommendation on the Ethics of Artificial Intelligence." November 23, 2021. https://unesdoc.unesco.org/ark:/48223/pf0000381137.

Vatican Council II. *Gaudium et Spes.* Rome: Vatican Library, 1965. https://www
.vatican.va/archive/hist_councils/ii_vatican_council/documents/vat-ii
_const_19651207_gaudium-et-spes_en.html.

Wall, James M. "Liberation Ethics: Insisting on Equality." *Christian Century*
99 (November 10, 1982): 1123–1124.

Walzer, Michael. *Radical Principles: Reflections of an Unreconstructed Democrat.* New York: Basic Books, 1980.

———. *Spheres of Justice: A Defense of Pluralism and Equality.* New York: Basic
Books, 1983.

———. *The Struggle for a Decent Politics: On Liberal as an Adjective.* New Haven,
CT: Yale University Press, 2023.

———. *Thick and Thin: Moral Argument at Home and Abroad.* Notre Dame,
IN: University of Notre Dame Press, 1994.

Welch, Sharon D. *Communities of Resistance and Solidarity.* Maryknoll, NY:
Orbis, 1985.

West, Traci C. *Disruptive Christian Ethics: When Racism and Women's Lives
Matter.* Louisville, KY: Westminster John Knox, 2006.

Williams, Preston. "James Cone and the Problem of a Black Ethic." *Harvard
Theological Review* 65, no. 4 (October 1972): 483–494.

Wolff, Robert Paul. *Understanding Rawls: A Reconstruction and Critique of A
Theory of Justice.* Princeton, NJ: Princeton University Press, 1977.

Wolgast, Elizabeth H. *The Grammar of Justice.* Ithaca, NY: Cornell, 1987.

Wolterstorff, Nicholas. *Journey toward Justice.* Grand Rapids, MI: Baker Academic, 2013.

———. *Justice in Love.* Grand Rapids, MI: Eerdmans, 2011.

———. *Until Justice and Peace Embrace.* Grand Rapids, MI: Eerdmans, 1983.

Woozley, A. D. "Injustice." In *Studies in Ethics,* American Philosophical Quarterly Monograph Series no. 7, edited by Nicholas Rescher. Oxford: Basil
Blackwell, 1973.

World Synod of Catholic Bishops. *Justice in the World.* 1971. https://www
.cctwincities.org/wp-content/uploads/2015/10/Justicia-in-Mundo.pdf.

Yee, Gale A., ed. *The Hebrew Bible: Feminist and Intersectional Perspectives.*
Minneapolis: Fortress, 2018.

Young, Iris Marion. *Justice and the Politics of Difference.* Princeton, NJ: Princeton University Press, 1990.

Yoder, John Howard. *The Politics of Jesus.* Grand Rapids, MI: Eerdmans, 1972.

Zagano, Phyllis. "'Fratelli Tutti' Does Not Include Women, and Neither Does
'Fraternity.'" *National Catholic Reporter,* September 21, 2020. https://www
.ncronline.org/opinion/just-catholic/fratelli-tutti-does-not-include
-women-and-neither-does-fraternity.

Zakaria, Fareed. "The ABCs of Communitarianism." *Slate,* July 26, 1996. https://slate
.com/news-and-politics/1996/07/the-abcs-of-communitarianism.html.

Zehou, Li, Paul J. D'Ambrosio, and Robert A. Carleo III. "A Response to Michael
Sandel and Other Matters." *Philosophy East and West* 66, no. 4 (2016):
1068–1147.

Index

in social conflict, 15
structures of, 134–135, 136
usefulness of, 13
utility and, 12–15, 16, 27
value and, 4
as vice, 56n48
as a virtue, 191
See also procedural justice; *specific theories*
justice as fairness, 34–35, 39–40, 41–42, 54n33
Justice in an Unjust World (Lebacqz), 182
Justice in the World (World Synod of Catholic Bishops), 108
justification, 39–41, 49–51, 102n3
just savings principle, 43–44

Kant, Immanuel, 14, 20, 34, 43, 55–56n48
Katie Geneva Cannon Center for Womanist Leadership (Center for Womanist Leadership), 188, 194
Katie's Canon (Cannon), 183, 189, 192
kidney analogy, 89
killing analogy, 110–111
King, Martin Luther, Jr., 120, 159, 164, 186, 189
kingdom of God, 130
knowledge, procedural requirement for, 62
Kohlberg, Lawrence, 180
Ku Klux Klan, 164

labor
contribution of, 202
in institutionalized injustice, 173n7
merit in, 92
ownership and, 73
protection of, 106

social product from, 48–49
taxes and, 66–67, 72
wages for, 108, 118, 141–142
labor analogy, 48–49
laissez-faire economy, 71
Langan, John, 72, 73
Latin America/Latin American
liberation theology, 5, 156–159, 165
Laudato Si', 113–114, 120, 126n31
least advantaged, identification of, 46. *See also* poor/vulnerable
Lebacqz, Karen, 165, 167, 178n102, 182, 198n76
legal right, injustice and, 13
Leo XIII (pope), 106, 111
lexical ordering, 44, 45–46
liberalism, 69, 74, 79n77, 97
Liberalism and the Limits of Justice (Sandel), 82–83
liberation, 163, 170–171, 212
liberation challenge
assessment of, 169–173
critique of, 165–169
new method in, 156–159
North American context and, 159–164
overview of, 5, 155, 203–204
review of, 164–165
liberation theology
Catholic social teaching (CST) and, 122
historical injustices and, 210
Latin American, 5, 156–159, 165
as new method, 156–159
origin of, 155
rationality in, 159
as "rice-roots" theology, 174n17
violence in, 158
weakness of, 168
libertarians, 86–87